LEADING TO THE 2003 IRAQ WAR

LEADING TO THE 2003 IRAQ WAR

THE GLOBAL MEDIA DEBATE

EDITED BY

ALEXANDER G. NIKOLAEV

AND

ERNEST A. HAKANEN

LEADING TO THE 2003 IRAQ WAR
© Alexander G. Nikolaev and Ernest A. Hakanen, 2006.

First published in 2006 by
PALGRAVE MACMILLAN™
175 Fifth Avenue, New York, N.Y. 10010 and
Houndmills, Basingstoke, Hampshire, England RG21 6XS
Companies and representatives throughout the world.

PALGRAVE MACMILLAN is the global academic imprint of the Palgrave Macmillan division of St. Martin's Press, LLC and of Palgrave Macmillan Ltd. Macmillan® is a registered trademark in the United States, United Kingdom and other countries. Palgrave is a registered trademark in the European Union and other countries.

ISBN 1–4039–7113–7

Library of Congress Cataloging-in-Publication Data

Leading to the 2003 Iraq war : the global media debate / edited by Alexander G. Nikolaev and Ernest A. Hakanen.
    p. cm.
Includes bibliographical references and index.
ISBN 1–4039–7113–7
    1. Iraq War, 2003—Mass media and the war. I. Nikolaev, Alexander G. II. Hakanen, Ernest A.

P96.I73L43 2006
070.4′4995670443—dc22   2005046288

A catalogue record for this book is available from the British Library.

Design by Newgen Imaging Systems (P) Ltd., Chennai, India.

First edition: January 2006

10 9 8 7 6 5 4 3 2 1

Printed in the United States of America.

CONTENTS

Part II   The Global Debate

Europe

The Middle East

Eurasia

Across the Globe

List of Graphs and Tables

Graphs

Tables

INTRODUCTION

Ernest A. Hakanen and Alexander G. Nikolaev

This volume is an edited book about the global media coverage of the coming of the 2003 Iraq war, written by media scholars from around the world. The main emphasis of the volume is the prewar media debate in different countries on whether to support or oppose the 2003 Iraq war.

The year leading up to the Iraq war witnessed a barrage of reasons to go to war given by the U.S. Administration, some reasonable, some unreasonable, some valid, some invalid, some factual, and some fictional. Reasons given for war changed almost daily. Americans and people around the world were undoubtedly confused. And the media clearly contributed to the confusion.

The Importance of the Event

The days leading to the 2003 Iraq war became an important moment in the history of international relations of the post–World War II era. For the first time since 1945, the doctrine of the preemptive war was not only openly proclaimed by the United States but actually put to practical use, encountering stiff political resistance even from its traditional allies and neighbors— France, Germany, Canada, Mexico, and others. It is not an exaggeration to say that the entire international security system was tested by this event. The future and the relevance of the United Nations—as a cornerstone of this system—were challenged by this war. Therefore, this event is being and will be thoroughly studied by scholars from different fields to assess the effects and future political consequences of this war. Since the media played an important role in the entire event, the analysis of the global media debate of this war is important and enlightening.

The Course and the Essence of the Debate

On January 29, 2002 President George W. Bush delivered his State of the Union Address, which would be later called the *"Axis of Evil"* speech.

President Bush for the first time revealed a new doctrine of preemptive action against America's enemies: "I will not wait on events, while dangers gather. I will not stand by, as peril draws closer and closer."[1] A phrase from that speech—"The United States of America will not permit the world's most dangerous regimes to threaten us with the world's most destructive weapons"—became the slogan for the entire anti-Iraq campaign.

The first media stories on serious preparations for war against Iraq didn't appear until April 2002. On April 28, The *New York Times* published an article "U.S. envisions blueprint on Iraq including big invasion next year."[2] At the same time, not only ordinary Americans but even many well-informed American journalists covering the White House kept asking the same question: "So what is President Bush's rationale?"[3]

Initially, the rationale for the war was in complete accordance with the slogan of the campaign: the presence in Iraq of weapons of mass destruction. Later, however, the scope of the threat was seemingly expanded. Iraq was said to present a threat not only to the United States, but also to its allies and interests in the region as well as to the world peace in general. There were also many attempts to connect Iraq to Al Qaeda and other terrorist organizations. President Bush presented these arguments for the first time in his September 12 speech to the UN General Assembly and later in his October 7 speech in Cincinnati:[4]

> In the attacks on America a year ago, we saw the destructive intentions of our enemies. This threat hides within many nations, including my own. In cells, in camps, terrorists are plotting further destruction and building new bases for their war against civilization. And our greatest fear is that terrorists will find a shortcut to their mad ambitions when an outlaw regime supplies them with the technologies to kill on a massive scale. In one place and one regime, we find all these dangers in their most lethal and aggressive forms [Iraq]. . . .[5]

But the very next day after the Cincinnati speech, the CIA released a document that directly contradicted the President. The report said, "Saddam is not a threat to the United States right now, but that the easiest way for him to become an immediate threat is to give him no options. Bush could well provoke the use of the very weapons he is trying to prevent."[6] *Newsweek* and *MSNBC* reported that intelligence pictures used by President Bush to support his case "were not convincing."[7] In addition, the 9/11 report did not support an Iraqi–Al Qaeda connection. *MSNBC* reported, "U.S. intelligence officials told NBC News the actual links between Saddam and Al Qaeda are sketchy. In fact, they believe Osama bin Laden views Saddam as too secular, not a true believer, and in some ways a threat to Islam."[8] In that same article, it was revealed that the Prague meeting between September 11 hijacker Mohammed Atta and an Iraqi spy, cited by

Cheney, never happened and that the President knew it. The *Washington Post* reported that "senior intelligence officials" told them that "the CIA had not found convincing proof, despite efforts that included surveillance photos and communication intercepts," of any connection between "Hussein and global terrorism."[9]

Considerable tensions started to form within the Bush administration between the "hawks" (Dick Cheney, Condoleezza Rice, Donald Rumsfeld, and Paul Wolfowitz) and the "internationalists" (Colin Powell, Richard Armitage, and Richard Haas).[10] And Bush sided with the hawks. However, his choice only energized the internal opposition and gave birth to what the British *Guardian* dubbed the "intelligence war."[11] "The past week has witnessed a behind-the-scenes revolt by U.S. intelligence and other government employees in sensitive positions, against the White House and Pentagon over the use of classified information about Saddam Hussein's activities."[12] "Officials in the CIA, FBI and energy department are being put under intense pressure to produce reports which back the administration's line, the Guardian has learned. In response, some are complying, some are resisting and some are choosing to remain silent."[13]

Bush did not have to fight for public support. The *Washington Post* and *USA Today* polls show that the level of public support for a military action against Iraq stayed at a steady 57–58 percent between early August and late November of 2002.[14] At the same time the American public assumed that Bush would get support from the United Nations and European allies. When that did not pan out, Bush's position on Iraq met a very active and widespread expression of public opposition in the form of antiwar rallies conducted all over the U.S. in January 2003. Ignoring international support and protests at home, the United States attacked Iraq on March 19, 2003.

Main Emphasis of the Volume

The months leading up to the 2003 Iraq war have become blurred in society's collective mind. It's important to note how the orchestration of arguments contradicted the facts and, often times, common sense. In this volume, we are concerned with illuminating these problems. However, we are specifically concerned with the months leading up to the war because once a war begins all history leading up to it is immediately based on the war itself, in other words the cause is explained by the effect. As William Dorman points out in chapter one, "the myth of war, once a war starts, has a power to overwhelm culture and public discourse, and therefore take over thought. Most of the arguments for or against war usually occur after the war has begun and will be in vain because rallying effects will win out." Therefore, our first purpose is to examine the actual reasons and arguments for war against Iraq as they were reflected in the prewar phase of the media debate. When a war or a conflict starts—the free and diverse media debate usually ends. But at the prewar stage the opposition is still vocal and not suppressed and the media deliberations are usually quite diverse and informative—not blurred by the rallying effects.

Our second purpose is to examine real reasons why certain countries supported or opposed the war. The national prewar debate within each country on the issue was inevitably reflected in each country's media. Consequently, if we look at the arguments used by the representatives of different nations for or against the war—we can understand the reasons behind their political stance on the issue and how and why their positions were formed. This kind of exploration will provide us with a deep insight into each nation's pattern of political reasoning. For many readers this material may be quite enlightening because for the first time they will be able to see the actual reasons behind other countries' actions and not the motives assigned or attributed (often falsely) to those countries by the domestic media seen by people within their own countries' borders.

Features and Structure of the Book

The structure and composition of the book reflect its main emphasis and purpose. First of all, this book will systematically cover the entire world. In this volume, the editors make sure that every corner of the Globe is covered. This is important in order not to get trapped in a traditional Eurocentric point of view and to show viewpoints of people living on all the continents of the Globe.

The second important feature of the book is that this volume is a collection of scholarly articles—not political essays. It became fashionable to publish collections of essays, that is, basically, the collections of personal political opinion pieces. This volume is a collection of scholarly research articles. There are no political favorites—countries that supported the war (United States of America, Great Britain, Spain, Australia, and Israel) are represented as well as the countries that opposed the war (France, Germany, Russia, China, Mexico, and the Arab countries). The main idea of the volume is to show and compare as objectively as possible all the types of arguments used throughout the world for as well as against the war. Although some contributions may have some small political biases, as a volume, this book does not have any political agenda.

Finally, only original articles—specifically written for the book—are included in this volume. The reader will be reading only original pieces of research not found anywhere else and not published previously anywhere.

Structurally, this book is divided into two parts. Part one is a collection of examinations of the media coverage of the days leading to war in the United States, Britain, and Australia—the core of "the coalition of the willing." Part two examines the global media outside this English-speaking alliance.

In the United States, the media did more than merely report the political events and actions. As we shall see in the chapters that follow, the media were slow to react, uncritical, some times ignorant, and often misleading. In many ways, the media are as culpable as the U.S. administration for Americans' confusion.

The second part of the book—The Global Debate—is structured not according to the pro-counter criterion but territorially: Europe, Eurasia, the Middle East, and the rest of the world. This type of structure allows for clear coverage of all the corners of the world, helps to avoid political grouping of the countries (pro- versus anti-), and, consequently, helps to tone down possible political undertones. In some cases, countries that supported and opposed the war are included in one chapter (for example, Mexico and Spain). This allows us to closely and objectively compare arguments highlighted in different countries as well as to highlight territorial and cultural similarities and differences in the patterns of political reasoning among different nations.

In general, it is important to examine the global media in their own right. First, we can learn what arguments for and against possible involvement in the war panned out in each country. Second, the international community through the UN did not support the war. Therefore, an examination of the rest of the world shows how the U.S. actions were seen vis-à-vis international relations.

Finally, the editors wish to thank Douglas Porpora, and Ronald Bishop, both of Drexel University for their support of this project. We also would like to thank Anthony Wahl and Heather Van Dusen of Palgrave Macmillan whose support and professionalism were invaluable in bringing this book into existence.

Notes

1. President George W. Bush, "The State of the Union Address," *The White House on the Web*, January 29, 2002 <http://www.whitehouse.gov/news/releases/2002/01/20020129-11.html> (accessed March 17, 2005).
2. T. Shanker, "U.S. Envisions Blueprint on Iraq Including Big Invasion Next Year," *The New York Times*, Sunday, April 28, 2002, A1.
3. "White House Daily Briefing," *The U.S. Department of State International Information Programs on the Web*, May 1, 2002 <http://usinfo.state.gov/regional/nea/iraq/text/0501wths.htm> (accessed March 26, 2003).

4. "George Bush's Speech to the UN General Assembly," *Guardian Unlimited*, Thursday, September 12, 2002 <http://www.guardian.co.uk/usa/story/0,12271,791155,00.html> (accessed March 17, 2005). And "Transcript: George Bush's speech on Iraq: An Address Given by President Bush in Cincinnati," *Guardian Unlimited*, Monday, October 7, 2002 <http://www.guardian.co.uk/usa/story/0,12271,806799,00.html> (accessed March 17, 2005).

5. "George Bush's Speech to the UN General Assembly," *Guardian Unlimited*, Thursday, September 12, 2002.

6. "Rosy Scenario: War Plans Are Supposed to Prepare for the Worst, not Hope for the Best," *Newsweek on the Web*, October 11, 2002 <http://stacks.msnbc.com/news/820163.asp?cp1=1> (accessed March 26, 2003).

7. Ibid.

8. A. Mitchell, "The Iraq and Al-Qaeda Connection: Bush Camp Says It's Clear, U.S. Intelligence Says It's Sketchy," *MSNBC.com*, Monday, October 21, 2002 <http://www.msnbc.com/news/824024.asp?cp1=1> (accessed March 26, 2003).

9. M. Allen, "Bush Asserts That Al Qaeda Has Links to Iraq's Hussein: President Cites Potential Cooperation as Concern," *The Washington Post*, Thursday, September 26, 2002, A29.

10. F. FitzGerald, "How Hawks Captured the White House," *Guardian Unlimited*, Tuesday, September 24, 2002 <http://www.guardian.co.uk/usa/story/0,12271,797608,00.html> (accessed March 17, 2005).

11. "Read between the lines," *Guardian Unlimited*, Wednesday, October 16, 2002 <http://www.guardian.co.uk/usa/story/0,12271,812829,00.html> (accessed March 17, 2005).

12. Ibid.

13. J. Borger, "White House 'Exaggerating Iraqi Threat,'" *Guardian Unlimited*, Wednesday, October 9, 2002 <http://www.guardian.co.uk/usa/story/0,12271,807286,00.html> (accessed March 17, 2005).

14. Poll numbers showing the level of public support for the war in the United States in 2002: August—57% (*Washington Post*); September—5–57% (*Washington Post*); September—23–57% (*USA Today*); November—58% (*USA Today*).

Part I

The English-Speaking Western Alliance—America, Great Britain, and Australia

THE UNITED STATES

CHAPTER ONE

A DEBATE DELAYED IS A DEBATE DENIED: U.S. NEWS MEDIA BEFORE THE 2003 WAR WITH IRAQ

William A. Dorman

There is no action of the state that can have a more immediate or dramatic impact on the lives of its citizens than the use of military force against an external foe: real or imagined. Consequently, in a democracy, public debate matters most over the question of whether to wage a war. I begin with two central propositions, the first and most important of which is that once a war begins critical thinking in any society, free or not, becomes virtually impossible. The thoughtful consideration of alternatives simply is unacceptable, suffocated as it were by nationalism and patriotism, not to mention fear and rage. The veteran war correspondent and journalist Chris Hedges has persuasively shown in his book, *War Is a Force that Gives Us Meaning*,[1] that the price we pay is the smothering of debate. Hedges learned this first-hand, when he shared with his audience his profound doubts about warfare and its effects on the civil voice in a college commencement address in spring 2003, just after the initial stage of the most recent war with Iraq had ended—and was promptly booed from the stage.

Given this, the only meaningful time to debate the need for war is before one begins; it is too late once it is under way. History is abundantly clear that the myth of war, once a war starts, has a power to overwhelm culture and public discourse, and therefore takes over thought to an extraordinary degree.

The second key proposition here is that the press is the only institution that can reasonably be expected to make possible a robust debate over foreign policy, in general, and the war option, in particular, in a timely enough way to make a difference in the choices made by policy elites. At least in theory, news-gathering organizations have the resources, both human and material, and the philosophic mission to investigate claims to truth by the state about the need for war, and are unfettered by either external government controls or (again, in theory) the concerns of partisan politics that limit other institutions, particularly Congress.

The general public, by contrast, has neither the inclination nor the wherewithal, for the most part, to open a genuinely serious debate on its own. At the same time, neither *non*mainstream media (e.g., public broadcasting, quality periodicals such as The *New Yorker* or small circulation opinion journals such as The *Nation*, the Internet, and so on) nor nonelite dissenting groups, think tanks, or academic specialists alone or in combination are sufficient for the task of creating a critical mass of doubt about official Washington's analysis sans questions about the policy options raised in the mainstream news media. To be sure, if a war goes on long enough, as did the Vietnam War, or a conflict is sustained at an obviously increasing cost and seems to have derailed, as is now the case of the American occupation of Iraq, the public can become alarmed and, eventually, a free-swinging debate can open up—but this almost always occurs long after terrible damage has been done. It is in this regard that a debate *following* a war is a case of too little far too late.

It was during the run-up to the war with Iraq that an authentic debate mattered most, the most critical time for a national discussion in which all sides could have had equal voice. Yet, as I hope to make plain, the press for a range of reasons failed to function, as democratic theory promises, and its passivity helped contribute to what arguably is a foreign policy fiasco of an unusual dimension.

The Press and an Ill-Informed Public

Never before in the annals of contemporary American foreign policy was so much evidence accumulated so quickly that the assumptions leading to a war were so questionable. Almost as soon as the president declared victory, the chaos and daily violence began on the ground in post-invasion Iraq and the failure of the U.S. military to find Weapons of Mass Destruction (WMDs) quickly became an embarrassment. Added to the mix, as time passed, were the final reports of David Kay, the administration's chief weapons inspector, the insider account of Richard Clarke, onetime White House's staff expert on terrorism, and the reports of the Senate Select Committee on Intelligence and the 9/11 commission. The only matter left in dispute by the summer of 2004 was whether President Bush and his advisors had *knowingly* misled Congress and the American people about the reasons for going to war.

As to how the press figures into all of this, the chain of logic is simple. Under democratic theory, a privately owned press unrestrained by government provides for a free-marketplace of ideas that makes it possible for *citizens* (as opposed to subjects) to debate alternatives, become aware of abuses of state power, and, ultimately, *hold government accountable.*

Understood in these terms, the *informed* consent of the governed is impossible without the mechanism of a free press. In the realm of foreign affairs, where under usual circumstances Americans tend to be least well informed and least interested, the press has a particularly important role to play, given the dynamics of the media's agenda-setting capacity and its power of representation. In other words, the media—especially television news—acts as the daily textbook for most Americans on what is happening in the world. In this sense, it provides the public with an agenda of concerns (e.g., Iraq versus Sudan), a vocabulary (e.g., "freedom fighters" versus "terrorists," or "peace process" versus "negotiated sellout"), and a sense of what dangers we face and from whom.

What Americans "learned" from the mainstream press in the run-up to the 2003 Iraq war had everything to do with what they came to *believe.* Couple this "learning curve" with other factors, not the least of which was Congressional passivity demonstrated most dramatically by the October 10–11, 2002 votes of both houses to approve the force resolution, and it was a relatively easy task for the Bush administration to go forward with its plans for war without fear of serious opposition from the general public.

The problem, of course, is that so much of what Americans came to believe was wrong. In this regard, I think the problem is not that the public is uninformed during times of international crisis, as so many observers lament, but rather that they are *ill informed.*

The study that most clearly demonstrated the gulf between "belief" and "knowledge"—a huge distinction always to keep in mind when thinking about any issue—was conducted by the Program on International Policy Attitudes (PIPA) in conjunction with Knowledge Networks.[2] The study was usefully discussed in the Winter 2003–04 issue of *Political Science Quarterly* by three of its principals.[3]

The PIPA surveys conducted before, during, and even after the war found that a significantly high percentage (in some instances as high as 68 percent) of Americans accepted one or more of the three most compelling administration claims, all of which were false.

The first "misperception" in the words of the survey, and the most important in a post–9/11 world in the American political context, was that there was a demonstrated connection between Saddam Hussein's Iraq and Al Qaeda, and that Iraq had played a key role in planning September 11. The second, very nearly equal in importance, is that Hussein possessed WMD. And the third misperception was that the war had international legitimacy, which is to say the support of world opinion, when the opposite was true.

Most significantly, the surveys demonstrated that there was a high correlation between this tendency toward misperception and Americans' support for the war, and, equally important these surveys provided evidence about the role played by the news media in giving currency to the false beliefs.

Most disturbingly, long after the war had ended and unbridled patriotism presumably had long since ebbed, not to mention that such experts on terrorism and WMDs as Richard Clarke, David Kay, and Hans Blix had been heard from at length, the false beliefs persisted. Almost a year after the major combat had ended, PIPA issued a follow-up study that indicated, despite an overabundance of evidence to the contrary, that a majority of Americans (57 percent) continued to believe that Saddam's Iraq had provided significant support to Al Qaeda. Of this, 20 percent believed Iraq was directly connected to the events of September 11, while 45 percent said they believed evidence of support for Al Qaeda had actually been found during the war. The results for belief about WMDs were quite similar.[4]

Why a sizeable percentage of Americans should persist in their mistaken beliefs about Saddam Hussein's connection to terrorism and the threat he posed to American security is not particularly difficult to comprehend. Once people have won a military victory in a war that they strongly believed was fought for honorable purpose and in the interests, indeed, of national survival, it will take far more than evidence after the fact to change their minds. In other words, it is not unusual that a large number of Americans should seek to avoid a kind of collective cognitive dissonance by holding on to false beliefs, which is yet another reason why the press needs to challenge such beliefs *before* a war begins, not after.

On the evidence included in studies such as those undertaken by PIPA as well as others to be discussed shortly, there is little to dispute the judgments of Kull, Ramsay, and Lewis that what "is worrisome is that it appears that the President has the capacity to lead members of the public to assume false beliefs in support of his position"[5] while at the same time "the media cannot necessarily be counted on to play the critical role of doggedly challenging the administration."[6] And, as the authors had observed earlier, there is striking evidence "that the readiness to challenge the administration is a variable that corresponds to levels of misperception among viewers,"[7] and I would hasten to add, presumably readers.

The Press and Connecting the Dots

As the PIPA and other studies suggest, the most noteworthy way in which the press contributed to tilting the prewar debate in favor of the Bush administration was to leave unchallenged the key assumptions and assertions of the proponents of war with Iraq. Perhaps because so many of

President George W. Bush's advisors had served in his father's administration in 1990 at the time of the invasion of Kuwait, they knew firsthand the potential dangers of not appearing to have a valid rationale for military action during the "establishing phase" of a war.[8] Unlike the first Bush administration, which wasted a period of valuable time casting about for a reason powerful enough to convince the public of the need for war with Iraq (e.g., it's a fight for democracy, it's about who controls the oil, it's about jobs, it's that Saddam is another Hitler, and so on), officials this time around chanted the same mantra from the moment the drums of war began to beat in August 2002.

According to this White House story line, the events of September 11 marked the beginning of a war on terror in which Iraq played a prominent role, both in the planning and execution of the attacks on the United States in 2001 and as a likely enemy in the near future armed with the most deadly WMDs. The only rational way to deal with such an adversary was through "regime change."

Why Americans should come so readily to accept this line of reasoning, and why only a sustained challenge from the press might have made a difference, is rooted in the impact that the events of 9/11 have had on most Americans. To say that Americans should have been less susceptible to manipulation or that they should have learned to be less fearful than other countries that have experienced terrorism over far longer periods of time and at much greater human cost is to ignore the simple reality that human beings do not live their lives by comparison, and Americans are certainly no exception. It is precisely because the trauma of 9/11 was so great that the mainstream media's deferential manner was most problematic.

And then there are those who wish to argue that the president or his advisors never actually encouraged false beliefs about Iraq and the war on terror, or who doubt journalism's role in reinforcing them. Such skeptics will first have to explain away such findings as those contained in the impressive study by Gershkoff and Kushner, which is based on a content analysis of all presidential speeches dealing with terrorism and/or Iraq delivered from September 11, 2001 to May 1, 2003, when the president famously delivered his end of hostilities speech from the deck of an aircraft carrier.[9] The researchers then looked at shifts in public opinion following key Bush addresses, as well as following the famous Powell presentation on Iraq and WMD before the United Nations.

According to the authors, while President Bush never publicly and explicitly connected Saddam Hussein and Iraq to 9/11, he used the "consistent technique of linking Iraq with the terms 'terrorism,' and 'al Qaeda' [that] provided the context from which such a connection could be made. Bush also never publicly connected Saddam Hussein to Osama bin Laden, the leader of al Qaeda. However, whether or not Bush connected each dot from Saddam Hussein to Osama bin Laden, the use of particular language and transitions in official speeches allowed, and indeed almost compelled, the listener to make this inference."[10]

As a result of their findings, Gershkoff and Kushner posit that the public responded to the "rhetoric it heard with impressively high levels of support for the war," citing as only one example the nine percent of Americans who switched from being antiwar to supporting it after the president's 2003 State of the Union message.[11]

On the assumption that to accept Bush's "Iraq as War on Terror" frame as legitimate "the American people had to hear it, understand it, and be faced with no other convincing frames,"[12] the authors also analyzed coverage of the president's speeches in The *New York Times* for the same time period. What they discovered is that "While at least some debate existed on the actual policy of war, almost none occurred within the *Times*' news coverage over the framing of the conflict in terms of *terrorism* [my emphasis]," and concluded that "the information flow remained one sided for the duration of the months preceding the war on Iraq."[13]

As a result, the authors say that during the period of their study, public opinion never fell below 55 percent and eventually achieved a level at or above 70 percent, despite the fact that polling revealed Americans were generally aware of the potential for a war to result in a large number of casualties, a weakened economy, and quite possibly a short-term increase in terrorism on the home front.[14]

Given that journalists are reluctant to take on a popular sitting president entirely on their own, the authors are careful to point out that one explanation for the muted questioning of the president's assertions in the press had to do with the tepid and cautious response of the Democratic Party to Bush. Such an explanation ignores that the press is popularly supposed to take its own initiative a priori, or that there were legions of academic experts and independent defense analysts who might have provided the basis for oppositional news frames, not to mention a large and vocal antiwar movement.

A particularly valuable part of the Gershkoff–Kushner study is their treatment of the effect on public opinion of Secretary of State Colin Powell's February 5, 2003 speech to the United Nations, an event that they and others, including myself, see as the pivotal moment in the run-up to the war. According to the authors, "Powell's speech provided more evidence than any other official administration speech about the links between Iraq with Al Qaeda and he made such links explicit."[15] The impact of Powell's case making was huge. According to Gershkoff–Kushner, there "was a *30-point jump* [their emphasis] in the number of Americans who felt convinced of a link between Saddam Hussein and al Qaeda" after he spoke.[16]

A piece in the *Columbia Journalism Review* argues that among Powell's most receptive audience members were editorial writers of some of the United State's most prominent newspapers. " 'Irrefutable,' declared The *Washington Post*. Powell 'may not have produced a *'smoking gun,'* added The *New York Times*, but his speech left 'little question that Mr. Hussein had tried hard to conceal one.' " Similarly enthusiastic were editorials in the *Chicago Tribune*, the *Los Angeles Times, USA Today*, and the *Wall Street Journal*, which rounded out the study.[17]

There were indeed occasional debunking pieces written about Powell's performance raising sharp questions about his "facts," but these pieces usually appeared in newspapers or periodicals in the hinterlands[18] and on OpEd pages rather than news columns. If it were written as a result of journalistic inquiry, it came too late in the game as public opinion had already been fixed.

As for how the press dealt with the matter of WMDs in general, the most thorough critique of this dimension is by Massing.[19] Given that U.S. news organizations in the months *following* the war were only too eager to examine the Bush administration's shortcomings, especially in terms of faulty intelligence about WMDs, Massing was moved to pose the question, "where were you all before the war?" and the detailed answer he provides is not a flattering one, as this quote from the beginning of his study foreshadows: "Some maintain that the many analysts who've spoken out since the end of the war were mute before it. But that's not true. Beginning in the summer of 2002, the 'intelligence community' was rent by bitter disputes over how Bush officials were using the data on Iraq. Many journalists knew about this, yet few chose to write about it."[20]

Among other things, in the period before the war, Massing argues, "US journalists were far too reliant on sources sympathetic to the administration. Those with dissenting views—and there were more than a few—were shut out,"[21] and he provides ample supporting detail to make his case. He also charges that the reporting of The *New York Times* was "especially deficient" but found that the *Times'* editorial page was frequently more "questioning."[22]

Massing was not the only critic to raise serious and compelling questions about press coverage of Iraq and WMDs. A study at the University of Maryland[23] and a piece in the *AJR (American Journalism Review)*[24] give persuasive and disturbing corroboration.

Admitted Lack of Criticism by the Press

In an editorial a year after the major combat ended, the *Times* announced the findings of an introspective survey of its own coverage, especially on the issue of Iraq and WMDs and its alleged ties to terrorism. After reviewing hundreds of articles written before, during, and just after the war, the *Times* came to conclude that in "a number of instances the coverage was not as rigorous as it should have been. In some cases, information that was controversial then, and seems questionable now, was insufficiently qualified or allowed to stand unchallenged."[25] While hardly an abject apology on the same scale as its reexamination of, say, the Jason Blair affair, the thrust of the editorial *mea culpa* for flawed foreign affairs reporting was more forthcoming than at any time previously. An even more detailed and pointed appraisal by the *Times'* public editor was published a week or so later.[26]

And some two months later in July, the *Times* went even further, pointing out that while it had been editorially skeptical of many aspects of President Bush's claims, it had "agreed with him on the critical point that Saddam Hussein was concealing a large weapons program that could pose a threat to the United States and its allies." It continued, "we should have been more aggressive in helping our readers understand that there was always a possibility that no large stockpiles existed." In an important admission, the *Times* wrote, "We did not listen carefully to the people who disagreed with us . . . we had a 'group think' of our own." Concluded the *Times*, "And even though this page came down against the invasion, we regret now that we didn't do more to challenge the president's assumptions."[27] The *Washington Post* followed with its own apologia in August of 2004.[28]

Why indeed didn't the *Times*, the *Post*, and the rest of the mainstream media challenge the president's assumptions about the need for a war that has had such extraordinary consequences for all concerned? How did a free press upon which Jefferson and Madison placed such high hopes come to such a pass? What could explain the failure of a press system that considers itself to be uniquely adversarial to power? As with many such matters, the reasons are both simple and complex.

A list of several of the most often heard explanations is topped by the belief that after 9/11 the press corps came to conclude collectively that in the interests of national unity it was untoward to criticize the commander in chief.[29] Two other possibilities frequently voiced were the fear of journalists of appearing unpatriotic, thereby alienating audience members, and the impact of such relatively new players on the journalistic scene as Fox News driving public discourse to the jingoistic right. Given the history of journalism since World War II, however, a more complex set of factors may be at work.

Study after study of mainstream press performance during periods of international conflict since 1946 involving U.S. interests, particularly where war is concerned, indicate that journalistic deference to Washington's official perspective is hardly a new phenomenon. In instances ranging from the Bay of Pigs to the Dominican Republic to Vietnam and the Iranian revolution, not to mention the invasions of Grenada and Panama, the first Gulf War, and the war against Yugoslavia, there was nothing unique about press behavior in 2003. What is new is that a policy came to ruin so quickly that the president's assumptions and strategies as well as the record of how poorly the press had covered them simply could not be ignored. Usually, years pass before the full extent of a policy disaster is known. Not so in the case of Iraq.

The press's behavior in 2003 has deep roots in the kind of national security journalism that emerged after World War II and prevailed throughout the cold war. The combination of economic and ideological competition for power between the United States and the Soviet Union, taken together with a fear of nuclear weapons, had transforming effects on American politics and institutions that have never been completely understood. In particular, it has never been fully appreciated that nuclear weapons are an inherently *undemocratic* technology that, out of necessity, concentrates power in the executive branch.

What does not seem to be generally grasped today is that while after 1989 the United States no longer possessed a powerful and coherent ideological schema to drive national security concerns, the national security state has neither withered away, nor has the military industrial complex suddenly found other work. Since September 11, 2001, the war on terror has taken care of this vacuum and driven a return to cold war norms. The national security state, as it were, had morphed into the Homeland Security State.

One of the institutions most dramatically transformed by the coming of the homeland security state has been the press, which before World War II could not dependably be counted on to defer to the executive's judgment on the need for war. Of course, once a war began, the press like the general public rallied to the cause, which is true of any press system at any time in any country. But at least before wars began, there frequently was an open and vigorous debate on the merits of military solutions. Not so after 1946 and the coming of the national security state.

Unlike the domestic arena, journalists and journalism simply lack the expertise or intellectual courage and self-confidence to dispute a sitting president on matters of national security, particularly when Congress remains compliant rather than combative. Moreover, they lack the *idiom*, not to mention supportive professional milieu, which is to say that they have yet to find a "clear and effective way to report incorrect impressions and untruthful statements, particularly those that emanate from the White House . . . Journalists are notoriously reluctant to use the word 'lie' when describing the statements of public officials."[30]

Compounding the problem is that just as the cold war got underway, the media in the United States moved from the periphery of the economy to dead center. This in turn led to concentration of ownership of media outlets on an unprecedented scale, and news organizations more often than not became part of conglomerates whose primary business interest was profit maximization—not the pursuit of truth.

In sum, after World War II, unbridled corporatism came to mix with an American quest for power and the result has been a journalistic deference to the statist perspective that was given new life by the events of 9/11. Such a combination produced the sort of journalism that preceded the 2003 war with Iraq.

It should be understood that "deference" means a yielding to the judgment of another. It does not mean abject submission, which is why journalism can and frequently does eventually turn on public officials. The problem is that such a turn occurs only *after* a policy is in deep trouble and policy elites have first opened the debate themselves.[31] Rarely, if ever, does this occur *before* a policy disaster occurs. And there is the rub.

The Future

What then are the prospects for coverage of the next decision by an American executive to pursue the path of war, whether in the best interests of the country or not? They are not promising, if Overholser's blunt appraisal is on the mark: "We [the press] are deflected from our driving purpose—to keep readers informed. Our newsrooms are marketing-driven and profit-oriented, our staffs are poorly trained and dispirited. We dread being called liberal, we hate to be seen as unpatriotic. We fear making our readers unhappy, we don't want to insult powerful people—indeed we seem to yearn for their favor."[32]

A more optimistic view is held by those who argue that the outpouring of studies, reports, and books dealing with the abject failure of intelligence preceding the 2003 war, taken together with ample evidence of the Bush administration's obsession with wrongheaded assumptions about the world in general and the Middle East in particular, will keep such a debacle from happening again. In sum, lessons will be learned.

I cannot help but remember a conference panel I participated on in Rome, in 1991, not long after the Gulf War. The other participants were retired *Times'* political columnist Tom Wicker, noted peace researcher Johan Galtung, and the *Times'* Judith Miller. Miller's remarks that day in a way presaged her work on WMDs and Iraq more than a decade later, a body of work that would come under sharp criticism by such as Massing. While Wicker and I politely begged to differ with Miller, it is what Galtung had to say that I remember most clearly. He closed the session with the judgment that all the well-reasoned critiques of press coverage and U.S. war policies in the world will not change journalistic behavior. No lessons from the Gulf would be learned anymore than they had been in Vietnam. The press would behave pretty much as it had in 1990–91 the next time around.

I thought Galtung unduly pessimistic at the time, but that was before the second war with Iraq. I have since been forced to reconsider.

Notes

1. C. Hedges, *War is a Force That Gives Us Meaning* (New York: Public Affairs, 2002).
2. S. Kull, "Misperceptions, the Media, and the Iraq War," *Report of the Program on International Policy Attitudes*, October 2, 2003 <http://www.pipa.org/OnlineReports/Iraq/Media_10_02_03_Report.pdf> (accessed October 28, 2003).
3. S. Kull, C. Ramsay, and E. Lewis, "Misperceptions, the Media, and the Iraq War," *Political Science Quarterly* 118: 4 (December 1, 2003): 569–598.
4. S. Kull, "U.S. Public Beliefs on Iraq and the Presidential Election," *Report of the Program on International Policy Attitudes*, April 22, 2004 <http://www.pipa.org/OnlineReports/Iraq/IraqReport4_22_04.pdf> (accessed May 3, 2004).
5. Kull et al., "Misperceptions," 596.
6. Ibid., 597.
7. Ibid., 593.
8. W. A. Dorman and S. Livingston, "The Establishing Phase of the Persian Gulf Policy Debate," in *Taken by Storm: the Media, Public Opinion, and U.S. Foreign Policy in the Gulf War*, ed. W. L. Bennett and D. L. Paletz (Chicago and London: University of Chicago Press, 1994), 63–81.
9. A. Gershkoff and S. Kushner, "The 9/11-Iraq Connection: How the Bush Administration's Rhetoric in the Iraq conflict Shifted Public Opinion," Paper presented at the Annual Meeting of the Midwest Political Science Association, Chicago, April 2004 <http://www.princeton.edu/~agershko/GershkoffKushnerIraqPaperJuly142004.pdf> (accessed July 21, 2004).
10. Ibid., 3.
11. Ibid., 13.
12. Ibid., 9.
13. Ibid., 11–12.
14. Ibid., 12.
15. Ibid., 14.
16. Ibid., 15.
17. C. Mooney, "Did Our Leading Newspapers Set Too Low a Bar for a Preemptive Attack"? *Columbia Journalism Review* March 2/April 2004 <http://cjr.org/issues/2004/2/mooney-war.asp> (accessed July 15, 2004).
18. G. Cranberg, "Colin Powell and Me: Tracking the Secretary's Crucial UN Speech," *Columbia Journalism Review* 1 (January/February 2004): 60–61.
19. M. Massing, "Now They Tell Us: The American Press and Iraq." *New York Review of Books* 51, no. 3 (February 26, 2004).
20. Ibid., 26.

21. M. Massing, "Now They Tell Us: The American Press and Iraq." *New York Review of Books* 51, no. 3 (February 26, 2004), 28.
22. Ibid., 61.
23. S. Moeller, "Media Coverage of Weapons of Mass Destruction," *Report* of the Center for International and Security Studies, University of Maryland, March 9, 2004 <http://www.cissm.umd.edu/documents/wmdstudy_full.pdf> (accessed July 7, 2004).
24. C. Layton, "Miller Brouhaha." *American Journalism Review* 6, (August/September 2003) <http://www.ajr.org/article.asp?id=3057> (accessed July 15, 2004).
25. Editors, "The Times and Iraq," *The New York Times*, May 26, 2004, A10.
26. D. Okrent, "The Public Editor—Weapons of Mass Destruction? Or Mass Distraction?" *The New York Times*, May 30, 2004, Sec.4, 2.
27. Editors. "A Pause for Hindsight," *The New York Times*, July 16, 2004, A20.
28. H. Kurtz, "The Post on WMDs: An Inside Story," August 12, 2004, A01.
29. P. Krugman, "To Tell The Truth," *The New York Times*, May 28, 2004, OpEd.
30. P. Waldman, "Why the Media Don't Call It As They See It," *The Washington Post*, September 28, 2003, B04.
31. W. L. Bennett, "The News About Foreign Policy," in *Taken by Storm: the Media, Public Opinion, and U.S. Foreign Policy in the Gulf War*, ed. W. L. Bennett and D. L. Paletz (Chicago and London: University of Chicago Press, 1994), 12–40.
32. G. Overholser, "If Only They Knew Cowed Media Can't Keep Americans Informed," *Columbia Journalism Review* 6, November/December 2002 <http://www.cjr.org/issues/2002/6/voice-over.asp> (accessed July 15, 2004).

Chapter Two

Strange Bedfellows: The Emergence of the Al Qaeda–Baathist News Frame Prior to the 2003 Invasion of Iraq

W. Lucas Robinson and Steven Livingston

In 1990, as the United States prepared for war with Iraq, the Bush administration launched a sophisticated communication campaign intended to convince a wary Congress and a concerned public that war with Iraq was necessary. The administration contracted with Hill & Knowlton, a public relations firm, and the Wirthlin Group, a polling and issue development firm, to help formulate a communication strategy that justified a war intended to drive Iraq from Kuwait, a country few Americans had heard of in 1990. As Dorman and Livingston recount, the 1991 Gulf War was framed around carefully selected and test-marketed themes taken from World War II.[1] Through a coordinated media communication campaign, Saddam was rhetorically paired with Hitler.

Different frames were used in the lead-up to the 2003 Iraq war. The second Bush administration emphasized rhetorical frames that highlighted Iraq's alleged possession of Weapons of Mass Destruction (WMDs) and its links with terrorism in general and the Islamist fundamentalist terrorist group Al Qaeda in particular.

This chapter argues that WMDs and Iraq's alleged ties to terrorist organizations were strategically selected justifications for invading Iraq in 2003, just as the Saddam-as-Hitler frame was strategically selected in 1990–91. Moeller has presented an exhaustive review of media coverage of the WMDs justifications for the war.[2] She found that the American news media generally accepted the administration's claims regarding Iraq's alleged possession of WMDs without critical evaluation. We are interested in asking similar questions about American news coverage concerning the other half of the administration's justification for war with Iraq. When did the Al Qaeda/ Baathist connection frame begin to appear in the media? Who were the primary proponents of the frame? How common were counterframes, that is, statements that tended to question or undermine the suggested links between terrorists and Saddam's regime? When counterframes appeared, who offered them? Political communication scholars call the appearance of two or more frames in tension with one another "framing contests." In these terms, we explore the robustness of the framing contest concerning the Baathist–Al Qaeda ties in the lead-up to the war in Iraq. We will track the emergence, depth, and prominence of the Iraq/terror frame and gauge the role of media in propagating the frame and any counterframes that might have appeared along the way.

Measuring Misconceptions

In October of 2003, the University of Maryland's Program on International Policy Attitudes released a report concerning "misperceptions" on Iraq.[3] In it, Steven Kull, the project director, listed a number of widely held myths concerning the war and the events leading up to it. He noted, for example, that in the run-up to the war significant portions of the public "believed that Iraq was directly involved in the September 11 attacks and that evidence of links between Iraq and al-Qaeda have been found, that weapons of mass destruction were found in Iraq after the war and that Iraq actually used weapons of mass destruction during the war, and that world public opinion has approved of the US going to war with Iraq."[4]

What explains these misperceptions? While available data do not allow us to offer a definitive answer to this question, we can suggest that part of the answer is found in the processes of news production routines and public knowledge dynamics. A long established axiom of state–media relations in the United States is that the news media provide a privileged position to officials as news sources. Most news most of the time comes from official sources. This position provides officials with ample opportunities to shape and frame public debate regarding war and other pressing policy matters.[5] This means that rather than being ill informed, Americans, holding the sort of erroneous views expressed in the survey results above, are quite possibly reflecting what they have heard and read in the news. It is important to keep in mind that frames do not necessarily populate the public mind with the truth. Rather, frames help a overwhelmed public organize and store information.[6] They help us "make sense of the world." Sense-making can just as well involve belief in far-fetched notions, as well as verified truths. More than one witch has been burned at the stake in the belief that she was the nefarious fount of some mysterious malady.

Following Robert Entman's definition, a frame involves "selecting and highlighting some facets of events or issues, and making connections among them so as to promote a particular interpretation, evaluation, and/or solution."[7] The most effective frames are not "truthful," per se, but "culturally congruent." As Entman notes, "The most inherently powerful frames are those fully congruent with schemas habitually used by most members of society." Conversely stated, "when it comes to news of matters incongruent with dominant schemas, common culture blocks the spread of many mental associations and may discourage thinking altogether."[8] Culturally congruent frames simply make sense, regardless of their verisimilitude. "Terrorists are bad guys. Terrorists attacked the United States on September 11, 2001. Saddam is a bad guy. Ergo, Saddam is a terrorist; Saddam must have been behind 9/11." The question before us in this chapter is whether news tended to reinforce this syllogism.

Going to War

The September 11, 2001 attacks marked a major shift in the Bush administration's focus in foreign affairs. Earlier discussions of ballistic missile defense and reducing the number of American peacekeepers gave way to a singular focus on terrorism. Although Afghanistan was the first war fought by the US in the new "war of terrorism," the long-simmering conflict with Iraq was almost immediately subsumed in the global war against terrorism. Exactly why this was the case remains unclear. To many observers, there were no obvious links between the 9/11 attacks and Iraq. As the *New York Times* stated in an editorial published following the release of the official report of the *National Commission on Terrorist Attacks Upon the United States*,[9] "It's hard to imagine how the commission investigating the 2001 terrorist attacks could have put it more clearly yesterday: there was never any evidence of a link between Iraq and Al Qaeda, between Saddam Hussein and Sept. 11."[10] In October 2004, Defense Secretary Donald Rumsfeld acknowledged that he too was unaware of any intelligence that linked the September 11 attacks and Iraq. Yet despite the unequivocal findings of the Commission Report and the occasional statement disassociating Iraq from the attack, the American public remained flummoxed. A *Newsweek* poll in September 2004—well after the release of the Commission Report—found that 42 percent of Americans, including 32 percent of Democrats, still believed that Saddam's regime was "directly involved" in the 9/11 attacks.[11] Again, we are left wondering how such a counterfactual assertion remained so firmly fixed in the consciousness of so many Americans.

One explanation is that contrary to the findings of the report, officials in the Bush administration were just as reluctant to believe—or at least publicly acknowledge—that Iraq was not involved in the 9/11 attacks. The *9/11 Commission Report* describes how President Bush speculated immediately after the attack whether Saddam Hussein's regime might have been involved. Richard Clarke, the former chief of counterterrorism for both Presidents Bush and Clinton, described how on the evening of September 12 President Bush told him to explore possible Iraqi links to 9/11. The president asked Clarke to "go back over everything, everything. See if Saddam did this." Clarke said he was "taken aback, incredulous." He told the president, "Al Qaeda did this." "I know, I know, but . . . see if Saddam was involved. Just look. I want to know any shred . . ." Responding to the president's directive, Clarke's office sent a memo to National Security Advisor Condoleezza Rice on September 18, titled "Survey of Intelligence Information on Any Iraq Involvement in the September 11 Attacks." Zalmay Khalilzad, the chief National Security Council staffer on Afghanistan, agreed with Clarke's assessment that only minimal anecdotal evidence linked Iraq to Al Qaeda. As the 9/11 Commission noted, "The memo found no 'compelling case' that Iraq had either planned or perpetrated the attacks."[12] This conclusion did not deter the administration from making repeated references to links between 9/11 and Saddam Hussein's regime. But what sort of references were made?

Our central point is that official rhetoric concerning the war in Iraq employed frames that reinforced mental associations between Iraq and the 9/11 attacks. Officials in the Bush administration, including the president himself, assiduously avoided using direct causal terms ("Saddam was responsible for the 9/11 terrorist attacks"). Instead, loose associative terms were used. An example of this occurred during the first presidential debate between President Bush and his Democratic Party challenger, Senator John Kerry, when Bush said the "enemy" attacked us and we had to go to war. The implied enemy was Iraq. In this instance, Senator Kerry responded by pointing out that Al Qaeda, not Iraq, attacked the United States. But this sort of rejoinder to the Bush administration's tendency to frame Iraq with 9/11 was rare. The question examined in this chapter is whether the news tended to reinforce this syllogism.

Methods

Using the Lexis-Nexis news archive, we analyzed 2662 articles that appeared in the *New York Times* between September 11, 2001 and December 31, 2002. The search was designed to count any story that mentioned both Iraq and "Al Qaeda or bin Laden or terrorism." Our unit of analysis is an individual story. This includes all *Times* articles, columns, and editorials mentioning both Al Qaeda and Iraq. In a limited number of cases the search protocol included erroneous "stories" that were actually tables of contents or correction indices. While these references find their way into our aggregate (quantitative) review of the newspaper (insignificantly affecting some of the cited percentages), they are not referenced as part of the qualitative discussion.

The qualitative analysis below draws on coding completed for this project during the spring of 2004. Each story was examined for frames that connected Osama bin Laden and/or Al Qaeda with Iraq and/or Saddam Hussein. We have called this the Baathist–Al Qaeda frame. We also examine where such a connection is refuted for information concerning the source and history behind the claim. Iraq's connections to generic or general "terrorism" are not counted. We are instead focusing more narrowly on specific associations with Al Qaeda and on the 9/11 attacks.

Iraq in the Press: September 2001–September 2002

Almost immediately, analysts quickly identified Al Qaeda and Osama bin Laden as the most likely perpetrators of the September 11 attacks. Feature length articles on bin Laden and Al Qaeda appeared as early as September 14, 2001. Many of these reports mentioned Al Qaeda's prior attacks on the American destroyer *USS Cole* in October 2000. But what about Iraq during this initial period following the attacks on New York and Washington? We found that, on the whole, very few assertions of a *direct* connection between Al Qaeda and the Baathist government in Iraq were made in the period reviewed. By direct links we mean statements that explicitly assert a connection between Al Qaeda, 9/11, and Iraq. Instead, what we found were frequent associational links among Al Qaeda, Saddam's Baathist regime, and the 9/11 attacks. In such a framing structure, the most efficient and culturally congruent logic suggested an operational collaboration between two otherwise ideologically antagonistic foes. The belief that two feared enemies of the United States were themselves friends makes sense. Our enemies must be friends. Indeed, in the eyes of some, they were one and the same. Al Qaeda and Saddam constituted an undifferentiated evil other.

But this sort of cognitively congruent but factually erroneous association did not materialize out of the ether. Instead, it was created and reinforced by frequent cues that subtly linked Al Qaeda with Saddam's regime. A close examination of the evidence suggests that the eventual mental associations between Iraq and 9/11–Al Qaeda developed over time. In September 2001 following the attacks, 100 articles appeared in the *New York Times* that dealt with both Iraq and the topic of terrorism (see graph 2.1).

Of those 100 articles, three made a direct connection between Iraq and the attacks or Al Qaeda, though nearly all referenced the assertion that Iraq

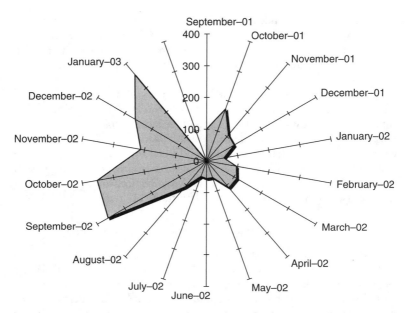

Graph 2.1   The chart represents the number of references to both Iraq and <Qaeda or Laden or Iraq> in the *New York Times*, from September 11, 2001, to January 31, 2003. The radial chart begins at the centre-top of the diagram (September-01, or the analogue clock position of "12:00") and reads clockwise. The data used to create this diagram is discussed in the text.

was known to "harbor" terrorists. In this same time, few Americans made a connection between Iraq and 9/11. On September 24, 2001, the *Times* reported that just six percent of Americans believed Saddam Hussein had something to do with the 9/11 attacks while better than 50 percent held Osama bin Laden responsible. It seems clear from these numbers that in the immediate aftermath of the 9/11 attacks most Americans understood that Iraq was not involved with the 9/11 attacks, either directly or indirectly. How then did nearly half of all Americans by March 2004 come to believe it did?

The Emergence of the Al Qaeda/Baathist Connection Frame

An alleged connection between Iraq and Al Qaeda was first described in the *Times* on Wednesday, September 19, 2001. David Johnston and James Risen reported that American intelligence officials said "Mohamed Atta, a suspected hijacker on American Airlines Flight 11, which struck the World

Trade Center North Tower, met several months ago with an Iraqi intelligence official in Europe."[13] Until the Johnston–Risen article, Iraq was generally referenced (at least in the *Times*) along with Al Qaeda and the Taliban in connection with states that "supported terrorism." Therefore, the Baathist–Al Qaeda news frame was incomplete for only eight days after the New York/Washington attacks.[14] Iraq's connection to Al Qaeda appeared again on September 20 when administration officials publicly discussed the impact of striking Iraq in response to September 11. Assistant Secretary of Defense Paul Wolfowitz argued at that time for a broad military response, which would have included Afghanistan, and "terrorist bases" in Iraq and Lebanon. Dick Cheney is described as having allied himself with Collin Powel when he said that the administration did not have evidence that linked Hussein with September 11. (For his part, President Bush avoided drawing any such links in his address to a joint meeting of Congress on the twentieth of September.)

In discussing Iraq in connection to the 9/11 attacks, officials folded Iraq into the rhetorical frame of terrorism. The editors and reporters at the *Times* clearly agreed, though they argued at the time that the correct course of action was to limit a military response to "those complicit in the World Trade Center and Pentagon attacks."[15]

The first discussion of the problematic nature of linking Saddam Hussein with Osama bin Laden (our counterframe) came on September 23, 2001, when Serge Schmemann[16] wrote that, ". . . this being the Middle East, there is the fact that many of the despots regarded as sponsors of terror, like Saddam Hussein of Iraq or Bashar al-Assad of Syria, are secularists who would not bemoan the eradication of Osama bin Laden, any more than Mr. Arafat would mourn the passing of Hamas, or Egypt's Hosni Mubarak that of the Islamic Brotherhood."[17] This was the first example of a counterframe to the Baathist–Al Qaeda frame propagated by the *New York Times*.

On September 24, William Safire's editorial ("The Ultimate Enemy") made the connection between Al Qaeda and Iraq (and WMDs) very clear. Having spoken with members of the Kurdish resistance in the north or Iraq, Safire concludes "the Iraqi dictator has armed and financed a fifth column of Al Qaeda mullahs and terrorists that calls itself the Jund al Islam ('Soldiers of Islam'). Its purposes are to assassinate the leaders of free Kurdistan, to sabotage the relief efforts of the U.N. and to whip up religious fervor in that free Muslim region. That is how Saddam plans to reconquer the no-flight zone that has been a thorn in his side for a decade."[18] Initially parameters for future discussions appear to have been defined by the members of the Bush administration—Powell on the one hand and Wolfowitz on the other. But the members of the press moved quickly, and soon made their own claims regarding the likelihood of a Saddam/bin Laden connection.

The arguments for war in Iraq moved ahead despite the fact that on October 11 intelligence officials found that Iraq was uninvolved with the September 11 attacks. ". . . intelligence agencies from a number of countries, including some with a strong desire to see Mr. Hussein fall, have concluded that Iraq was not involved in the attacks, nor has he given harbor to al Qaeda, Mr. bin Laden's organization."[19] A former Clinton official is citied in the same article as having said that, "We would have loved to have found an Iraqi connection."[20] Despite these findings, the possibility of such a link persisted.

By mid-October, the press had latched on to the dichotomy of opinions that supposedly existed between the Powell (described as the "seasoned diplomat") and Wolfowitz (labeled the "hard liner") camps. The tit-for-tat public debate as to whether the war on terrorism should be expanded to include Iraq begins with a debate as to whether Hussein had anything to do with the September 11 attacks but eventually switches to accusations concerning involvement in terrorism in general, which has been accepted by all since the attacks took place (and even earlier, as described by Livingston and Dorman[21]).

With the anthrax bioterrorism scare, a focus on Iraq's "bioterrorist" past reemerged. Once again, the CIA claims that they have no evidence pointing to Iraq's involvement in the present domestic issue, though this is generally reported following a discussion of Iraq's history with such substances. Richard Butler, then ambassador in residence at the Council on Foreign Relations, makes the most direct connection between Al Qaeda and Iraq that had, up to that point, been made:

> If the scientific path leads to Iraq as the supporter of the anthrax used by the terrorist mailers in the United States, no one should be surprised. Meetings between Mohamed Atta, who is thought to have been an organizer of the Sept. 11 attacks, and an Iraqi intelligence official in Prague in June 2000 may have been an occasion on which anthrax was provided to Mr. Atta. There have also been reports of meetings between senior Iraqi intelligence officials and members of Al Qaeda.[22]

Butler's comments are important for two reasons: first, they make a reference to the (by then commonly alleged) Mohamed Atta meeting—a theme that is picked up repeatedly in the weeks and months to come; second, they suggest that even if Iraq wasn't responsible for the Anthrax attacks, they had the capacity to be responsible for future attacks.

The Atta meeting was also discussed by Safire on October 22. He asked, "Does this web of eavesdropped-upon communication provide proof positive of Saddam's participation in the Sept. 11 attack? No indisputable smoking gun may ever be found, but it is absurd to claim—in the face of what we already know—that Iraq is not an active collaborator with, harborer of, and source of sophisticated training and unconventional weaponry for bin Laden's world terror network."[23]

The Atta meeting was "confirmed" by Czech authorities on October 26, 2001. A 2000 word, page 1 article by Patrick Tyler and John Tagliabue is led by the following headline: "Czechs Confirm Iraqi Agent Met with Terror Ringleader."[24] The article is the most comprehensive account of any potential connection between Al Qaeda and the Baathist government in Iraq. The article is exceptional because the authors make various attempts to balance the possibility that such a link does not exist. But the headline gives away the story's primary message: raising "fresh questions about whether Iraq's foreign intelligence arm in recent years established secret ties with Al Qaeda, Osama bin Laden's organization." In fact, these comments grossly overstate "what was known." The *9/11 Commission Report* eventually discounts the meeting between Atta and the Iraqis.[25] But earlier, this story provided the clearest link between 9/11 and Iraq.

Our search criteria netted 174 articles in October 2001. The vast majority of these articles once again made only a general connection between Iraq and the issue of terrorism (this time often relating to Anthrax) and frequently touched on Al Qaeda in the same article. But connections were once again limited: we found six articles that present the Baathist–Al Qaeda news frame and five articles that present a counter frame (suggesting that such a link was unlikely). In short, in October the Baathist–Al Qaeda frame and its counterframe were almost at parity.

Yet by November 2001, survey results reported by Gallup found that that 74 percent of the American public favored sending American troops back to the Gulf to remove Hussein. This was up 22 percent from February 2001.[26] On November 8, reports of new evidence of a Baathist–Al Qaeda link were presented in a relatively lengthy (1300 words) page-1 article in the *Times*. In an interview with two Iraqi defectors set up by Iraqis in the United States who were seeking to overthrow Saddam Hussein, Chris Hedges reported on terrorist training camps that were said to have trained Islamic radicals.[27] The story garnered serious public attention, including this response from a reader in Vermont: "The news from credible defectors that Iraq is training terrorists (front page, November 8) should remove any doubts about the dangerous nature of the Iraqi regime and the need to eliminate it."[28]

The Al Qaeda–Baathist frame grew more common in November, though it must be said that the counterframe was just as common. We found six stories that cite a connection in November and seven that disputed it. But once again the most common mentions of Iraq and terrorism were indirect rather than causal. In November, a total of 107 stories discuss Iraq and the subjects of terrorism and/or Al Qaeda.

In December 2001, 100 *New York Times* articles met our search criteria. By December the news began to reflect the administration's emphasis on Iraq. The links between WMD, Iraq, and terrorism were by this time made with growing frequency. In one of the articles, at that time Russian President Vladimir Putin is quoted twice as doubting a connection between Iraq and the type of terrorism that Americans need to be concerned with. Two other articles appearing toward the end of the month point out the counter-intuitive connection between Osama bin Laden and Saddam Hussein: one discusses the radically different leadership styles and religious beliefs of the two men.[29] The second outlines Osama bin Laden's rise to power in the Arab world, and goes on to suggest that he in fact proposed to oust Hussein from Kuwait himself, to "avoid the indignity of allowing an army of American unbelievers to enter the kingdom."[30]

By March, the American public was solidly supportive of a second war with Iraq. Public opinion polling found that 88 percent of Americans believed that it was an important (very and/or somewhat) to remove Hussein from power.[31] The politics in Europe, in particular Great Britain, were also shifting slightly by the end of the year. Once strongly opposed to war in Iraq, "Mr. Blair said there was a clear need to deal with weapons of mass destruction but also an imperative to move forward only 'within the deliberation and consultation of key allies.' "[32]

References to connections between Iraq and terrorism decline slightly in the early winter of 2002, but began to climb again between February and April, after the president's "State of the Union" address, on January 27, 2002. The Pew Research Center reported on January 17, 2002, "the president will have the nation's full attention on Jan. 29 when he delivers his first official State of the Union address. Fully 54% of Americans say the speech is more important than such speeches in past years."[33]

This speech, delivered before Congress, and heard live by millions of Americans, clearly linked the issues of weapons of mass destruction and terrorism to Iraq. Bush said, after brief mentions of Iran and North Korea, that:

> Iraq continues to flaunt its hostility toward America and to support terror. The Iraqi regime has plotted to develop anthrax, and nerve gas, and nuclear weapons for over a decade. This is a regime that has already used poison gas to murder thousands of its own citizens—leaving the bodies of mothers huddled over their dead children. This is a regime that agreed to international inspections—then kicked out the inspectors. This is a regime that has something to hide from the civilized world.
>
> States like these, and their terrorist allies, constitute an axis of evil, arming to threaten the peace of the world. By seeking weapons of mass destruction, these regimes pose a grave and growing danger. They could provide these arms to terrorists, giving them the means to match their hatred. They could

attack our allies or attempt to blackmail the United States. In any of these cases, the price of indifference would be catastrophic.[34]

Bush's speech—now widely known as the "Axes of Evil" speech—is one the clearest examples we find of the administration linking the subject of terrorism with Iraq, though efforts were obviously made to do so throughout the fall (of 2001). The 2002 State of the Union address was followed by an appearance by George Tenet before Congress where he made similar remarks. Colin Powel found himself in the limelight early in February 2002, as he made his strongest statements to date on the role of Iraq in the War on Terrorism. Even General Tommy Franks, the head of the military's Central Command, referenced Iraq in testimony before the Armed Services Committee (cited in the *Times*).

Collectively these events are reflected by the *Times* coverage, as the incidence of Iraq and Al Qaeda/bin Laden/terrorism climbs to 96 in February, 110 in March, and 110 again in April, 2002 (see graph 2.1). In May, there are 56 such stories; another 55 appeared in June, and 52 in July. While nearly all of these stories spend significant time discussing the issue of terrorism, and frequently referencing that subject in connection to Iraq (and vice versa), focus on Al Qaeda–Baathist frame is not commonly employed between February and July of 2002. There are three stories in February that do so, and three stories that refute the claim. In March there are two stories that suggest an Al Qaeda–Baathist link, and one that provides a counter argument. In April there are five stories, in May there are two, in June none, and in July two (and no counterframes).

Our analysis has found that—contrary to popular perception—in the year after 9/11 there were very few direct links made (as a statement by either reporters or officials) between Iraq and Al Qaeda. However, we have shown that the suggested and stated links to terrorism in general are very frequent (2662 stories between September 11, 2001 and December 31, 2001). But this in itself is not new, as Iraq has for years been associated with terrorist activity. All the same, it is somewhat alarming that in August 2002, a "near-unanimous majority [86 percent of the U.S. public] believes that the Iraqi government trains and supports terrorists."[35] In September of that year, *Newsweek* reported that 75 percent of Americans believed that "Saddam Hussein's regime in Iraq is harboring al-Qaeda terrorists and helping them to develop chemical weapons."[36]

One explanation for this is that the American people who were misinformed did not receive their misinformation from the *New York Times*. This is likely partially true, as Kull shows that television viewers (*Fox* in particular) were more likely to draw a link between Al Qaeda and Iraq. That only explains part of the story: 40 percent of those who say they receive most of their information from print media associate Iraq with Al Qaeda.[37] Thus, one cannot blame the significant misconception regarding Iraq's role in 9/11 on *Fox* News alone.

What we believe may actually be happening here is a syllogism of associative blame. The "terrorist" Americans generally know is Osama bin Laden and, more generally, Al Qaeda. The *Times*, and the Administration, made thousands of loose references to Iraq in articles that are primarily on the subject of terrorism, bin Laden, and/or Al Qaeda. Importantly, this happens in the reverse scenario as well (a story about Iraq that loosely deals with Terrorism and/or Al Qaeda). The newspaper also makes reference to the subjects of terrorism, Al Qaeda and Iraq in a diverse array of articles. In the new world of post–September 11, everything relates to terrorism, "Osama," and Iraq; stories on the environment, education, religion, economics, local politics, energy consumption, travel, and insurance premiums have all at one point (or many) referenced these two subjects. Also, as shown by Livingston and Dorman, the public has experienced over a decade of media and institutional references to Iraq as a terrorist state.[38] Furthermore, the American public has been told that biological and chemical weapons are the weapons of terrorists and terrorist states—Iraq, thanks to Anthrax and WMD more generally, is consistently referenced on this subject.[39]

The *New York Times'* Mea Culpa

Throughout the spring of 2004, the news media engaged in an unprecedented evaluation of their own news coverage of Iraq. The *New York Times* was no exception. On May 26, 2004, the *Times* published a critical evaluation of its own coverage; it found that its reporting was, "not as rigorous as it should have been." "In some cases, information that was controversial then, and seems questionable now, was insufficiently qualified or allowed to stand unchallenged. Looking back, we wish we had been more aggressive in re-examining the claims as new evidence emerged—or failed to emerge."[40] As critical as this self-assessment was, the analysis places little emphasis on the issue of an Al Qaeda–Baathist connection. It seems the journalists were duped by "informants" with an agenda, much the same way American Intelligence officials were.

Both the *Times'* self-assessment and the *Times'* ombudsman Daniel Okrent find that no one individual or group was responsible for the credulous reporting that appeared in the paper leading up to (and during) the war in Iraq. Okrent writes that, "The failure was not individual, but institutional."[41] Okrent does however delve deeper into these institutional errors than the editorial board commited. He cites five ailments that appear to have afflicted the paper, much of which rightly lands on the doorstep of the editors, not the reporters. In general, Okrent argued that the misconceptions concerning Iraqi links to 9/11 were as much a result of what was not said as it is of what was said. Our findings broadly support this conclusion.

Erroneous links were also allowed to stand because of a political environment that discouraged dissent. As Paul Krugman commented, "After 9/11 much of the press seemed to reach a collective decision that it was necessary, in the interests of national unity, to suppress criticism of the commander in chief."[42] But, importantly, he continues: "After 9/11, if you were thinking of saying anything negative about the president, you had to be prepared for an avalanche of hate mail. You had to expect right-wing pundits and publications to do all they could to ruin your reputation, and you had to worry about being denied access to the sort of insider information that is the basis of many journalistic careers."[43] Krugman even more bluntly ties the issue of Iraq to September 11 than either the editorial board or Okrent.

It is likely that all of these explanations come into play when looking at the *Times'* coverage of the lead-up to war in Iraq.[44] Our analysis of the *Times'* coverage suggests that there were additional issues at play: the commingling of references (essentially overly simplistic news frames) reinforced the erroneous impression that Saddam was behind the 9/11 attacks on Washington and New York. Sadaam was deemed guilty by the American public by verbal association—propagated both by the Bush administration and the *New York Times*. This finding is supported by polling data, which indicates that the public responded by shifting both their stated understandings and opinions concerning the war with Iraq, in the name of countering terrorism.

Notes

1. S. Livingston and W. Dorman, "Historical Content in the News: Policy Consequences for the 1990/91 Persian Gulf Crisis," in *Taken By Storm: The Media, Public Opinion, and U.S. Foreign Policy in the Gulf War*, ed. W. Lance Bennett and David L. Paletz (Chicago: University of Chicago Press, 1994).
2. S. Moeller, *Media Coverage of Weapons of Mass Destruction* (Maryland: Centre for International and Security Studies at Maryland, 2004) <http://www.cissm.umd.edu/documents/WMDstudy_full.pdf>
3. S. Kull, *Misperceptions, the Media and the Iraq War*, Maryland: Program on International Policy Attitudes (PIPA), 2003. <http://www.pipa.org/OnlineReports/Iraq/Media_10_02_03_Report.pdf>
4. Ibid.
5. L. Sigal, *Reporters and Officials* (Lexington, MA: D.C. Heath, 1973); S. Livingston, *The Terrorism Spectacle* (Boulder, CO: Westview Press, 1994); W. L. Bennett, "Toward a Theory of Press-State Relations," *Journal of Communication* 40:2 (1989): 103–125; S. Livingston and W. L. Bennett,

"Gatekeeping, Indexing and Live-Event News: Is Technology Altering the Construction of News?" *Political Communication* 20:4 (2003): 363–380.
6. D. Graber, *Processing Politics: Learning from Television in the Internet Age* (Chicago: University of Chicago Press, 2001).
7. R. Entman, *Projections of Power: Framing News, Public Opinion, and U.S. Foreign Policy* (Chicago: University of Chicago Press: 2004), 5.
8. Ibid., 14.
9. 9/11 Commission, *The 9/11 Commission Report*, Washington, DC: 2004.
10. Editorial, "The Plain Truth," *The New York Times*, June 17, 2004, section A.
11. R. Rich, "This Time Bill O'Reilly Got it Right," *The New York Times*, September 19, 2004, section 2.
12. 9/11 Commission, *The 9/11 Commission Report*, 2004.
13. D. Johnston and J. Risen, "Officials Say 2 More Jets May Have Been in the Plot," *The New York Times*, September 19, 2001, section B.
14. Not insignificantly, Iraqi state-run television immediately hailed the New York and Washington attacks as the "operation of the century," lending weight to the (now generally dismissed) argument that Hussein and bin Laden were closely linked.
15. Editorial, "Calibrating the Use of Force," *The New York Times*, September 22, 2001, section A.
16. S. Schmemann, "Aftermath: The Target; Israel as Flashpoint, not Cause," *The New York Times*, September 23, 2001, section 4.
17. Schmemann is now the Editorial page editor in the *International Herald Tribune*, and has received a Pulitzer Prize (International Affairs) for coverage of the reunification of Germany.
18. W. Safire, "The Ultimate Enemy," *The New York Times*, September 24, 2001, section A: Safire repeats this claim a week later, in W. Safire, "For a Muslim Legion," *The New York Times*, October 1, 2001, section A.
19. R. Bonner, "A Nation Challenged: Baghdad; Experts Doubt Iraq had Role in Latest Terror Attacks," *The New York Times*, October 10, 2001, section B.
20. The issue comes up again, on October 12, 2001: "British officials emphasize that there is no evidence to link Iraq to the Sept. 11 attacks, although they acknowledge that any such evidence would put Mr. Blair in an awkward position. 'I know it's a common right-wing view in Washington that Iraq must be involved,' a senior British official said. 'But it's a big jump in logic, and to go bomb Iraq for this attack would be daft. We need to deal with the job in hand first, Osama bin Laden and his organization, Afghanistan and its future.' " S. Erlanger, "Britain Presses U.S. for 'Nation Building' in Afghanistan," *The New York Times*, October 12, 2001, section A.
21. Livingston and Dorman, "Historical Content in the News."
22. R. Butler, "Who Made Anthrax," *The New York Times*, October 18, 2001, section A.
23. W. Safire, "Advance the Story," *The New York Times*, October 18, 2001, section A.
24. P. Tyler and J. Tagliabuem, "Czechs Confirm Iraqi Agent Met with Terror Ringleader," *The New York Times*, October 27, 2001, section A.
25. 9/11 Commission, *The 9/11 Commission Report*, 2004.
26. Polling Report.com, "Iraq, page 7" <http://www.pollingreport.com/iraq7.htm>

27. C. Hedges, "Defectors Cite Iraqi Training for Terrorism," *The New York Times*, November 8, 2001, section A.
28. D. Katcoff, Letter to the Editor, *The New York Times*, November 10, 2001, section A.
29. E. Sciolino and A. Mitchell, "Calls for New Push Into Iraq Gain Power in Washington," *The New York Times*, December 3, 2001, section A.
30. D. Jehl, "A Nation Challenged: A Critic; After Prison, a Saudi Sheik Tempers His Words," *The New York Times*, December 27, 2001, section B.
31. Gallup Poll, from Polling Report.com <http://www.pollingreport.com>
32. W. Hoge, "Blair and Putin Agree to Begin Exchange of Intelligence Data," *The New York Times*, December 23, 2001, section A.
33. The Pew Research Center For The People & The Press, *Unusually High Interest in Bush's State of the Union: Public Priorities Shifted by Recession and War*, January 17, 2002 <http://www.pewtrusts.com/ideas/ideas_item.cfm?content_item_id=886&content_type_id= 18&issue_name=Public%20Opinion%20and%20Polls&issue=11&page=18&name=Public%20Opinion%20Polls%20and%20Survey%20Results>
34. G. W. Bush, "The President's State of the Union Address," Washington, DC, 2002 <http://www.whitehouse.gov/news/releases/2002/01/20020129-11.html>
35. PIPA, Program on International Policy Attitudes, *Conflict With Iraq* <http://www.americans-world.org/digest/regional_issues/Conflict_Iraq/linkstoTerr.cfm>
36. Ibid.
37. S. Kull, "Misperceptions, the Media and the Iraq War," 2003.
38. Livingston and Dorman, "Historical Content in the News."
39. S. Moeller, *Media Coverage of Weapons*.
40. Editorial, "The Times and Iraq," *The New York Times*, May 26th, 2004, section A.
41. D. Okrent, "Weapons of Mass Destruction? Or Mass Distraction?" *The New York Times*, May 30, 2004, section A.
42. P. Krugman, "To Tell the Truth," *The New York Times*, May 28, 2004, section A.
43. Ibid.
44. All of this self-loathing attracted the attention of other pundits in Washington and around the world. The United Kingdom's left leaning *The Guardian* reported on both the editorial boards and Okent articles, concluding that the "latest act of self-flagellation has further bruised *The New York Times's* reputation. The newspaper is still struggling to recover from the revelation last year that a reporter, Jayson Blair, invented elements of dozens of stories." D. Teather, "New York Times says it was duped by Pentagon 'cunning,'" *The Guardian*, May 31, 2004 <http://www.guardian.co.uk/international/story/0,3604,1228111,00.html>

CHAPTER THREE

THE WHOLE WORLD IS WATCHING,
BUT SO WHAT? A FRAME ANALYSIS
OF NEWSPAPER COVERAGE OF
ANTIWAR PROTEST

Ronald Bishop

Introduction

In his landmark book, *The Whole World is Watching*, Todd Gitlin argues that journalists at mainstream news organizations "process" activism; they control and diffuse the image they create of it, "absorb what can be absorbed into the dominant structure of definitions and push the rest to the margins of social life."[1] Journalists "undermine whatever efforts movements make to present a general, coherent political opposition." Reporting suggests that activists focus on "single grievances which the system, however reluctantly, can correct without altering fundamental social relations."[2]

Further, since the attacks on New York and Washington, the federal government, in its zeal to end terrorism, has circumscribed protest and made it more difficult for journalists to cover the military. Perhaps the government's efforts were unnecessary. Journalists tripped over each other to try and show their patriotism. MSNBC, for example, now promotes itself as "America's News Channel." Journalists defended the practice of wearing and displaying flags during newscasts in the name of bringing the nation together.

Gitlin concluded in 1980 that reporters undermined efforts by Students for a Democratic Society (SDS) to "present a general, coherent political opposition." Activists focused on "single grievances," which the significant institutions in society could address, without "altering fundamental social relations"—in other words, without real change. Editors at the *Times* were concerned that conservatives would charge that the paper was sympathetic to Communism, Gitlin claims. Reporters also suggested that SDS was intent on persuading young people to avoid the draft.

True to their job routines, reporters covered "the event, not the condition; the conflict, not the consensus; the fact that 'advances the story,' not the one that explains it," as Gitlin argues.[3] Reporters paid significant attention to spokespeople who "most closely matched prefabricated images of what an opposition leader should look and sound like: theatrical, bombastic, and knowing and inventive in the ways of packaging messages"[4] for maximum media exposure. The group's goals and ideas were less important because they made for less than compelling stories.

This drive to find compelling stories is echoed in Jack Lule's contention that news is composed of what Lule believes are "enduring, abiding stories."[5] In covering what goes on in the world, journalists tap "a deep but nonetheless limited body of story forms and types." This reliance on certain story forms is no surprise, writes Lule, given our love for and dependence on stories. "We understand our lives and our world through story," he argues.[6]

Perhaps more important for our journey, Lule contends that familiar myths—"the great stories of humankind"[7] regularly come to life in news reporting. Lule defines myth as "a sacred, social story that draws from archetypal figures to offer exemplary models for human life."[8] Myths empower society to express its "prevailing ideals, ideologies, values, and beliefs." They are, Lule writes, "models *of* social life and models *for* social life."[9] Myths are not evident in every news story, as Lule cautions, but in many instances journalists draw upon "the rich treasure trove of archetypal stories" to revisit those shared stories that help us make sense of the world in which we live.

Lule's analysis of news produced seven of what he calls "master myths" found in news—the *victim*, whose life is abruptly altered by "the randomness of human existence"; the *scapegoat*, deployed in stories to remind us of "what happens to those who challenge or ignore social beliefs"; the *hero*, there to remind us that we have the potential for greatness; the *good mother*, who offers us "a model of goodness in times when goodness may seem in short supply"[10]; the *trickster*, a crafty figure who usually ends up bringing "on himself and others all manner of suffering," thanks to his crude, boorish behavior; the *other world*, that enables us to feel good about our way of life by contrasting it, sometimes starkly, with ways of life elsewhere (as when reporters wrote of life in the former Soviet Union during the cold war); and the *flood*, in which we see the "destruction of a group of people by powerful forces," often because they have "strayed from the right path."[11]

Lule's assessment meshes with Richard Campbell's claim that while we talk a good game when it comes to dissent, we truly recognize it only when it is situated in what John Fiske calls our "communal allegiances."[12]

Our path in life should not be so unique that we forget how to conform, or that journalists are unable to make it seem like we conform. While journalists routinely criticize powerful institutions, they do so by "personalizing" issues or casting them as battles between individuals. This shift comes with a cost. "The social origins of events are lost," he writes.

In his excellent book on the mythic structure of the CBS newsmagazine *60 Minutes*, Campbell argues that the program's reporters and producers managed to portray former president Ronald Reagan as embodying Middle American values despite the fact that they he and his wife Nancy were wealthy, powerful people. Similarly, in a story on Joyce Brown, a homeless person from New York, the program symbolically moved her from the "periphery" to "a central location more in line with a consensual middle ground."[13]

Those from the periphery fare better with journalists, Campbell argues, if they are able to make their arguments in a "common sense" fashion. Thus, reporters tend to draw nonconformist arguments "back into the consensus," as Stuart Hall argues.[14] By doing so, these individuals manage to reaffirm the communal allegiances noted by Fiske. Individuals who espouse excessively radical viewpoints are "not allowed to speak directly, but are reported, that is, mediated if their point of view is represented at all," argues Fiske.[15]

It is against this backdrop that I explore print coverage of organized opposition to President Bush's decisions to go to war with Afghanistan and with Iraq. I sought answers for a single research question: What new frames of protest activity have emerged from newspaper coverage of protests against wars in Afghanistan and in Iraq?

Method

A series of Lexis-Nexis searches performed between December 2002 and May 2003, and my own collection efforts, produced 178 articles on antiwar protest in the United States from the nation's major daily newspapers that appeared between September 12, 2001, the day after the terrorist attacks on the United States, and May 1, 2003, the day President Bush announced the end of the War on Iraq from the deck of the USS *Abraham Lincoln*, a Navy aircraft carrier.

I performed a frame analysis on the work of these print journalists. Erving Goffman wrote that a frame is a "principle of organization which governs events—at least social ones—and our subjective involvement in them."[16] Frames enable us to "locate, perceive, identify, and label a seemingly infinite number of concrete occurrences."[17] We use frames to make sense of the world around us. Journalists create news frames to help them "simplify, prioritize, and structure the narrative flow of events."[18]

As Oscar Gandy explains, frames "are used purposively to direct attention and then to guide the processing of information so that the preferred reading of the facts come to dominate public understanding."[19] Jamieson and Waldman contend that frames are "the structures underlying the depictions that the public reads, hears, and watches."[20] Framing takes place when journalists "select some aspects of a perceived reality and make them more salient in a communicating text." By attempting to organize experiences for readers, journalists "highlight some bits of information about an item that is the subject of communication, thereby elevating them in salience."[21]

At the heart of my analysis is the use by reporters of "keywords, stock phrases, stereotyped images, sources of information, and sentences that provide reinforcing clusters of facts or judgments" about protestors[22] and their actions. My analysis has at least some of its roots in the constructionist paradigm most recently discussed by D'Angelo. Through their reporting, D'Angelo argues, journalists provide "interpretive packages" of the positions of parties who have a political investment in an issue. In so doing, journalists "both reflect and add" to what Gamson and Mogdiliani call the "issue culture"[23] of a topic. Of particular relevance for my research are the constructionist contentions, summarized by D'Angelo, that frames limit our political awareness, hamstring activists, and "set parameters for policy debates not necessarily in agreement with democratic norms." Journalists select sources because they are credible, and believe that even a longstanding frame has value because it contains "a range of viewpoints that is potentially useful" to our understanding of an issue.[24]

While I agree that frames can lead to a preferred reading of a story, I am not convinced that these frames are arrived at consciously by journalists. Frames are more a product of a story's unruliness and the reporter's need to meet deadlines than of a journalist flexing a particular ideology. While the framing elements identified by Gitlin (e.g., trivialization, disparagement, reliance on official sources) were evident throughout the coverage, the goal of this research was to track the emergence of significant new frames. As Carey notes, it is vital to explore "how the media of communication enter a ceaseless temporal process of change rather than a static snapshot of having or not having an effect."[25] Each article was reviewed line-by-line; I looked for recurring themes, and developed a set of new frames that were fine-tuned as the analysis progressed.

Domestication

In the weeks immediately following the September 11 attacks, journalists suggested that the antiwar movement was limited to, and contained by, college campuses. Lawrence led a *USA Today* article this way: "Remember the peace movement? It's back on campus."[26] But where protest was more passionate in the 1960s, today's would-be student activists are more cautious. Lawrence reminded readers that protestors "are a distinct minority," and that their initial efforts represented only a single "wave of antiwar sentiment." College students across the country "are being taught to question and analyze," as if professors had only recently begun to encourage their students to think critically.[27] In interviews, Todd Gitlin urged students to offer "realistic alternatives" to the use of military force. Students took Gitlin's words to heart, treating protest like a resume entry. "Protesting is a niche activity," said a professor interviewed by Kate Zernike of the *New York Times*. "There are some people who do drama, some people who do protest, other people who drink too much."[28]

Washington University on September 20 closed an antiwar rally to the media in order to protect students, despite claims that rallies at more than 140 other schools had been "completely peaceful,"[29] as Susan Thomson wrote in the *St. Louis Post-Dispatch*. Organizers did not contest the decision out of the desire "to keep a good relationship with the administration." As war with Iraq loomed, even college campuses saw a drop-off in peace activism. Kevin Fagan of the *San Francisco Chronicle* interviewed a man who was taken aback by the lack of protest activity at Berkeley. He "expected to see strident action at the nation's most famous fount of war protests past— not the placid vision of students milling around tables offering information on meditation, dance concerts, and business associations."[30] The lack of activism seemed to disappoint reporters, if only because protest was not taking place where they expected.

By the late fall of 2002, campus protest activity had escalated. But reporters emphasized that the teach-ins and Internet-driven protests were a different brand of activism, decidedly less antagonistic than campus protest during the 1960s—"scrappy but impassioned,"[31] wrote Amy Argetsinger of the *Washington Post* in March 2003. Nine months earlier, the *New York Times'* Tamar Lewin described a student who "never showed the faintest interest in political protest,"[32] but yet found himself taking part in a walk for peace. Teach-ins and coalition building replaced violent clashes with police. Today's student, suggests Lewin, has no experience with political protest. One activist found support for the antiwar cause, but also unwillingness to get involved. "They're so used to feeling helpless that it doesn't occur to them to be outraged."[33] This line of reasoning suggests that this kind of activism did not occur in the 1960s, or was drowned out by more aggressive antiwar protestors.

This is evidence of a new frame: *domestication*—docile, cooperative protestors who want to get their message out, but want to do it without challenging authority. The mood on campus, wrote Dick Reavis of the

San Antonio Express-News was "milder" than during the Vietnam War.[34] The *San Francisco Chronicle*'s Tyche Hendricks, writing a month after the 9–11 attacks, noted that the mood of antiwar protestors was "circumspect and less militant"[35] than in the past. Manny Fernandez of the *Washington Post* told readers that protestors at one 2003 rally had "done a good job of policing themselves."[36] Reporter Terry Rodgers described protestors at San Diego peace rally as "a bit lethargic in the brilliant sunshine and balmy weather."[37]

A key part of this frame is the suggestion that activists were either young or old—and thus inexperienced, or unable to generate the same passion as in protests past. A group of protestors at a Boeing plant in St. Louis "peered through the plant's gates to check for tractor-trailers," as if they were children. The *Chronicle*'s Rob Morse wrote in October 2002 about "a bunch of people (OK, a bunch of old ladies, mostly)"[38] protesting in San Francisco. "All ages were represented" there, "but the predominant hair color was gray." Older protestors were willing, but not always able. At least one, suggested Brian Albrecht of the *Cleveland Plain Dealer* in his story about a Washington DC protest, had "to sit this one out."[39] A *New York Times* reporter wrote about an 83-year-old woman on her way to her "regular gig"[40]—a vigil outside a local post office. "What they lack in number, they make up for in dedication,"[41] wrote a *New York Times* colleague.

Colleges and universities were, for a time, hotbeds of protest, but the protestors there, at least initially, were tame. Protestors felt "powerless,"[42] wrote Dick Reavis of the *Express-News*. Even the Anti-Capitalist Convergence, identified by the *Washington Post*'s Manny Fernandez and Petula Dvorak in 2001 as "one of the most radical" anti-globalization groups, agreed to "tone down their tactics to emphasize their theme."[43] To draw more mainstream supporters, "organizers from groups on the far left . . . have downplayed some of their potentially alienating political positions,"[44] wrote the *Post*'s Monte Reel.

By the time larger protests were underway, the domestication was complete. Reporter Chris Jenkins described a protestor's attempt to find hot chocolate at a march held on a frigid day in January 2003. "Toe and foot warmers, triple-layered thermal underwear and rabbit-fur hats were as common as 'No War for Oil' and 'Money for Jobs, Not For War' signs and antiwar leaflets,"[45] he wrote. Within the domestication frame, journalists suggest that activists lack the hardiness and aggressiveness of their predecessors. They're too cold, too concerned about finding food, and too willing to cooperate with law enforcement authorities to have any impact.

Anachronism

Protestors, young and old, took their cue, wrote journalists, from protests against the Vietnam War, signaling the emergence of an *anachronism* frame.

This new round of antiwar protests was "like a trip down protest lane,"[46] noted Michael Sneed of the *Chicago Sun-Times*. "All that's missing are Peter, Paul, and Mary singing 'Blowin' in the Wind' and Dr. Benjamin Spock urging them on,"[47] added Don Feder of the *Boston Herald* in November 2001. A little more than two years later, Peter, Paul, and Mary entertained at a protest vigil. The trio "mused that folk songs are always apt for political demonstrations,"[48] wrote Ian Shapira of the *Washington Post*.

Students at Berkeley were ready to protest, said one to Tyche Hendricks of the *San Francisco Chronicle*, because "it's kind of what you do when you're here."[49] Mark Brown, a columnist for the *Chicago Sun-Times*, wrote that support for retaliation "is a pretty strong insult to a child of the 60's with sympathies in the antiwar movement of the Vietnam War era."[50] Reporter Kevin Fagan noted that protestors "hauled their protest signs out of the closet"[51] when the United States attacked Afghanistan. The possibility of mass protest caused a *Cleveland Plain Dealer* reporter to remember "the scent of burning draft cards."[52]

By spending so much time talking about the past, reporters enabled President Bush to ram home the point that protestors were outside the mainstream. By challenging the president, protestors were clearly "going against the national tide." Marginalization was furthered by name calling: "liberal-leaning activists";[53] "these people,"[54] or "the usual suspects," to use Brown's words.[55] Bob Dart, a reporter for *Cox* Newspapers, said the protestors were "out of step with most of their fellow citizens."[56] James Sweeney of the *Cleveland Plain Dealer* mimicked Dart: "[n]ever have they seemed more out of step with the general public."[57] In many instances, it was just name-calling, later, it turned into a frame all its own: the methods used by protestors were outdated. Either protestors were old farts or they were technologically savvy, emotionally detached young people.

Journalists made only passing references to protests that have taken place between the end of the Vietnam War and the beginning of the War in Iraq.[58] This created the impression that the protests against the wars in Afghanistan and Iraq came from out of the blue and that opponents of our involvement in the wars were coming together just for this purpose. This approach mutes protest by failing to recognize ongoing opposition to government policy. A *Washington Post* article reported that "peace activism, often a faint presence among recent protests,"[59] was pushing aside anti-globalization protests, as if these efforts could not coexist.

A protestors' length of service to the cause of peace became a tool of denigration in the hands of some journalists.[60] "Veterans of peace groups from the past," wrote Dick Reavis, "acknowledged that their reconstituted movement 'has grown a bit rusty.' "[61] James Sullivan of the *San Francisco Chronicle* wrote about "a coterie of veteran underground newspaper publishers" who banded together to print an antiwar newspaper. Two of the publishers ran into each other, Sullivan wrote, the day after the September 11 attacks, and realized "that it was time to crank up the old counterculture presses." Sullivan described one of the publishers "shuffling around the bookstore in his stocking feet while a friend pasted up pages in the back."[62]

Such a description suggests that the publishers, while energetic and dedicated, are hopelessly outmanned and hampered by antiquated methods and equipment. They may be wasting their time, suggested Fagan of the *San Francisco Chronicle in 2002*, since protests "have become so old that some police officers privately call the usual crowds 'professional protestors' who show up no matter what the cause."[63]

Ambivalence

Along with domestication comes another frame: *ambivalence*. Many protestors struggled with their opposition to war. The *New York Times'* Elizabeth Becker noted that a "mostly young crowd" of protestors were trying to "walk a fine line"[64] between respecting September 11 victims and their families and opposing Bush's plans to go to war. In many stories, activists were forced to defend their patriotism.[65] "We are all hit in our Americanness,"[66] said a Berkeley professor to a *San Francisco Chronicle* reporter. Protestors grappled with the tension between their reactions to the September 11 attacks and their desire to work for peace. Ann McFeatters of the *Pittsburgh Post-Gazette* commented that activists were "torn between their desire for justice and their aversion to military strikes to get it."[67]

Tyche Hendricks of the *San Francisco Chronicle* described protestors who were "uncertain how the United States should be responding to the terror." The director of the American Friends Service Committee told a reporter that "being antiwar doesn't make us anti-American,"[68] a sentiment echoed by a protestor interviewed by Valerie Schremp of the *St. Louis Post-Dispatch*: "I'm not anti-American. I would be the first one to go to war if my country were attacked."[69]

The ambivalence of protestors made it harder for them to get their message across. Reporters suggest that they struggle with the supposed failure of anti-Vietnam War activism. For example, Kevin Fagan of the *San Francisco Chronicle*, noted in 2002 that it was difficult for protestors "to attract a wide following when you try to explain how you can oppose attacking enemies of America while still feeling patriotically supportive of the country."[70] Interviewed by a *Chicago Sun-Times* reporter, Todd Gitlin said protestors would be done in by their radicalism, a fate that befell antiwar protestors in the 1960s. Activists should be trying to recruit "people to a banner that looks more like the American banner and doesn't appear to be a slap at patriotism."[71] Thus, even Gitlin is suggesting that 1960s antiwar activism, was almost always violent and certainly not mainstream. This makes it harder for today's protestors to put on even a slightly aggressive, slightly anti-American face. After all, as one high school junior and ROTC member put it in an interview with two *Sun-Times* reporters, "if you're proud of your country, you have to defend it."[72]

A key theme within the ambivalence frame was the assertion by journalists that protestors were not patriotic. This is certainly not a new idea, but a few of the features that accompany the emergence of this theme set it apart. Supporters of the war were portrayed as simplistically as the protestors. Opponents defended the country in a tame and controlled manner; many articles described equal parts support and rejection. "They have been met with a mix of thumbs ups and thumbs down,"[73] wrote the *New York Times'* Jane Gordon about some diehard Connecticut protestors. In many cases, confrontations between protestors and their adversaries often were reduced to a series of physical gestures. Howie Padilla of the *Minneapolis Star-Tribune*, for example, wrote of "jeers of profanity" and "looks of disdain and disbelief."[74] A man quoted by San Diego reporter Dana Littlefield called the protestors "quasi-hippies."[75]

Several journalists recalled how opponents made obscene gestures at protestors.[76] "Some onlookers waved their middle fingers at the protestors, but others raised their fists in solidarity,"[77] wrote a reporter for the *Seattle Times*. "Attack Iraq, you Girl Scouts!"[78] shouted a man at protestors during a rally covered by the *San Francisco Chronicle*. Douglas Belkin of the *Boston Globe* told of activists sharing stories "of peace signs being ripped off doors and extended middle fingers being proffered through windshields in response to peace-nik bumper stickers."[79] A woman in an SUV rolled down the window of her SUV to ask protestors at the Golden Gate Bridge, wrote Jim Zamora and Kelly St. John of the *Chronicle*. "Why did you do this? You ruined my day. What was the point?"[80]—casting the act of protest as an inconvenience.

Most striking was the fact that reporters allowed that the "protest means that you don't support the troops" line of reasoning to entrench itself in their stories, often unchallenged. Thus, those who opposed the war were automatically in a defensive position. Opponents of the war, wrote *Wilmington News Journal* reporter Cris Barrish, recognized that their views were not popular. "But they bristle at the suggestion they are disloyal Americans,"[81] he wrote. Some chose to speak out, others kept their opinions to themselves. A student interviewed by Columbus, Ohio, reporter Alice Thomas said that she and her fellow activists were labeled terrorists "because our government equates dissent with terrorism."[82]

Many of those who opposed the protestors sided with the government, but showed their support not by attacking the protestors directly, but by playing the unity card. Protests, wrote the *Columbus Dispatch*'s Andy Netzel, quoting an individual critical of the protestors, "did a disservice to the country by dividing it when everybody should be pulling together."[83] Others, like a 19-year-old Coast Guard seaman apprentice interviewed by the *Chronicle*'s Elizabeth Fernandez, exaggerated the age of the protestors and of their ideas: "There's a generation gap going on here. I see a lot of old people who probably haven't been protesting since Vietnam."[84] Thus, journalists suggest protestors' lack of patriotism stemmed as much from the fact they were rusty as from their radical ideology.

Selfishness

Coverage of protest also revealed a *selfishness* frame, in which protestors were depicted as self-indulgent—the "me" generation and the baby boomers fresh from the therapist's couch. For some protestors, their activism was "an emotional outlet,"[85] as one reporter told a reporter for the *San Francisco Chronicle*. "As for why people do it," said one protestor, "I think it's 50 percent for themselves and 50 percent for other people." Don Feder of the *Boston Herald* chided "professional pacifists" for resurrecting "the moldy clichés and self-righteous pieties of the 1960's."[86] Protestors were described as self-indulgent. "It's group therapy in a way, but what's the point?"[87] said one protestor interviewed by the *San Francisco Chronicle*. The antiwar sentiment in the Bay Area, wrote reporter Laurel Wellman, "is as much a product of pop psychology as it is of reality."[88] Lacking a viable solution, activists "tell us we need to examine our own attitudes."

Such a suggestion is not portrayed as constructive criticism; instead, it is "therapy-derived." The "pop psychology of personal empowerment," wrote Wellman, led activists to believe that they could impact America's foreign policy. Today's activists see September 11 "as an unprecedented opportunity for personal growth."[89] In a 2001 editorial, Debra Saunders of the *San Francisco Chronicle* wrote, "It's all about their feelings. Their superior feelings."[90] Everyone should "bow because they experience doubt, sadness, revulsion" toward the Taliban, but "manage to throw in a kind word about the Afghan civilians for whom they claim to be champions," Saunders noted. "Because they are so special, others should not rain on their orgy of self-congratulation."[91]

After the orgy, suggested Don Feder, protestors returned home "in their VW buses to well-heated homes, paid for with jobs dependent on reliable energy supplies."[92] Liz Bowie of the *Baltimore Sun* wrote about "peaceniks" who "now own SUV's and fly antiwar car flags."[93] One wonders if reporters would suggest that the activists described by Gitlin would abandon their cause when they realized they were missing classes and were cold, as journalist

Alice Thomas noted.[94] Without the threat of a draft, a point made by several journalists,[95] young protestors were reduced to calling their parents on cell phones to let them know where they were, noted Jim Kirksey of the Denver Post.[96]

Younger protestors, wrote Michele Melendez of the *Seattle Times*, came from "the first generation to value the needs of the individual over the good of the group."[97] Protest, said a professor to reporter Vikki Ortiz, is "more personal and private and community-oriented, a little less policy-oriented."[98] One college student, in an article by the *Pittsburgh Post-Gazette's* Bill Schackner, offered advice to organizers on how to drum up interest: "You give people free food. It doesn't matter what kind."[99] For others, being able to fit a protest rally into one's travel itinerary was of paramount importance. Tourists emailed an organizer interviewed by the *Washington Post's* Evelyn Nieves in 2003, were "thrilled that they'll be able to squeeze in an antiwar rally while they're in town."[100]

Whatever their itineraries hold, wrote Nieves, protestors "want to be a part of the antiwar events taking place this weekend around the globe."[101] This frame undermines protest by making it seem as thought protest is just another entry on a resume, or a stop on a tour—something to do, rather than something to actually believe in. It also converts protest into a theme park attraction, as if stopping to see an antiwar rally will be the high point of a vacation.

Diversity

By discussing such a wide range of people and organizations, reporters gave the impression that the antiwar effort was too broad, too *diverse*—there were too many competing points of view to form a coherent action plan.[102] Writing about organized labor's burgeoning opposition to the war, Joe Garofoli of the *San Francisco Chronicle* described a January 2003 rally this way: "Marching side-by-side in Saturday's antiwar rally in San Francisco: pro-Palestinian supporters, Earth-loving environmentalists. And Joe Six-Pack?"[103]

In an editorial, Michelle Goldberg of the *Chicago Sun-Times* wrote that the International Action Center's website was "a cornucopia of left-wing rhetoric,"[104] suggesting that the arguments were dated and ideologically out of reach. "It was quite a mix,"[105] wrote Rob Morse about the range of people at a San Francisco rally. Zamora and St. John described a coalition of activists that "represents a variety of left-wing causes."[106]

To Matt Stearns of the *Pittsburgh Post-Gazette*, protestors "seemed to be a combination of kids on a lark and committed idealists."[107] Michele Ames and Vladimir Kovalev of the *Rocky Mountain News* described protestors who "came in diamond rings and nose rings. They wore spike hair and pinstriped suits." Their ranks ranged "from the bizarre to the brash."[108] And while hip-hop artists were lending their talents to activism, "it is by no means a united front,"[109] wrote two reporters from the *New York Daily News*. Bob Dart of Cox Newspapers wrote that an early protest in Washington included "[a]ngry, black-clad activists and gray-bearded hippies" as well as "possessors of earnest young faces with multiple piercings."[110]

About one of the first antiwar protests, the *Chicago Sun-Times*' Mark Brown wrote that the "participants were young and old and in between, many of them veterans of past antiwar efforts or other social justice protest."[111] Ann Rodgers-Melnick of the *Pittsburgh Post-Gazette* noted that protestors "ranged from multiple-pierced college students to white haired nuns."[112] In short, protestors could not decide what they wanted. They had no focus. An *Omaha World-Herald* editorial told readers that "some elements of an antiwar movement kicked off their protest with statements that almost anyone could agree with."[113] Protestors "demanded everything from a Palestinian homeland and an end to racial profiling to better public hospitals and rights for Afghan women,"[114] wrote Dart. Taken together, these comments suggest that protestors were mercenaries, opportunistically shifting ideological gears.

Reporters discounted protestors' ability to rally a variety of people to their cause; instead, they focused on how this variety might make it difficult to achieve their goals. An activist quoted by Alice Thomas said "[S]ome folks are antiwar, and some are pro-peace. They sometimes meld well together and sometimes don't."[115] As a result, "the coalition doesn't always speak with one voice." Several journalists noted that protestors who had been planning demonstrations at a meeting of the International Monetary Fund (IMF) and the World Bank easily shifted their focus to the threat of war. The *Washington Post*'s Fernandez and Dvorak reported that the IMF/World Bank protests "have taken a new form as antiwar rallies."[116] Said one protestor to reporter Matt Stearns, "the antiwar stuff has become a lot more urgent."[117] And protestors observed by Fernandez and Dvorak soon traded in their gas masks for "guitars and banners."[118] These impressions suggest that activists are vagabonds, setting up shop at every opportunity.

When tensions escalated in the Middle East in March 2002, activists began demonstrating for peace. "And not long after," wrote Kevin Fagan of the *Chronicle*, "a loud, new element started picketing right alongside them: general peace activists."[119] Again, this suggests that activists are looking for a fight, no matter what it is, and do so without a sense of direction.

Strong, vocal antiwar organizations were replaced by Act Now to Stop War and Racism (ANSWER), an off-campus consortium that lacked direction, suggested San Antonio reporter Dick Reavis. The group's "origins and ultimate objectives are unclear to many in the peace movement."[120] Descriptions of the multigenerational nature of protest suggested that protestors were either longtime, frustrated protestors (veterans of Vietnam War protests) or just starting out. Older protestors were too busy teaching their young charges and softening their messages, and younger protestors too busy learning from the veterans and flashing their computer skills, to have significant impact. Where Gitlin argued that journalists undercut protest in part by suggesting protest was the province of angry white middle- and upper-middle-class college students, today's reporters achieve the same effect by suggesting that everyone is encouraged to find a place in the protest tent. Such breadth dilutes the impact of activism.

Self-Reflexivity

As the war with Iraq approached, reporters wrote more frequently about themselves—how they failed to offer sufficient coverage of protest, and how protestors schemed to use the media to spread their message. As part of this *self-reflexivity* frame, reporters detailed discussions among protestors about tactics and strategies. Martha Mendoza of the *Wilmington News Journal* invoked military terms, describing how activists used "buildup time" to "coordinate 'emergency response plans' to disrupt domestic military activity, tie up commerce,"[121] and get out their message. Since "many of the new techniques occur online and in closed-door meetings, organizers are aware that they need to increase the visibility and volume of their protests"[122] wrote Lynette Clemetson of the *New York Times in* 2003.

Andy Netzel of the *Columbus Dispatch* reported that protestors were concerned about how their actions would play with the public. "There are a lot of things in the newspapers and on TV showing how angry people are about the World Trade Center attack,"[123] said one protestor. Protestors in Boston "strove to be noticed" by "using jugglers, drums, cowbells, megaphones, and waves of chanting,"[124] noted Ellen Silberman of the *Boston Herald*. The *Philadelphia Inquirer's* Chris Gray took a more hi-tech tone, telling readers that the Internet, discussion groups, and chat rooms had converted protestors into "smart mobs,"[125] able to coordinate activities from their computers.

A veteran protestor, whose quote appeared more than halfway through the story, worried that technology was taking the community out of protest. Gray called this a part of the "generation gap" that separated old and young activists. Law enforcement officials matched protestors step for step, suggested reporters. Stories detailed preparations by police to keep a close eye on protest activity. "We've been preparing for this for a long time," said one.[126]

This frame includes discussion by reporters of the news media's role in helping—and hindering—the protests. "I learned at Monday's protest that

I'm just one of the 'corporate reporters' who is supporting" Bush "while glossing over the root causes in misguided American foreign policy,"[127] wrote Mark Brown of the *Chicago Sun-Times*. Protestors would not have the media to help them, as they did in Vietnam by sending home night after night of graphic images. The "kind of gut-wrenching TV that sustains protests"[128] would be missing from news media coverage, wrote the *Denver Post*'s Dave Curtin. "There may be no nightly news TV footage to rally protestors,"[129] wrote Joe Garofoli of the *San Francisco Chronicle*. Douglas Belkin of the *Boston Globe* commented that "the television cameras that breathe life into any demonstration"[130] did not make it to a January 2002 protest in Boston.

It was never made clear if protestors actually mastered how to attract the media, only that they had to learn how to do it. Garofoli quoted a Berkeley professor as saying that protest "will take innovative strategies that have to respond to situations that will be very fluid."[131] According to reporters, protestors could maximize their message only after developing appropriate skills. Large-scale protests "can be more easily organized today because of the spread of air travel and the rise of the internet,"[132] wrote Richard Louv of the *San Diego Union-Tribune*. The *New York Times*' Thomas Lueck noted that Internet-organized vigils offered protestors an alternative to more raucous street protests. Advances in communication enabled these organizations to "grow up overnight."[133] With the advent of CNN and the 24-hour news cycle, noted Louv, "public opinion can turn on a dime, for a war or against it."[134]

Until celebrities got involved, anyway. By October 2002, a growing number of artists, including actors Susan Sarandon, Tim Robbins, and Martin Sheen, came together to protest the war, signing a "Not in Our Name" declaration that appeared as an ad in major newspapers. Their involvement may have raised awareness of the antiwar cause, but it also per-suaded journalists to talk a great deal about their involvement, rather than the issues it raised. We learned that being an antiwar protestor was not good for one's career. "I would advise my clients to stay away from the topic,"[135] said a publicist interviewed by the *USA Today*'s Cesar Soriano.

Eventually, some protestors felt they had no choice but to adopt a more outrageous stance in order to attract media attention. One group of women, calling themselves "Unreasonable Women Baring Witness" used their bod-ies to spell out antiwar slogans, according to a story by the *Chronicle*'s Joe Garofoli. "They are bypassing mainstream media outlets they say are ignor-ing their pleas" for a more peaceful end to the Iraqi crisis. After CBS, the BBC, and several other broadcast journalists paid attention to their efforts, other groups of activists "have stripped from Montana to Florida."[136] Thus, this frame could just as easily have been called *process*.

Fits and Starts

Journalists described a movement that went through *fits and starts*. Even as war with Iraq loomed, protestors would begin, then stall, then start up again. Early on, protests were portrayed as scattered, small, and poorly organized. The *Washington Post* described "a loosely organized series of rain-soaked demonstrations that disrupted traffic, drew heavy police presence and resulted in few arrests."[137] "I think people haven't quite regeared,"[138] said one protestor interviewed by Dick Reavis. A college student from St. Louis told Susan Thomson of the *St. Louis Post-Dispatch* that the antiwar effort at his school was "just kind of people hanging out."[139] James Sweeney noted that protests in the Cleveland area were "small and muted."[140] And when protests drew more people, journalists sometimes failed to report that they were connected to the larger movement. Tara Burghart of the *Wilmington News Journal* described a "fresh round"[141] of protests in March 2003.

As protestors welcomed people from all walks of life, reporters suggested that this, too, caused sluggishness in the antiwar movement. Protesters at an antiwar rally hosted by Washington labor unions "were new to the antiwar scene—teachers in high heels, union bosses carrying briefcases and steel-workers in satin baseball jackets embroidered with union logos. The familiar protesters with drums and wild hair were there, too, but they were in the minority,"[142] wrote Petula Dvorak of the *Washington Post*.

Disorganization was another key theme within this frame. John Wildermuth of the *San Francisco Chronicle* noted that organizers of an early protest had not decided on a route for a September 2001 march.[143] The *Washington Post* reported in September 2002 that protestors had not yet selected a military installation for an upcoming protest.[144] Kevin Fagan of the *Chronicle* wrote that activist groups "that have carried the torch of nonviolence for decades have found a voice once again."[145] Still, it would take some time for that voice to be heard. "Their message will be tough to get across,"[146] wrote Fagan in a 2002 article about protests against the war in Iraq. As late as October 2002, wrote Maggie Haberman of the *New York Daily News*, "the activists are outnumbered by the apathetic"[147] on college campuses.

Coverage informed readers that protestors were gaining and then losing, momentum. Dick Reavis described "the revival of calls for antiwar activity."[148] One protestor told the *Washington Post* that apathy about the war was ending and that "what you see is a social consciousness and awareness that is beginning to spread."[149] A Berkeley alumnus interviewed by the *San Francisco Chronicle*'s Tyche Hendricks said that he believed "the antiwar movement is going to become quite substantial."[150] Hector Saldana of the *San Antonio Express-News* told his readers that "the current incarnation of the peace movement"[151] was taking shape.

But when President Bush was considering an attack on Iraq, journalists suggested that protestors had to once again start over. Richard Louv wrote that "a nascent antiwar movement has emerged."[152] Dave Curtin reported that demonstrations "are percolating"[153] on local campuses. Said one protestor quoted by Ames and Kovalev, "the feeling is starting to get out that this is truly a dangerous war."[154] Tanya Schevitz cited speculation that "over time, the antiwar activity could evolve into a movement like that opposing Vietnam."[155] Elizabeth Fernandez of the *Chronicle* wrote that "antiwar fever awoke over the weekend"[156] during an October 2002 march in San Francisco. Along the way, however, readers learned that an organization set up by activists in Ohio, "once the only speck of antiwar sentiment" at Ohio State, "has packed up and left, leaving peaceniks without a visible presence,"[157] noted Alice Thomas of the *Columbus Dispatch*.

Once the larger protests began, reporters suggested that protestors were not sure their efforts would change President Bush's mind. "Whether fatalistic or feeling they could still make a difference, Americans came from great distances"[158] to a March 2003 protest in Washington, noted Calvin Woodward of the *Wilmington News Journal*. A protestor told the *New York Times'* Lynette Clemetson in 2003 that "the government is going to do what they are going to do regardless"[159] of the impact generated by protest. "But at least we can try to make sure that people in other countries know that all Americans are not down with this war." By the winter of 2002, however, journalists were still reporting on "a new phase of coalition building around the antiwar movement,"[160] according to the *Times'* Clemetson. All the while, readers are encouraged to be on the lookout for activism that will truly make a difference. This frame suggests that it will never materialize.

Tabulation

Stung by criticism of their tendency to undercount protestors, reporters covering the massive antiwar protests in the winter of 2002 and spring of 2003 placed great importance on crowd estimates and the number of cities in which protests occurred, signaling the emergence of a *tabulation* frame. Instead of undercounting, they just counted; the size of the marches, both large and small, became a distraction to the issues raised by protestors. Reporters seemed to jump from suggesting the antiwar protest movement could not get started to describing it in fully realized form.

The *New York Times'* Robert McFadden described "throngs of chanting, placard-waving demonstrators" who protested in New York "and scores of cities across the United States, Europe, and Asia."[161] The *Times* reporter called it a "global daisy chain" of protests. On March 16, 2003, the *Washington Post* reported that "tens of thousands of protestors . . . surrounded the

Washington Monument and later the White House."[162] One Associated Press article turned the turnout into a contest, pointing out that Rome had the most protestors as part of a "global outpouring of antiwar sentiment."[163]

The *USA Today's* John Ritter told readers that a march in San Francisco drew 50,000.[164] Evelyn Nieves described 1,400 arrests, an attempt by 100 protestors to block the entrance to a Bechtel facility, and 1,000 protestors marching outside a government building in Los Angeles in 2003.[165] Norm Parish of the *St. Louis Post-Dispatch* described the efforts of 20 protestors to raise awareness of the antiwar side. Nearby, he noted, "about a dozen people proudly backed the war effort."[166] The number of arrests made during rallies is also a key element in this frame.

In the first six paragraphs of his story, the *New York Daily News'* Bob Kappstatter rattled off cities and numbers of protestors—"tens of thousands" in Melbourne, Australia, 50,000 in Berlin—leaving the reasons for the protests for later in the piece.[167] Robert McFadden of the *Times* blamed the undercounting on law enforcement officials and the protestors: "Crowd estimates are often little more than politically tinged guesses."[168]

By responding to early accusations of undercounting, journalists have again introduced themselves into the story. More than once, they quote protestors as saying that they realize they won't have any impact, but that they still feel motivated to do something—reinforcing the suggestion, raised earlier, that protest is somehow a casual activity. It is as if journalists are covering a fund-raiser for a nonprofit group or politician; the focus is on the race to raise money, not on real exploration of ideas.

Conclusions

I have explored the "issue culture" of protest that emerges from the frames developed by print reporters. Several important impressions stand out. First, the movement is large and encompasses a diverse range of people, but its diversity is just as much a weakness as it is a strength. Antiwar activism is too broad, lacks focus, and is on a never-ending quest to define itself. The movement was partially driven by an eclectic mix of aggressive young people and Vietnam War protest veterans whose zeal and computer-savvy on the one hand, and a tendency to go through the motions for old times sake on the other, hampered the movement's progress. Those from the "middle ground" who protested came to the movement suddenly, and at times did so only when protest fit their schedule. These frames suggest that activism is undertaken because it is fashionable.

Second, journalists went from undercounting protestors to focusing on the number of protestors at each rally and on the range of their activities. By the time the United States attacked Iraq, reporters were doing little more than telling readers how many protestors were protesting, where they were protesting, and how many were arrested. Missing was intelligent discussion of the issues raised by the protestors. Their arguments were reduced to chants, signs, and the phrase "no blood for oil." Further, protests against the Vietnam War served as an anachronistic springboard for reporters to discuss the diversity in the ranks of protestors, and at the same time, took the ideological teeth out of the ideas that motivated protest in the 1960s.

The "veterans" interviewed by reporters are stuck in the 1960s. They are still devoted to the cause, but are irrelevant. The use by journalists of Gitlin as a source is a somewhat disconcerting nod to the fact that 1960s style protest is not relevant, a device deployed by reporters to distract readers from their failure to explore the viewpoints offered by the protestors. Despite covering efforts by protestors to attract "middle America," stories tended to focus on preachers (veteran protestors) and students (their contemporary counterparts). Reporters also isolated antiwar protest, creating the impression that these sentiments spring up out of the blue and lack continuity with earlier antiwar activism. There was little discussion of demonstrations against the Persian Gulf War and none about antiwar sentiment directed toward Grenada, Somalia, Bosnia, or Kosovo.

Third, coverage suggests that the ambivalence felt by protestors about challenging their government lends at least some support to the idea that this round of protests was unpatriotic. Reporters give ample space and time to angry individuals who, in sometimes profane terms (and using profane gestures), question the patriotism and love of country shown by protestors. The pursuit of peace, at least as it was undertaken by the protestors, was unpatriotic. Exacerbating this tendency was the impression conveyed by reporters that celebrities damage the credibility of activists. For example, reporters wondered what qualified singer Sheryl Crow to use her guitar strap to make known her feelings about the war, and criticized more vocal celebrities like Barbra Streisand for being so vocal. Some news organizations asked us in polls whether we thought celebrities should speak out. Focusing on celebrities in this fashion trivialized and further domesticated opposition to the war.

Fourth, if protestors aren't old and irrelevant, they are faceless and violent. We can't identify with them because they are too busy running through the streets, joining themselves together with PVC pipe, chaining themselves to things and to each other, and blocking traffic. Further, today's protestors are well versed in how to use the media and technology to get their message across and to mobilize support.

Thus, while journalists provided a significant amount of protest coverage (speculation that must be confirmed by future research), they did so by developing a set of frames that extends the marginalization of antiwar protest first discussed by Gitlin. Even Gitlin has been domesticated.

Antiwar protest is still not patriotic, and is practiced by older, eccentric people. But the radicals still can't reach the suburban families—only the larger, faceless organizations like ANSWER can. These groups can generate attendance, journalists suggest, but have no real impact on policy. It is as if protestors are either going through the motions, are worried about fitting activism into their busy lives, or are protesting only because it is fashionable. Whatever the motivation, their efforts are colorful and well-organized, but fruitless. At least the frames explored by Gitlin in the 1960s were built, at least partially, on the idea that activism was having some impact.

Today, journalists suggest that protest has been, as John Thompson suggested in 1969, "infected by the worm of self-consciousness" by focusing in their coverage on how aware protest is "of its own technique and method."[169] Reporters treated these protests as if they appeared out of nowhere, not as an ongoing journey toward truth. This should not be a surprise, given the growing tendency of reporters to report on themselves and their performance. It is as if journalists place themselves and protestors in competing, though never touching, rhetorically drawn zones, like those seen at the Masters golf tournament and the 2004 political conventions. Protestors share the blame here—they are as self-reflexive and media conscious as the reporters who cover them. The positions of the protestors and the government are cobbled together by journalists to form a social drama—a good story, as Jack Lule would argue, one that continues to marginalize protestors. But that drama now includes a portrayal of protestors as going through largely anachronistic, largely fruitless motions.

Notes

1. Todd Gitlin, *The Whole World is Watching* (Berkeley: University of California Press, 1980), 5.
2. Ibid., 35.
3. Ibid., 122.
4. Ibid., 154.
5. Jack Lule, *Daily News, Eternal Stories* (New York: Guilford, 2001), 3.
6. Ibid., 3.
7. Ibid., 15.
8. Ibid., 17.
9. Ibid., 15.
10. Ibid., 24.
11. Ibid., 25.
12. Quoted in Richard Campbell, *60 Minutes and the News: A Mythology for Middle America* (Urbana, IL: University of Illinois Press, 1991), 242.
13. Ibid., 151.
14. Quoted in Campbell, *60 Minutes and the News*, 151.
15. Ibid.

16. Erving Goffman, *Frame Analysis: An Essay on the Organization of Experience* (New York: Harper Colophon, 1974), 11.
17. Ibid., 21.
18. Pippa Norris, "The Restless Search: Network News Framing of the Post-Cold War Period," *Political Communication*, 12 (1995): 357–370.
19. Oscar Gandy, "Epilogue," in *Framing Public Life*, ed. Stephen Reese, Oscar H. Gandy, and A. Grant (Mahwah, NJ: Lawrence Erlbaum, 2001), 365.
20. Kathleen Hall Jamieson and Paul Waldman, *The Press Effect: Politicians, Journalists, and the Stories that Shape the Political World* (New York: Oxford University Press, 2002), xii.
21. Robert Entman, "Framing: Toward Clarification of a Fractured Paradigm," *Journal of Communication*, 43 (1993): 51–58.
22. Ibid., 52.
23. William Gamson and Anthony Modigliani, "The Changing Culture of Affirmative Action," in *Research in Political Sociology (Vol. 3)*, ed. R.D. Braungart (Greenwich, CT: JAL, 1987).
24. Paul D'Angelo, "News Framing as a Multiparadigmatic Research: A Reponse to Entman," *Journal of Communication*, 52 (2002): 870–888.
25. James Carey, "The Press, Public Opinion, and Public Discourse: On the Edge of the Postmodern," in *James Carey: A Critical Reader*, ed. Eve Munson and Catherine Warren (Minneapolis, MN: University of Minnesota Press, 1997), 240.
26. Jill Lawrence, "Students Rally Against War," *USA Today*, September 20, 2001, 8A.
27. Ibid.
28. Kate Zernike, "With Current War, Professors Protest, as Students Debate," *The New York Times*, April 5, 2003, A1.
29. Susan Thomson, "Washington University Closes Campus During Peace Rally; Police Bar Reporter From Observing Event," *St. Louis Post-Dispatch*, September 21, 2001, B1.
30. Kevin Fagan, "Groups Prepare for Protests Against Military Action in Iraq," *San Francisco Chronicle*, September 17, 2002, A15.
31. Amy Argetsinger, "Campus Protests Show Passions, Divisions," *The Washington Post*, March 22, 2003, A29.
32. Tamar Lewin, "Seeds of Protest Growing on College Campuses," *The New York Times*, October 12, 2002, A4.
33. Ibid.
34. Dick Reavis, "New Antiwar Movement Slowly Takes Shape," *San Antonio Express-News*, September 20, 2002, 16A.
35. Tyche Hendricks, "Strikes Bring Long Muted Responses in Former Hotbed of Activism," *San Francisco Chronicle*, October 11, 2001, A17.
36. Manny Fernandez, "Antiwar Protests Continue in Capitol," *Wilmington News Journal*, January 20, 2003, A3.
37. Terry Rodgers, "Hundreds Protest Bombing by U.S.," *San Diego Union-Tribune*, October 14, 2001, B3.
38. Rob Morse, "Gray Hair, Canes on Front Line of Antiwar Protest," *San Francisco Chronicle*, October 9, 2002, A2.

39. Brian Albrecht, "Veteran Antiwar Activists Rejoin Fold," *Cleveland Plain Dealer*, October 20, 2002, A1.
40. Jane Gordon, "Antiwar Protests Spread Across State," *The New York Times*, March 30, 2003, 3.
41. Debra West, "Song of Antiwar Protests Rises in County," *The New York Times*, February 16, 2003, 14WC.
42. Reavis, "New Antiwar Movement," 16A.
43. Manny Fernandez and Petula Dvorak, "Without IMF, Protesters Giving Peace a Chance," *The Washington Post*, September 28, 2001, B1.
44. Monte Reel, "Organizers Aim for Loud Protest of War in Iraq," *The Washington Post*, October 25, 2002, B1.
45. Chris Jenkins, "In the Heat of Protest, Some Cold Discomfort," *The Washington Post*, January 19, 2003, A14.
46. Michael Sneed, "Anti-war Protest Just Like the Good Old Days," *Chicago Sun-Times*, September 29, 2002, 9.
47. Ibid.
48. Ian Shapira, "On the Mall, Songs of Old Carry Current Plea for Peace," *The Washington Post*, March 17, 2003, B1.
49. Hendricks, "Strikes Bring," A17.
50. Mark Brown, "Dissenters' Antiwar Slogans Just Don't Fit," *Chicago Sun-Times*, September 25, 2001, 2.
51. Kevin Fagan, "Israel-Palestine Issues Energizes Bay Area Peace Movement," *San Francisco Chronicle*, May 5, 2002, A3.
52. Albrecht, "Veteran Antiwar Activists," A1.
53. "Peace Advocates Oppose Calls For Retaliation; Campus Groups, Religious Leaders Urge Alternatives to Military Action," *Milwaukee Journal-Sentinel*, September 21, 2001, 8A.
54. "A Multi-Fronted War," *Omaha World Herald*, September 23, 2001, 12B.
55. Brown, "Dissenters' Antiwar Slogans," 2.
56. Bob Dart, "Washington Peace Rally Spotlights Minority View; America Prepares," *Atlanta Journal and Constitution*, September 30, 2001, 3A.
57. James Sweeney, "Giving Peace a Hand; Small Groups in Northeast Ohio Campaign Against Afghan Conflict," November 28, 2001, E1.
58. See Reavis, "New Antiwar Movement," 16A; Richard Stevenson, "Antiwar Protests Fail to Sway Bush on Plans for Iraq," *The New York Times*, February 19, 2003, A1.
59. Fernandez and Dvorak, "Without IMF," B1.
60. See Gwen Florio, "2,000 Protest Plans for War on Iraq," *Denver Post*, September 29, 2001, B4 and Valerie Schremp, "Anti-war Demonstrators Target Boeing Missile Plant in St. Charles," *St. Louis Post-Dispatch*, October 2, 2002, B2.
61. Reavis, "New Antiwar Movement," 16A.
62. James Sullivan, "Antiwar Press Cranks Up," *San Francisco Chronicle*, September 28, 2001, C1.
63. Fagan, "Israel-Palestine Issue," A3.
64. Elizabeth Becker, "Marchers Oppose Waging War Against Terrorists," *The New York Times*, October 1, 2001, B7.

65. See Samuel Autman, "UCSD Crowd Rallies in Support of Bush; Conservatives Say War is Right Action," *San Diego Union-Tribune*, October 24, 2001, B3.
66. Tanya Schevitz, "Targeting Terrorism; Campus Reaction," *San Francisco Chronicle*, October 7, 2001, A9.
67. Ann McFeatters, "What Does Loyalty Really Mean?" *Pittsburgh Post-Gazette*, October 7, 2001, A18.
68. Rodgers, "Hundreds Protest Bombing," B3.
69. Schremp, "Anti-war Demonstrators Target," B2.
70. Fagan, "Israel-Palestine Issue," A3.
71. Michelle Goldberg, "Antiwar Groups Too Extreme?" *Chicago Sun-Times*, October 20, 2002, 21.
72. Ana Mendieta and Kate Grossman, "Local Antiwar Protests Attract Thousands," *Chicago Sun-Times*, March 21, 2003, 11.
73. Gordon, "Antiwar Protests Spread," 3.
74. Howie Padilla, "About 300 Minneapolis Marchers Seek End to 'Immoral and Illegal War,'" *Minneapolis Star-Tribune*, November 16, 2001, 11A.
75. Dana Littlefield, "Crowd Protests Preparations for War in Iraq," *San Diego Union-Tribune*, October 28, 2003, B3.
76. See, for example, Jaclyn O'Malley, "Antiwar Protestors Line Busy Intersection," *Omaha World Herald*, October 10, 2002, 8B.
77. "500 Protest War in Portland Rally," *Seattle Times*, December 17, 2001, B6.
78. Kathleen Sullivan, "1,000 March Against Iraq Invasion Plan," *San Francisco Chronicle*, September 15, 2002, A25.
79. Douglas Belkin, "For Protestors, No Sight of President During Visit," *Boston Globe*, January 9, 2002, A9.
80. Jim Zamora and Kelly St. John, "Cops Stop Traffic to Make Arrests at Golden Gate," *San Francisco Chronicle*, May 26, 2002, A19.
81. Cris Barrish, "Opponents of War Feel Pressured to Keep Quiet," *Wilmington News Journal*, April 5, 2003, A4.
82. Alice Thomas, "Campers Wanted to Give Peace a Chance," *Columbus Dispatch*, January 21, 2002, 3C.
83. Andy Netzel, "Hundreds Protest at Kent State," *Columbus Dispatch*, May 5, 2002, 3C.
84. Elizabeth Fernandez, "Antiwar Rallies Across U.S.," *San Francisco Chronicle*, October 7, 2002, A16.
85. Joe Garofoli, "Labor Finds an Issue to March For," *San Francisco Chronicle*, January 16, 2003, A3.
86. Don Feder, "Pacifism Isn't Wrong," *Boston Herald*, November 2001, 25.
87. Hendricks, "Strikes Bring Long," A17.
88. Laurel Wellman, "Looking Inward Won't End War," *San Francisco Chronicle*, October 16, 2001, A2.
89. Ibid.
90. Debra Saunders, "Give War a Chance," *San Francisco Chronicle*, October 28, 2001, C6.
91. Ibid.
92. Feder, "Pacifism Isn't Wrong," 25.
93. Liz Bowie, "Antiwar Protests Take Center Stage," *Baltimore Sun*, March 3, 2003, 1B.

94. Thomas, "Campers Wanted," 3C.
95. See, for example, "Seeds of a Movement," *San Francisco Chronicle*, October 29, 2002, A22.
96. Jim Kirksey, "Cherry Creek High Students Fast to Protest Potential War With Iraq," *Denver Post*, October 25, 2002, B2.
97. Michele Melendez, "Multiple Generations Join for Latest Antiwar Protests," *Seattle Times*, January 13, 2003, E7.
98. Vikki Ortiz, "On Campuses Where Antiwar Protests Once Reigned," *Milwaukee Journal-Sentinel*, November 28, 2002, 25A.
99. Bill Schackner, "Specter of War Treads Lightly on Campuses," *Pittsburgh Post-Gazette*, November 24, 2002, A1.
100. Evelyn Nieves, "Protests Take Some Unlikely Routes; Rallies Planned in Smaller Cities," *The Washington Post*, February 15, 2003, A3.
101. Ibid.
102. See, for example, Karen Crummy, "Protestors Call for Peace; Activists Blame Attacks on U.S. Policy," *Boston Herald*, September 30, 2001, 5.
103. Garofoli, "Labor Finds," A3.
104. Goldberg, "Antiwar Groups," 21.
105. Morse, "Gray Hair," A2.
106. Zamora and St. John, "Cops Stop," A19.
107. Matt Stearns, "Protests Target War, Finance," *Pittsburgh Post-Gazette*, September 28, 2002, A6.
108. Michele Ames and Vladimir Kovalev, "Protestors Take to the Streets," *Rocky Mountain News*, September 28, 2002, 8A.
109. George Rush and Joanna Malloy, "Patriotism and Protest From Rappers," *New York Daily News*, February 4, 2002, 16.
110. Dart, "Washington Peace Rally," 3A.
111. Brown, "Dissenters' Antiwar Slogans," 2.
112. Ann Rodgers-Melnick, "100 Protest U.S. Strikes," *Pittsburgh Post-Gazette*, October 21, 2001, B6.
113. "A Multi-Fronted War," B12.
114. Dart, "Washington Peace Rally," 3A.
115. Thomas, "Campers Wanted," 3C.
116. Fernandez and Dvorak, "Without IMF," B1.
117. Stearns, "Protests Target," A6.
118. Fernandez and Dvorak, "Without IMF," B1.
119. Fagan, "Israel-Palestine Issues," A3.
120. Reavis, "New Antiwar Movement," 16A.
121. Martha Mendoza, "Protesters Ready to Rise Against War," *Wilmington News Journal*, December 24, 2002, A3.
122. Lynette Clemetson, "Protest Groups Using Updated Tactics to Spread Antiwar Message," *The New York Times*, January 15, 2003, A9.
123. Andy Netzel, "Hundreds Protest at Kent State," *Columbus Dispatch*, May 5, 2002, 3C.
124. Ellen Silberman, "Demonstrators Protest Against War With Iraq," *Boston Herald*, October 5, 2002, 4.
125. Chris Gray, "Protestors Get Crowds With a Few Keystrokes," *Philadelphia Inquirer*, March 11, 2003, A1.

126. Mary Otto and Christian Davenport, "Protests, Protection, Care Packages; Activists Walk for Peace, Ft. Meade Unfurls Ribbons and Security Increases," *The Washington Post*, March 27, 2003, T3.
127. Brown, "Dissenters' Antiwar Slogans," 2.
128. Dave Curtin, "Students Rallying 'Round Antiwar Demonstrations," *Denver Post*, October 17, 2002, A1.
129. Joe Garofoli, "Activists to Appeal; Rallies Planned in S.F., D.C.," *San Francisco Chronicle*, September 28, 2001, A20.
130. Belkin, "For Protestors," A9.
131. Garofoli, "Activists to Appeal," A20.
132. Richard Louv, "The Wrong Way to Protest the War," *San Diego Union-Tribune*, October 13, 2002, G3.
133. Thomas Lueck, "Candlelight Vigils Held Around the World to Oppose Military Action against Iraq," *The New York Times*, March 17, 2003, A14.
134. Louv, "The Wrong Way," G3.
135. Cesar Soriano, "Celebrities Mobilize for Peace," *USA Today*, October 7, 2002, 3A.
136. Joe Garofoli, "Bay Area Antiwar Activists Go Nude in Surge of Creative Vigils," *San Francisco Chronicle*, September 28, 2001, A20.
137. Manny Fernandez and Dan Wilgoren, "Few Arrests in D.C. Area Protests," *The Washington Post*, March 21, 2003, A26.
138. Reavis, "New Antiwar Movement," 16A.
139. Thomson, "Washington University Closes," B1.
140. Sweeney, "Giving Peace a Hand," E1.
141. Tara Burghart, "Another Round," *Wilmington News Journal*, March 2003, A7.
142. Petula Dvorak, "D.C. Marchers Protest War, Rising Joblessness," *The Washington Post*, April 5, 2003, A7.
143. John Wildermuth, "Anti-war Rallies Planned Saturday in Washington, S.F.," *San Francisco Chronicle*, September 25, 2001.
144. "In Brief," *Washington Post*, September 5, 2002, B3.
145. Fagan, "Israel-Palestine Issue," A3.
146. Fagan, "Groups Prepare," A15.
147. Maggie Haberman, "Slow Going for War Protests," *New York Daily News*, October 27, 2002, 28.
148. Reavis, "New Antiwar Movement," 16A.
149. Manny Fernandez, "War Protesters Take to Neighborhoods; D.C. Demonstrators Get Mixed Reception," *The Washington Post*, October 1, 2001, B3.
150. Hendricks, "Strikes Bring," A17.
151. Hector Saldana, "Attacks, Retaliation Spur Peace Groups to Link Up; Agendas Vary But Their Goal is the Same—No War," *San Antonio Express-News*, October 21, 2001, J1.
152. Louv, "The Wrong Way," G3.
153. Curtin, "Students Rallying," A1.
154. Ames and Kovalev, "Protesters Take," 8A.
155. Schevitz, "Targeting Terrorism," A9.
156. Fernandez, "Antiwar Rallies," A16.
157. Thomas, "Campers Wanted," 3C.

158. Calvin Woodward, "Hopeful or Not, Protesters Speak Up," *Wilmington News Journal*, March 16, 2003, A9.
159. Lynette Clemetson, "Thousands Converge in Capital to Protest Plans for War," *The New York Times*, January 19, 2003, 12.
160. Lynette Clemetson, "Protests Held Acorss the Country to Oppose War With Iraq," *The New York Times*, December 11, 2002, A22.
161. Robert McFadden, "From New York to Melbourne, Cries for Peace," *The New York Times*, February 16, 2003, A1.
162. Tony Pugh and Tosin Sulaiman, "Antiwar Protests Growing Larger," *The Washington Post*, March 16, 2003, A11.
163. "Millions Stand Against War," *Wilmington News Journal*, February 16, 2003, A1.
164. John Ritter, "Antiwar Movement Broadening," *USA Today*, January 17, 2003, 3A.
165. Evelyn Nieves, "Demonstrations Stepping Up," *Wilmington News Journal*, March 23, 2003, A5.
166. Norm Parish, "Antiwar Protest is Staged Next to Group Demonstrating in Support of Troops," *St. Louis Post-Dispatch*, March 15, 2003, 7.
167. Bob Kappstatter, "Antiwar Protests Ring Globe," *New York Daily News*, March 20, 2003, 6.
168. McFadden, "From New York," A1.
169. Quoted in James Carey, Editor's Introduction. In *Media, Myths, and Narratives: Television and the Press*, ed. James Carey (Newbury Park, CA: Sage, 1988), 9.

CHAPTER FOUR

THEIR MORALS ARE OURS: THE AMERICAN MEDIA ON THE DOCTRINE OF "PREEMPTIVE WAR"

Marilyn G. Piety and Brian J. Foley

The performance of the U.S. corporate commercial news media after 9/11 has been the most profound and dangerous failure of journalism in my lifetime.
—Robert Jensen, "Highjacking Catastrophe: A Review," *Counterpunch*

Introduction

What should a nation do when it fears an old foe is arming itself to the teeth? Should it sit by waiting to be attacked, or should it strike first in the hope of thwarting, or at least weakening the force of the attack? International law requires that an attack be either underway or imminent before a nation can strike in self-defense. Military action in the absence of an imminent threat has been traditionally considered as military aggression, which the Nuremburg Tribunal called "the supreme international crime."[1] Yet almost 60 years later, in the run up to the U.S. invasion of Iraq, the American media accepted without question the Bush administration's doctrine of "preemptive war."

One could expect such unreflective acceptance of the "Bush doctrine" from the general public. After all, we think of military aggression as something that other countries do—countries led by dictators. We think of military aggression as waged for imperialistic reasons, that is, to expand an empire rather than merely to preserve it. We tend to tolerate action in the name of self-preservation that we would otherwise not tolerate in the name of self-aggrandizement. But what counts as self-preservation? Can any sort of action be undertaken in its name? That is, does the end of self-preservation justify the means of military aggression—the taking of perhaps thousands of innocent lives, the devastation of the environment, and the creation of social, political, and economic disorder both at home and abroad? These are the sort of questions that ought to have been examined in detail by the American media during the period leading up to the Iraq war, yet were left unasked.

The United States prides itself on having the freest, most independent, and critical media in the world, and yet the American media, ever since the attacks of 9/11, have toed the line of the Bush administration in an uncritical manner that one would normally associate with state-controlled media such as that in the former Soviet Union.[2] What happened? Did the 9/11 attacks frighten the American public, or more particularly, American journalists, into accepting the kinds of constraints on free and open debate that one normally associates with totalitarian states?

Much has been written about the behavior of the American media since 9/11.[3] Little attention has been paid, however, to the philosophical import of this behavior. This chapter is intended to detail a disturbing shift in the nature of the basic assumptions of both print and television journalists, a shift away from the egalitarian Enlightenment principles on which the country was founded and toward a kind of totalitarian elitism.

Totalitarianism can take many forms. It is thus possible to compare the shift in the basic assumptions of the American media since 9/11, or the new assumptions that appear to characterize them, with those of any one of a variety of totalitarian regimes throughout history. There is one comparison that seems to us to be particularly poignant and that is the one between these new assumptions and those of the architects of the former Soviet Union. We argue that in uncritically accepting the doctrine of preemptive war, the media committed the same sin that American philosopher John Dewey accused the Bolsheviks of committing in their uncritical acceptance of violence as a legitimate means of bringing about the end of socialism. As Trotsky argued in his essay "Their Morals and Ours"[4] socialism was such a supremely good end that it justified the use of any means necessary to bring it about.

Dewey countered, however, with the observation that one can never be certain what will result from one's actions. The desirability of the end was thus irrelevant to the issue of the justification of the means chosen to achieve it. Only objective evidence of efficacy, Dewey argued, could serve to justify the means one chose to bring about a given end and this evidence needed to be carefully, coolly, and painstakingly collected beforehand.[5] We argue that the American media, in failing to examine the issue of whether preemptive war could reasonably be assumed to reduce the threat of terrorism or increase national security, appears to have fallen under the spell of the same kind of group think that has characterized totalitarian movements throughout history and that is coming increasingly to characterize political discourse in the United States.

"The Bush Doctrine"

In June 2002, President Bush, in his graduation speech at the U.S. Military Academy at West Point, New York, announced a new U.S. foreign policy: preemptive war. The attacks of the previous September demanded that the United States proactively seek out and destroy nations that might pose a danger in the future. President Bush declared, "[i]f we wait for threats to fully materialize, we will have waited too long . . . our security will require all Americans to be forward-looking and resolute, to be ready for preemptive action when necessary to defend our liberty and to defend our lives."[6] Three months later, the official, written *National Security Strategy of the United States* was released, declaring that the United States would use its military "preemptively" against "terrorists," because "we recognize that our best defense is a good offense." Approval by the United Nations, or anyone else for that matter, would be nice but not necessary. The *Strategy* states, in part:

> We will disrupt and destroy terrorist organizations [and the rogue nations that support them] by . . . defending the United States, the American people, and our interests at home and abroad by identifying and destroying the threat before it reaches our borders. While the United States will constantly strive to enlist the support of the international community, we will not hesitate to act alone, if necessary, to exercise our right of self defense by acting preemptively against such terrorists, to prevent them from doing harm against our people and our country . . . [7]

The *Strategy* further states:

> The purpose of our actions will always be to eliminate a specific threat to the United States or our allies and friends. The reasons for our actions will be clear, the force measured, and the cause just.[8]

The *National Security Strategy* claims the moral high ground. Because the American cause is just, the United States may use force. Terrorists, on the other hand, will suffer the full fury of American might if they seek to acquire a single nuclear weapon—weapons that the United States has in thousands.

This announcement that the United States would be justified in waging preemptive wars startled many observers.[9] The policy shift was enormous and rejected not only previous U.S. policy but also international law, which allows nations to use force only under the direction of the U.N. Security Council, or in self-defense as a response to an attack.[10] There are no other exceptions to this collective control over the use of force in international affairs.

The U.S. invasion of Iraq was the first preemptive war launched pursuant to the new Strategy. There was evidence that the rest of the world did not see Iraq as a threat or otherwise believe that military force was justified: the United States had tried, but failed, to win U.N. Security Council approval to invade, and the U.N.-led weapons inspections of Iraq had turned up no conclusive evidence that Iraq had begun, or even intended, to restart its Weapons of Mass Destruction (WMD) program. It was not certain that Iraq would use any of these weapons against the United States, either directly or by handing them off to terrorists. There were actual protections in place: Iraq was already under a weapons inspections regime that the United Nations was enforcing, which included embargoes of materials that could be used to make chemical, biological, or nuclear weapons, a grip that could have been strengthened if necessary.[11] And there was common sense that suggested that the Iraqi government would never use or even threaten to use WMD against the United States, because doing so would spark an overwhelming, destructive response.[12] That Iraq would attack the United States was merely speculation built upon speculation—a house of cards.

In his speech on the eve of war, President Bush seemed to drive home that this war was a war of choice, a result of the new Strategy. He explained that conquering Iraq would prevent dangers *at some point in the future*: "We are now acting because the risks of inaction would be far greater. In one year, or five years, the power of Iraq to inflict harm on all free nations would be multiplied many times over."[13] The United States would start the war, President Bush said, "at a time of our choosing."[14]

Media "Group Think"

"[T]here may be no higher duty," writes Chris Mooney in the *Columbia Journalism Review*, "for an editorial page than to set a high bar for war, particularly a preemptive war that most of the world is against."[15] Yet none of the nation's largest and most prestigious newspapers, not The *New York Times,* The *Wall Street Journal*, The *Washington Post*, nor *Chicago Tribune*, questioned the doctrine of preemptive war in the crucial time period between Colin Powell's speech to the U.N. Security Council on February 5, 2003, in which he detailed claims of, among other things, Iraqi mobile WMD laboratories, and the launching of the war on March 19, 2003.[16]

The *New York Times* and *Los Angeles Times* appeared to have reservations about the idea of launching a war without U.N. approval. Neither appeared, however, to have a problem with the idea of preemptive war in principle. The *Wall Street Journal* was actually an enthusiastic proponent of the idea, asserting that "[s]omeone has to prevent the emergence of nuclear and biological-armed chaos."[17] The *Chicago Tribune* agreed that "the US had no choice but to deal militarily with Iraq's 'lethal menace.' "[18]

The media failed to question the doctrine that the previous section shows was an enormous shift in U.S. policy and one that could have catastrophic results. The media also failed, as Michael Massing, among others, has pointed out,[19] to sufficiently scrutinize what proponents of the war argued was evidence that Iraq represented a threat to American security.[20] And the media failed to apply common sense, to question the basic assumption that attacking Iraq, or any country that represented a threat to American security, would be an effective way of dealing with that threat.[21]

Blame for the war has been placed on the intelligence community's purportedly falling victim to the impersonal forces of "group think."[22] It is not clear, however, that the intelligence community was at fault. The Pentagon and the White House appear to have pressured the CIA to produce reports that would support the view that Iraq was a threat to U.S. security.[23] However, to the extent that the result was the widely held conviction that it was necessary to conquer Iraq to protect the security of the American people, all proponents of this view could be described as having been caught up in group think.

The question is how could the delusion that Iraq represented an imminent threat to U.S. security claim so many "victims"? There were plenty of individuals, including some in the intelligence community, who argued before the war that Iraq posed no serious threat.[24] Why were they ignored? More pointedly, why were they ignored by the mainstream media whose purpose is purportedly to serve as a check on what would otherwise be the unrestrained ambitions of government? The answer would appear to be that not only did both the Bush adminiistration and the intelligence community fall victim to group think, but the media also appeared to fall victim to it. This is perhaps part of the reason the media simply reported that "group think" had been behind the Iraq war without investigating what "group think" actually was. "Group think," as described by social psychologist Irving Janis, who is credited with having come up with the expression, is a frightening phenomenon. When the various characteristics of group think are looked at closely, it becomes apparent that it is nothing but decontextualized totalitarianism. It outlines the basic characteristics that all totalitarian movements throughout history have shared.

These characteristics, paraphrased from Janis, are as follows:

1. An illusion of invulnerability coupled with excessive optimism and a tendency to take extreme risks.
2. A tendency to rationalize, rather than scrutinize basic assumptions and decisions made on those assumptions.

3. An unquestioned belief in the group's inherent moral rectitude that inclines members to ignore the ethical and moral consequences of their decisions.
4. A tendency to stereotype adversaries as too evil to negotiate with or as too weak and stupid to thwart efforts against them.
5. A tendency to put pressure on members of the group to make them feel disloyal if they question any of the group's stereotypes, illusions, or commitments.
6. A tendency toward self-censorship that minimizes individual doubts and questions.
7. An assumption of unanimity concerning the group's basic beliefs.

And most importantly perhaps in this instance,

8. A tendency to ignore information that would appear to go against the group's stereotypes, illusions, or commitments or to shatter their complacency about the effectiveness and morality of their actions.

Group think is an expression of the kind of unquestioning conformism and authoritarianism that is an essential part of totalitarian political regimes. There have been many examples of it throughout history. One of the most conspicuous examples in the twentieth century was arguably Bolshevism. In one of the most ironic twists in recent history, political conservatives in the United States are coming increasingly to resemble Bolsheviks.[25]

The *Apparat*

The political spectrum in the United States has shifted steadily to the right since the 1970s. This is unquestionably a complicated phenomenon with a variety of causes.[26] As an organized political movement, however, it can be traced to a small group of private foundations. These foundations included the Lynde and Harry Bradley Foundation of Milwaukee, the John M. Olin Foundation of New York City, several foundations controlled by Richard Mellon Scaife of Pittsburgh, the Smith Richardson Foundation (Vicks), the Castle Rock Foundation (Coors), and the Koch family foundations (energy).[27] These foundations spawned numerous conservative think tanks such as the Heritage Foundation, the Cato Institute, and the American Enterprise Institute.[28] These think tanks exercise enormous influence over the mainstream media. They promote their members as "experts" on topics such as economics, education, foreign and domestic political policy, even religion and ethics. So-called "analysts" from the Heritage Foundation, for example, published more than 8,000 newspaper and magazine articles and were featured in more than 1,600 television and radio broadcasts.[29] Many of these articles and broadcasts were attacks on journalists who were considered "too liberal." Journalists who were critical of the Bush administration were regularly targets of organized hate mail campaigns in which they were accused, among other things, of being "traitors."[30] There are even three conservative organizations, Accuracy in Media (AIM), the Center for the Study of Popular Culture (CSPC), and the Media Research Center (MRC), whose main purpose is to neutralize the purported liberal bias of the mainstream media. The MRC, for example, "issued a broadside to its rank-and-file against CBS anchor Dan Rather, for tossing what it alleged were soft questions at Democratic primary candidates—a marked contrast, it maintained, to the 'rough' treatment Rather allegedly dishes out to Republicans."[31]

Group think appears not to have been restricted to the intelligence community, or even to those who relied uncritically on its findings. It appears, in fact, to be an essential characteristic of political conservatism in the United States.[32] "The potency of right wing politics and opinion molding," argues Jerry M. Landay in "The *Apparat*: George W. Bush's Back-Door Political Machine,"

> lies in the architecture of the movement. That is, its constituent organizations think and act *strategically*. Agendas, priorities, and propaganda are directed from the center. Members are disciplined and dedicated to the narrow theology of the right. . . .
>
> The disparate streams of conservative thought and action—social, economic, religious, libertarian, and corporate—set aside major differences and march to a single drummer—with the tempo set at weekly tactical conferences in Washington. . . .
>
> This cohesion has undeniably had a large impact on the American body politic. The far right coalition now effectively controls the three branches of the federal government, overriding the checks-and-balances against rampant political power built into the Constitution. Conservatives now also set the terms of the national political debate through their dominance of the unofficial "fourth estate," the media.[33]

This is how the media succumbed to the group think of right-wing hawks. Efforts to resist this development were answered by well-orchestrated harassment campaigns. The media had long been subject to such campaigns. Even the White House appears to have joined in.[34] The 9/11 attacks served to accelerate the effectiveness of these campaigns. That is, after 9/11, much of the American public felt that national security was genuinely at risk, and that criticism of the government further threatened this security. In this climate, branding journalists as "traitors," one of the favorite terms of abuse used by conservatives as part of these campaigns,[35] could damage their careers. Several journalists were actually fired for appearing too critical of the government.[36] Journalists must thus have legitimately feared appearing too critical of the Bush doctrine of preemptive war.

The justification for the war was a relatively straightforward utilitarian calculus: A few innocents would be killed, but this evil was well worth suffering if the end was securing the United States against another 9/11. No one in the mainstream media seriously questioned the claim that Iraq represented an imminent threat to the United States or whether if it did, attacking the country would be an effective way of reducing this threat. There was little speculation about just how many people were likely to be killed or about the increased threat to global security the precedent such a preemptive war would set. Whatever evils one could expect to be attendant upon invading Iraq were considered justifiable in the name of national security. The end of increased U.S. security was considered by the Bush administration, much of the general public, and, most importantly here, nearly everyone in the mainstream media, to justify the means of preemptive war. No serious consideration was given to the issue of whether the means in question could reasonably be expected to lead to that end.

To say that journalists have fallen under the spell of group think is, of course, not to say that the mainstream American media are themselves a deliberately designed, or self-consciously styled propaganda machine. With the exception, perhaps, of the Fox network,[37] such a claim would be unsupportable. When, however, the media abandon their critical role and begin merely to repeat what they are told by official sources, they become a de facto propaganda machine. The effect is the same as if they had been set up for that purpose.

Their Morals Are Ours

Landay's argument that the various conservative groups that influence public rhetoric and policy in the United States resemble the "*apparat*" of the ruling Communist Party in the former Soviet Union is persuasive. It is not merely the value placed on conformity of thought, however, or the authority attributed to the vision of a small handful of leaders that causes the collection of conservative groups in the United States to resemble Soviet power brokers. That is, it is not merely the *form* of the conservative propaganda machine that resembles its now deceased communist counterpart; there is a chilling similarity in the *content* as well. The American "apparat" has effectively appropriated the old Bolshevik rationale that the end justifies the means famously propounded by Leon Trotsky in his essay "Their Morals and Ours."

The idea that there are abstract moral norms that are universally binding on all people is to a large extent a product of the Enlightenment.[38] It is this period in the history of thought that profoundly influenced the thinking of the founding fathers, the framers of both the Declaration of Independence and the U.S. Constitution.[39] It is this idea that provides the foundation for the view that all human beings are possessed of certain inalienable rights, the most significant of which is undoubtedly the right to life, which in this context can be interpreted to mean, the right not be killed in a war whose end is guaranteeing someone else's freedom from the threat of death by military aggression.

Leon Trotsky attacked the idea of universally binding abstract moral norms as merely an "element in the mechanism of class deception."[40] The end of Marxism, according to Trotsky, was to abolish "the power of one person over another,"[41] and that end was deemed so desirable by the Bolsheviks that any means necessary, including lying, torture, and killing, were justifiable if they helped achieve that end. Trotsky argued that "amoralism in any given case is only a pseudonym for higher human morality."[42] Bolsheviks did not recognize any such thing as rights as being inherent in individuals. Rights, if there were such things in their view, inhered in the collective, in humanity in general and in the Communist Party in particular. Like political conservatives in the United States, Bolsheviks valued conformity. "[T]o a Bolshevik," asserted Trotsky, "the party is everything."[43] There could be "no contradiction," he argued, "between personal morality and the interests of the party, since the party embodies . . . the very highest tasks and aims of humanity."[44]

Again, like political conservatives in the United States, Bolsheviks were elitist.[45] Trotsky argued that although communism was inherently egalitarian, aiming as it did to abolish the power of one person over another, he also tacitly acknowledged that, at least during the revolutionary period, it tended toward a certain elitism. The Bolsheviks, he explained, believed that people did not always understand what was best for them, but tended at different times to be "inspired by different moods and objectives"[46] and that, for this reason, "a centralized organization of the vanguard [was] indispensable."[47] It was this vanguard, who knew better than the masses what was good for them, who had license to lie, torture, and kill as a means of "building a bridge" to "a society without lies and violence."[48]

Trotsky, like political conservatives in the United States argued that war, which he acknowledged included the killing of innocents, was a defensible means to the end of liberating an oppressed people. "[W]ar," argued Trotsky, "is better than . . . slavery. But this . . . merely signifies that the end (democracy or socialism) justifies under certain conditions such means as violence and murder. Not to speak about lies! Without lies war would be as unimaginable as a machine without oil."[49]

Liberating an oppressed people was precisely one of the rationales that was used in the American media in defense of the invasions of both Afghanistan and Iraq, whose official names were, respectively, "Operation Enduring Freedom" and "Operation Iraqi Freedom." This was not the only justification, of course, and was not even initially the primary justification for either invasion. The idea that the desirability of the end justified whatever means were necessary to bring it about was also essential, however, to the initial justification of both invasions as necessary to protect American security. Lies were deemed justifiable if they were necessary to get sufficient support for the war.[50] Lies and the killing of innocents were deemed necessary in the service of the higher morality of defending our way of life, our "freedoms."[51]

There is just one small difficulty with the argument that acts one would normally consider immoral, such as lying and killing, are justifiable as a means to a higher moral end, as the American philosopher John Dewey pointed out to Trotsky in 1938.[52] There is no guarantee that one will succeed in bringing about what one aims to bring about through such means. Dewey pointed out that means and ends were "interdependent"[53] and that the recognition of this fact must lead to the "scrupulous examination of the means that are used, to ascertain what their actual, objective consequences will be as far as it is humanly possible to tell—to show that they do 'really' lead to" the desired end.[54] "What has given the maxim . . . that the end justifies the means a bad name," explains Dewey,

> is that the end-in-view, the end professed and entertained (perhaps quite sincerely) justifies the use of certain means, and so justifies the latter that it is not necessary to examine what the actual consequences of the use of [the] chosen means will be. An individual may hold, and quite sincerely as far as his personal opinion is concerned, that certain means will "really" lead to a professed end. But the real question is not one of personal belief but of the objective grounds upon which it is held: namely, the consequences that will actually be produced by them.[55]

Means must be chosen, continued Dewey, based on "an examination of measures and policies with respect to their actual, objective consequences."[56]

But just as the Bolsheviks, because they sincerely desired to bring about an egalitarian utopia, did not need to worry about what lying, torturing, and killing were likely to do, so were the proponents of the recent American invasions of Afghanistan and Iraq prone to assume that because they sincerely desired to protect the United States (and to liberate an oppressed people), they did not need to trouble themselves with the issue of whether war and its attendant lying, torturing, and killing were likely to do.[57]

Objective evidence supporting the efficacy of one's chosen means is the only justification for choosing means that would otherwise violate the abstract moral norms against lying, torturing, and killing that the West holds dear. Few in either the Bush administration or the Pentagon troubled ahemselves, however, with the issues of the likelihood that war would be an effective means either of making us safer from terrorism or of liberating the peoples in question from their oppressive political regimes.[58] More importantly, however, the mainstream media failed to alert the public to the absence of any serious consideration of these crucial issues. The overwhelming majority of articles in the mainstream media simply assumed that preemptive war (otherwise known as military aggression) would achieve what its proponents aimed to achieve.[59]

What happens to the justification of lying, torturing, and killing if the good they were supposed to foster never materializes? What happens if lying and torturing and killing does not lead to "the abolition of the power of one person over another"? What happens if lying and torturing and killing does *not* reduce the threat of terrorism or preserve the American way of life in the sense of the freedoms associated with it? What then? Then it looks like a nation that employs such means is simply a lying, brutal, murderous power that is either seriously self-deluded, downright despicable, or both. Such denunciations of the Soviet Union were common among U.S. politicians and journalists. Yet no one in the mainstream media has, to use a phrase made famous after 9/11, "connected the dots" and similarly denounced recent U.S. behavior.

Most Americans would probably be disturbed to discover that the purported defenders of American freedom are in bed, ideologically, with the Bolsheviks. Most Americans would probably react quite negatively to the revelation that we have abandoned our morals for theirs, that although the Soviet Union is no more, the morals of the Bolsheviks, of Lenin, Trotsky, and Stalin, have triumphed, here, over those of the founding fathers. Their morals are now our morals.

Few in the general public appear to know enough history or philosophy to be able to identify this catastrophic defeat of the Enlightenment ideals of freedom and individualism on which this country was founded.[60] Journalists should know this much history, though, and this much moral philosophy. Yet our mainstream media have failed to report this defeat. How could they when they never reported the mobilization of the apparat and the war of ideas that led to it?

Notes

Though this paper is, as a whole, the product of a joint effort, it is perhaps important to point out the nature of the contribution of the two authors. M.G. Piety conceived the idea for the paper and is responsible for every section except for the one on the doctrine of preemptive war. Brian J. Foley reviewed the paper, made extensive editorial suggestions, supplied many of the references contained in the footnotes and is the sole author of the section on preemptive war.

1. United Nations, *Historical Review of Developments relating to Aggression* (United Nations Publication, 2003), 8.

2. CBS anchor Dan Rather remarked, e.g., when he appeared on the *Late Show with David Letterman* on September 17, 2001, that "George Bush is the President. He makes the decisions. As just one American, wherever he wants me to line up, just tell me where" (as quoted in David Dadge, *Casualty of War: The Bush Administration's Assault on a Free Press* [New York: Prometheus Books, 2004], 120).

3. See, e.g., Steve Chermak, Frankie Bailey, and Michelle Brown, *Journalism After September 11* (Westport, CT: Praeger, 2003); Alison Gilbert, Robyn Walensky, Melinda Murphy, Phil Hirschkorn, and Mitchel Stephens, *Covering Catastrophe: Broadcast Journalists Report September 11* (New York: Bonus Books, 2002); Bradley S. Greenberg, *Communication and Terrorism: Public and Media Responses to 9/11* (Norwood, NJ: Hampton Press, 2002); William A. Hachten and James F. Scotton, *The World News Prism: Global Media in an Era of Terrorism* (Ames, IA: Iowa State Press, 2002); Nancy Palmer, *Terrorism, War and the Press* (Cambridge, MA: Joan Schornstein Center, 2003); and Barbie Zelizer and Stuart Allan, *Journalism after September 11* (New York: Routledge, 2002).

4. Leon Trotsky, "Their Morals and Ours," in *Their Morals and Ours: Marxist Versus Liberal Views on Morality*, ed. Leon Trotsky, John Dewey, and George Novak (New York: Pathfinder Press, Inc., 1973), 13–52.

5. John Dewey, "Means and Ends," *Their Morals*, 67–73.

6. President George W. Bush, "Remarks by the President at 2002 Graduation Exercise of the United States Military Academy, West Point, New York," <http://www.whitehouse.gov/news/releases/2002/06/20020601-3.html> (accessed September 9, 2004).

7. *The National Security Strategy of the United States of America*, September 17, 2002, chapter VIII <http://www.whitehouse.gov/nsc/nss3.html> (accessed September 9, 2004).

8. Ibid., chapter V <http://www.whitehouse.gov/nsc/nss5.html> (accessed September 9, 2004).

9. T.E. Ricks and V. Loeb, "Bush Developing Military Policy of Striking First: New Doctrine Addresses Terrorism," *The Washington Post*, June 10, 2002, A1. ("[T]here is general agreement that adopting a preemption doctrine would be a radical shift from the half-century-old policies of deterrence and containment that were built around the notion that an adversary would not attack the United States because it would provoke a certain, overwhelming retaliatory strike. Administration officials formulating the new doctrine said the United States has been forced to move beyond deterrence since September 11 because of the threat posed by terrorist groups and hostile states supporting them.")

10. UN CHARTER art. 2(3–4) (nations must use peaceful means to solve international disputes and refrain from using force); art. 24(1) (nations confer primary responsibility on the Security Council for use of force in international affairs); art. 51 (nations may use force in self-defense if there is an armed attack but

must report to Security Council immediately). The rule governing self-defense, known as the *Caroline Rule*, named after the rule used to resolve an 1837 dispute between the United States and Great Britain involving a ship of that name, keeps this exception a limited one: "There must be a necessity of self-defense, instant, overwhelming, leaving no choice of means, and no moment for deliberation. [The means of self-defense must involve] nothing unreasonable or excessive; since the act, justified by the necessity of self-defense, must be limited by that necessity, and kept clearly within it." P. Malanczuk, *Akehurst's Modern Introduction to International Law* (New York: Routledge, 1997), 314. Many politicians and legal scholars have argued to expand this right of self-defense to include less-than-imminent attacks, a doctrine known as "anticipatory self-defense." This expansion—notably less permissive than preemptive war—is controversial and has not prevailed generally. Ibid., 311–314.

11. M. Walzer, *Arguing About War* (New Haven, CT: Yale University Press, 2004): 147–151, 157–159 (arguing, in essays before the invasion, that the threat Iraq would go nuclear was best solved with increased worldwide cooperation, punishing countries that supply Iraq with proscribed material, a robust inspections program that would include surprise inspections and expanded no-fly zones, backed up, if necessary, by limited uses of military force rather than a full-scale military invasion).

12. J.J. Mearsheimer and S.M. Walt, "Can Saddam Be Contained? History Says Yes." Paper (Cambridge, MA: Belfer Center for Science and International Affairs, November 2002) <http://bcsia.ksg.harvard.edu/publication.cfm?Program=CORE&ctype=paper&item_id=361> (accessed September 17, 2004).

13. President George W. Bush, "Speech on Iraq," *CBS News*, March 17, 2003 <http://www.cbsnews.com/stories/2003/03/17/iraq/main544377.shtml> (accessed September 9, 2004).

14. Ibid.

15. Chris Mooney, "The Editorial Pages and the Case for War," *Columbia Journalism Review*, March/April 2004, 29.

16. Mooney notes that the *Los Angeles Times* devoted "a single paragraph" to questioning the doctrine in this crucial time period (Mooney, "The Editorial Pages," 33). Although the mainstream media were not entirely silent regarding this doctrine, which was announced in 2002 (see the previous section of this paper), the discussion was not deep and searching. As Arthur Schlesinger Jr. wrote, "The press and television in effect set the agenda for public opinion. They were reluctant to add to the low esteem in which they are held by questioning the presidential war. This reluctance aborted the national debate that should have taken place over changing the basis of our foreign policy from containment and deterrence to preventive war, and then over the waging of such a war against Iraq" (Arthur Schlesinger Jr., "The Making of a Mess," The New York Review of Books, 51: 14 [September 23, 2004], 42). It is important to note, however, that the doctrine was regularly, if not even routinely, criticized in alternative media such as the *Nation,* the *Progressive, Z Magazine, Tikkun*, and *Counterpunch* as well as the various stations in the Pacifica radio network.

17. As quoted in Mooney, "The Editorial Pages," 29.

18. Ibid.

19. See Michael Massing, "Now They Tell Us," *New York Review of Books*, 51: 3 (February 26, 2004), and "Unfit to Print," *New York Review of Books*, 51: 11 (June 24, 2004).

20. When the media did report on those who questioned the Bush administration's factual claims regarding Iraq, the story was relegated to pages deep inside the newspaper. "The press," asserts Schlesinger, "seems to have spontaneously decided that they would not give equal time to skeptics about the war" (Schlesinger, "The Making of a Mess").

21. Strangely, nearly everyone, including the Bush administration, the general public, and the media, seem to appreciate the wisdom of not provoking an unfriendly nation about which we have more solid evidence of nuclear capability, namely North Korea. This ideological incoherence is, in the words of Søren Kierkegaard, "both to be laughed at and to be wept over." See Søren Kierkegaard, *Works of Love*, trans. Howard V. Hong and Edna H. Hong (Princeton: Princeton University Press, 1995), 242.

22. See William Branigin and Dana Priest, "Senate Report Blasts Intelligence Agencies' Flaws," *The Washington Post*, July 9, 2004 <http://www.washingtonpost.com/ac2/wp-dyn/A38459-2004Jul9> includes links to Senate report (accessed September 13, 2004).

23. See, e.g., Robert Dreyfus, "The Pentagon Muzzles the CIA," *American Prospect*, 13: 22 (December 16, 2002); Massing, "Now They Tell Us"; and Walter C. Uhler, "Preempting the Truth," *Bulletin of the Atomic Scientists* (September/October 2004).

24. See, e.g., Michael Massing, "Now They Tell Us"; Ambassador Joseph Wilson, *The Politics of Truth: Inside the Lies that Led to War and Betrayed My Wife's CIA Identity* (New York: Carroll & Graf, 2004); Richard A. Clarke, *Against All Enemies: Inside America's War on Terror* (New York: Free Press, 2004); Hans Blix, *Disarming Iraq* (New York: Pantheon, 2004); and Sheldon Rampton and John Stauber, *Weapons of Mass Deception: The Uses of Propaganda in Bush's War on Iraq* (New York: Tarcher/Penguin, 2003).

25. What makes this particularly ironic is that today's conservatives are the ideological offspring of Reagan conservatives, the most vehemently anti-Soviet group in recent history. It was the Reagan administration that pressured the CIA to come up with intelligence that would be damning of the Soviet Union. (Cf. Dreyfuss, "The Pentagon.")

26. This shift has been the subject of much recent scholarship. See, e.g., Thomas Frank, *What's the Matter With Kansas: How Conservatives Won the Heart of America* (New York: Metropolitan Books, 2004); Dan T. Carter, *The Politics of Rage: George Wallace, the Origins of the New Conservativism, and the Transformation of American Politics* (Baton Rouge, LA: Louisiana State University Press, 2000); Paul Krugman, *The Great Unraveling: Losing Our Way in the New Century* (New York: W.W. Norton & Company, 2003); Kevin Phillips, *Wealth and Democracy: A Political History of the American Rich* (New York: Broadway Books, 2003); Richard Sennet, *The Corrosion of Character: The Personal Consequences of Work in the New Capitalism* (New York: W.W. Norton & Company, 1998); and Richard A. Viguerie, David Franke, and Tim LaHaye, *America's Right Turn: How Conservatives Used New and Alternative Media to take Power* (Chicago: Bonus Books, 2004).

27. The title of this section and much of the information contained here comes from Jerry M. Landay's excellent article, "The *Apparat*: George W. Bush's backdoor political machine," <http://www.mediatransparency.org/stories/apparat.html> (accessed September 13, 2004). We are indebted to Rob Laymon for bringing this article to our attention. See, e.g., Jerry M. Landay, "The *Apparat*," and Lewis Lapham, "Tentacles of Rage: The Republican propaganda mill, a brief history," *Harpers* (September 2004).

28. Other conservative think tanks include the Manhattan Institute, the Hudson Institute, the Hoover Institution, the Federalist Society, the Reason Foundation, Citizens for a Sound Economy, the American Legislative Exchange Council, the Intercollegiate Studies Institute, The Foundation to Defend Democracy and the National Association of Scholars.

29. Cf. Landay, "The *Apparat*."

30. See, e.g., Massing, "Unfit to Print."

31. Landay, "The *Apparat*."

32. In the spirit of fairness, we should perhaps point out that in the extremely polarized political climate of the United States, even "progressives" sometimes fall victim to group think. Like the Mensheviks, however, progressives in the United States often evince a tendency to think for themselves and thus lack the unanimity and moral certainty that drives the conservative movement.

33. Landay, "The *Apparat*."

34. See, e.g., Ken Auletta, "Fortress Bush," *The New Yorker*, January 19, 2004.

35. See, e.g., Ann Coulter, *Treason: Liberal Treachery from the Cold War to the War on Terror* (New York: Crown Forum, 2003).

36. See Dadge, *Casualty of War*, 103–117. See also David Brock, September *The Republican Noise Machine: Right-Wing Media and How It Corrupts Democracy* (New York: Crown Publishers, 2004), 141–42.

37. See, e.g., "Not Necessarily the News," *Harpers* (September 2004).

38. The idea actually goes back through the history of Western philosophy to the thought of the ancient Greeks. It was in the Enlightenment, however, that it received both its clearest articulation and its widest acceptance.

39. See, e.g., Adrienne Koch, *Power, Morals and the Founding Fathers: Essays in the Interpretation of the American Enlightenment* (Ithaca, NY: Cornell University Press, 1961); Paul Merrill Spurlin, *The French Enlightenment in America: Essays on the Times of the Founding Fathers* (Athens, GA: University of Georgia Press, 1984); Bernard Bailyn, *The Ideological Origins of the American Revolution* (Cambridge, MA: Belknap Press, 1992); and Gordon Wood, *The Creation of the American Republic 1776–1787* (Chapel Hill, NC: University of North Carolina Press, 1998).

40. Trotsky, "*Their Morals* and Ours," Their Morals, 22.

41. Ibid., 48.

42. Ibid., 45.

43. Ibid., 44.

44. Ibid.

45. On the elitism of political conservatives in the United States see, e.g., Kevin Phillips, *American Dynasty: Aristocracy, Fortune and the Politics of Deceit in the House of Bush* (New York: Viking, 2004), and Paul Suskind, *The Price of Loyalty: George W. Bush, the White House, and the Education of Paul O'Neill*

(New York: Simon and Shuster 2004). This elitism is actually a theme that runs through much recent scholarship referred to in the notes of the present paper.

46. Trotsky, "Moralists and Sycophants," *Their Morals*, 59.
47. Ibid.
48. Trotsky, "Their Morals and Ours," *Their Morals*, 36.
49. Ibid. It is interesting to note that although proponents of the recent U.S. invasion of Iraq have cited Churchill's famous defense of lies in wartime, none of these proponents mention that Trotsky also defended the use of lies in war.
50. See, e.g., Dilip Hiro, *Secrets and Lies: Operation "Iraqi Freedom" and After* (New York: Nation Books, 2004), Rampton and Stauber, *Weapons of Mass Deception*; and Uhler, "Preempting the Truth."
51. We have put "freedoms" in quotation marks here because although this claim has been part of the rhetoric of proponents of both invasions, the greatest threat to the freedoms that have characterized the American way of life has so far come from these very same proponents. See, e.g., James Bovard, *Terrorism and Tyranny: Trampling Freedom, Justice and Peace to Rid the World of Evil* (New York: Palgrave/Macmillan, 2003); David Dadge, *Casualty of War*; and Nat Hentoff, *The War on the Bill of Rights and the Gathering Resistance* (New York: Seven Stories Press, 2003).
52. See John Dewey, "Means and Ends," *Their Morals*.
53. Ibid., 68.
54. Ibid., 69.
55. Ibid., 69–70.
56. Ibid., 70.
57. Opinion seems to be shifting, in fact, toward the view that attacking Iraq has not made us safer from terrorism. See, e.g., Tom Maertens, "Asserting This War Has Made Us Safer Won't Make It So," *Minneapolis Star Tribune*, July 27, 2004 <http://www.commondreams.org/views04/0727-04.htm> (accessed September 13, 2004); Christopher Dickey and John Barry, "Has the War Made Us Safer?" *Newsweek*, 2004 <http://www.msnbc.msn.com/id/46661300/site/newsweek/> (accessed September 13, 2004); "Has Iraq War Made U.S. Safer? That's questionable," *USA Today*, <http://www.usatoday.com/news/opinion/editorials/2004-07-15-our-view_x.htm> (accessed September 13, 2004); Gary Langer, "Was It Worth It? Poll: More Americans Think Iraq War Raises Risk of Anti-U.S. Terror," *ABC News*, September 8 2004 <http://abcnews.go.com/sections/wnt/World/poll030908_iraq.html> (accessed September 13, 2004); and Bertus Hendrix, "Not a safer world," *Radio Netherlands Wereldomroep*, September 10, 2004 <http://www.rnw.nl/hotspots/html/us040910.html> (accessed September 13, 2004).
58. See, e.g., Richard K. Betts, "Suicide From Fear of Death?" *Foreign Affairs*, January/February 2003, discussing the possibility that Iraq, if it were indeed armed with WMD, would have the incentive to use such weapons given the Bush administration's clear, bellicose intentions in the months preceding the actual invasion.
59. Articles on this issue did begin to appear, however, after the invasion and subsequent declaration of victory in Iraq. That is, articles began to appear only

after the failure of the war was conspicuous even to the relatively uninformed and it was too late for the American public to use the information contained in the articles to pressure their elected officials to oppose the war.

60. See, e.g., "Knowing Enough of Our History to Save Our Future," in *The War on the Bill of Rights*, ed. Hentoff, 127–29.

THE UNITED KINGDOM

CHAPTER FIVE
POSTMODERN WAR ON IRAQ*

Philip Hammond

The French philosopher Jean Baudrillard achieved a certain notoriety with his trilogy of articles on the 1991 Persian Gulf War, declaring in advance that the war would "not take place"; asking, once it had started, if it was "really taking place"; and maintaining afterward that it "did not take place."[1] His hyperbolic claims attracted much criticism.[2] Yet, as a number of commentators have remarked, Baudrillard's analysis of the 1991 conflict seems even more pertinent to the 2003 invasion of Iraq.[3] In 1991, for instance, Baudrillard described how Saddam Hussein's military strength was exaggerated by:

> [B]randishing the threat of a chemical war, a bloody war, a world war—everyone had their say—as though it were necessary to give ourselves a fright, to maintain everyone in a state of erection for fear of seeing the flaccid member of war fall down.[4]

His account of this "futile masturbation" seems even more applicable to the talking up of Iraq's nonexistent Weapons of Mass Destruction (WMD) in 2003, and to the way that both the anti- and pro-war lobbies tried to frighten the public into agreement by issuing dire warnings of the dangers either of action or of inaction against Iraq. Similarly, Baudrillard's remark that "the war ended in general boredom, or worse in the feeling of being duped. . . . It is as though there were a virus infecting this war from the beginning which emptied it of all credibility"[5] stands equally well as a description of the efforts to build public support for the 2003 invasion, such as the British government's publication of unconvincing dossiers of "evidence." In the United Kingdom, both opponents and supporters of the war ended up feeling they had been duped, accusing Prime Minister Tony Blair of having led the country to war on a "false prospectus."

Baudrillard wrote of the 1991 conflict as a "non-war," a war that "never began," the outcome of which was "decided in advance":

> We should have been suspicious about the disappearance of the declaration of war, the disappearance of the symbolic passage to the act, which already presaged the disappearance of the end of hostilities, then of the distinction between winners and losers (the winner readily becomes the hostage of the loser . . .)[6]

Even before foreigners started literally being taken hostage in Iraq in 2004, the winners could be said to have become hostages of the losers: coalition forces quickly became bogged down in a chaotic and unstable situation with no clear prospect either of an imminent exit nor of being able to bring order to the country. The second time around, the allies' "victory" looked even more suspect. President George W. Bush's speech on May 1, 2003 announcing the "end of major combat operations" was the nearest thing to a declaration of victory, but many took the symbolic toppling of Saddam's statue on April 9 as marking the moment when the regime fell. The fact that the image was staged in front of the hotel housing the international media, and that a year later the coalition troops admitted they were "no longer in control"[7] of some parts of the country, suggested that this was a victory on television only.

This chapter argues that the concept of "postmodern war" can offer some insights into the nature of contemporary conflict and illuminate both the reasons for the invasion of Iraq and the problems that the coalition encountered. The invasion was an attempt to restore a sense of meaning and purpose to Western societies that have, since the end of the cold war, become acutely aware of their lack of a "grand narrative." This was attempted by linking the war on Iraq to the two major themes of post–1989 Western foreign policy: humanitarian intervention and the war on terrorism. The effort, however, has been a failure: all the coalition has succeeded in doing is exporting the hollowness of its own political institutions somewhere else.

Postmodernity and War

Postmodernism began as a rejection of left-wing politics by a minority of French intellectuals, but has become the generalized outlook of our times. When Jean-Francois Lyotard defined postmodernism as an "incredulity towards metanarratives," he primarily meant that he no longer believed in the traditional Left commitment to progress and liberation.[8] As Perry Anderson has observed: "Just one 'master narrative' lay at the origin of the term: Marxism."[9] Significantly, however, the rejection of Marxism took the form of a repudiation of the entire inheritance of the Enlightenment. Where Marxism had traditionally claimed to be the Enlightenment's true heir, upholding values of reason, progress, and emancipation as the bourgeois order could not, postmodernists rejected those values as complicit with power.

Baudrillard voiced precisely these sentiments when he wrote, for instance, of "All these events, from Eastern Europe or from the Gulf, which under the colours of war and liberation led only to political and historical disillusionment. . . ."[10] His attempted critique of the West was a rejection of "the Enlightenment, the Rights of Man, the Left in power . . . and sentimental humanism."[11] Baudrillard could not see, in the Persian Gulf War, any possibility of an alternative grand narrative to challenge the hegemony of the West: his essays are littered with references to the decline of Arab nationalism, the containment of radical Islam, the collapse of communism in Eastern Europe, and the defeat of the "revolutionary potential"[12] of the Algerian uprising against colonial rule in the 1950s. As James Heartfield argues, it was the last of these events that was the formative experience in the development of the postmodern sensibility.[13] In France, both the Establishment and the Left justified the suppression of Algerian claims for independence in the name of the Enlightenment, leading some radical thinkers—including Lyotard and Baudrillard—to draw the conclusion that Enlightenment humanism itself was flawed.

For the Left, the defeats of the 1980s, culminating in the fall of communism after 1989, consolidated this mood of pessimism. As the Berlin Wall tumbled, Margaret Thatcher's famous insistence that "There Is No Alternative" to capitalism seemed to have been borne out by events. From this perspective of disillusionment, the only option seemed to be the "ironic" postmodern attitude: refusing to get excited by the propaganda, dismissing it all as only images. Baudrillard's advice was to

Resist the probability of any image or information whatever. Be more virtual than events themselves, do not seek to re-establish the truth, we do not have the means, but do not be duped . . .[14]

Without any means to establish the truth, not being duped can only mean disbelieving everything. For this reason, postmodernism is an inadequate critique: it is premised on the death of political agency.

The notion of a "postmodern condition" is nevertheless useful in seeking to understand the present, precisely because the period since the end of the cold war has been characterized by the dissolution of the political sphere. Whereas the tough pro-capitalist ideology of the Thatcher–Reagan era gained coherence by defining itself against the Left and the labor movement, since

1989 the old politics of Left and Right have become irrelevant. Where once politics was about competing visions of the future, it is now reduced to a technical managerialism. Incredulity toward grand narratives is no longer merely the subjective outlook of a few disillusioned former radicals: it captures the mood of societies in which the political sphere is emptied of substance, traditional allegiances seem worthless, and there is no longer any shared framework of meaning. As former patterns of social and political engagement have broken down, leaders have sought new ways to engage with an atomized public and to recreate a sense of purpose. It is this search for alternative sources of legitimacy that has led successive Western governments to turn repeatedly to the international sphere, despite periodic assertions that they wish to prioritize domestic issues.

The post–cold war international arena has presented both opportunities and problems in this respect. Initially, the end of the cold war seemed to open up the possibility of a brighter future. Wildly optimistic claims were made: a revivified UN, no longer hampered by the Soviet veto, would henceforth be able to act on moral principles; there would be a "peace dividend" as money formerly spent on the arms race was put to better use; there would, in President George H. W. Bush's phrase, be a "New World Order." There was no longer any ideological alternative to Western capitalism, and no Soviet deterrent to the exercise of U.S. military power. "In the life of a nation, we're called upon to define who we are and what we believe,"[15] declared Bush Sr.: the Persian Gulf War provided a new source of meaning; a way to redefine what America stood for. This was the President who famously had difficulties articulating what he called "the vision thing," but the war seemed to offer moral clarity: "It's black and white. . . . The choice is unambiguous. Right vs. Wrong."[16]

Yet the success was only temporary. In the post–cold war era, though there are fewer restraints than ever on the open use of military force and the pursuit of U.S. interests and influence around the globe, the overarching rationale for action has also collapsed. Having intensified the cold war in the 1980s, the implosion of Soviet communism left the West without an enemy and without any reason why "the West" should have any coherent existence. As former president Ronald Reagan noted in a 1992 speech, the end of the cold war "robbed much of the West of its uplifting, common purpose" (*Sunday Times*, December 6, 1992). At the very moment of its victory, the West lost the ideological cement that had cohered an international alliance against the common enemy of the "Evil Empire" and provided the elite with a sense of purpose at home. In the post–cold war era, military actions are undertaken by temporary "coalitions of the willing," rather than the more stable cold war alliance under assumed U.S. leadership. Already in 1990–91, the Bush administration had to bully and cajole other countries into supporting its war on Saddam.

As Zaki Laïdi suggests, the end of the cold war "buried two centuries of Enlightenment," leaving us in "a world without meaning."[17] Although it is driven to use war and international intervention to offset the absence of shared meaning and purpose at home, the Western elite has some difficulty in constructing a coherent grand narrative to make sense of its foreign adventures. Despite having the most powerful military machine ever, there is no framework of meaning within which to use it; no metanarrative to allow the projection of power. Baudrillard repeatedly emphasized this point in his Gulf War essays, when he wrote of "the profound self-deterrence of American power and of Western power in general":[18]

> Unlike earlier wars, in which there were political aims either of conquest or domination, what is at stake in this one is war itself: its status, its meaning, its future. It is beholden not to have an objective but to prove its very existence. . . . In effect, it has lost much of its credibility.[19]

Without a grand narrative to make sense of the enterprise, war is unable to inspire belief or enthusiasm. Instead, he argued, war becomes meaningless and empty, a mere image.

Since 1991 Western leaders have pursued two main themes in an attempt to rediscover meaning and purpose in the international arena. The first is humanitarian intervention. In the speech quoted above, Reagan went on to argue that "evil still stalks the planet," and offered a "noble vision" that would provide a new "cause" for the post–cold war generation. He asked rhetorically:

> [M]ight we not now unite to impose civilised standards of behaviour on those who flout every measure of human decency? Are we not nearing a point in world history where civilised nations can in unison stand up to the most immoral and deadly excesses against humanity?

His proposed solution to the West's loss of purpose was "a humanitarian velvet glove backed by a steel fist of military force," through which "the world's democracies must enforce stricter humanitarian standards of international conduct" (*Sunday Times*, December 6, 1992). As Reagan spoke these words, his successor, Bush Sr., was putting the doctrine into practice by sending the U.S. marines into Somalia on a "humanitarian" mission. Indeed, the first "humanitarian intervention" of the post–cold war period was Bush's effort to set up "safe havens" for Iraqi Kurds at the end of the Persian Gulf War. The most ideologically successful instance of humanitarian military intervention was the 1999 Kosovo conflict, which is why, as discussed below, references to Kosovo featured prominently in attempts to justify war on Iraq in 2003.

Since September 11, 2001, a second theme has been the "war on terrorism." Notwithstanding claims that "the world changed" on 9/11, there has been considerable continuity in the attempt to discover meaning in the international sphere. As President Bush put it in a May 2000 speech:

> This is a world that is much more uncertain than the past. In the past we were certain, we were certain it was us versus the Russians in the past. . . . You see, even though it's an uncertain world, we're certain of some things. We're certain that even though the "evil empire" may have passed, evil still remains. We're certain there are people that can't stand what America stands for. . . . We're certain there are madmen in the world, and there's terror, and there's missiles . . . .[20]

It is striking how much of the post–9/11 outlook—evil, madmen, terror, missiles, and threatened American values—was already in place in this speech, delivered while Bush was campaigning for the presidency. Like his predecessors, Bush has looked to the international stage for a new inclusive cause for people to rally round. Hence when he addressed Congress after the World Trade Center attacks, he invoked not just U.S. national interests but a broader mission: "This is the world's fight. This is civilization's fight. This is the fight of all who believe in progress and pluralism, tolerance and freedom." Like the humanitarian interventions of the 1990s, the war on terrorism has been presented as a titanic struggle between Good and Evil. The new element is that, since 9/11, risk-averse Western publics and their political leaders have regarded the world with an even greater sense of fear. Politicians still regularly issue calls to "reorder the world," as Blair put it in an October 2001 speech to the Labour Party conference, but the notion seems less plausible than before as the world appears increasingly chaotic and dangerous.

While both humanitarian interventionism and the war on terrorism are attempts to reconstitute a sense of purpose internationally and forge new connections with an individualized and depoliticized electorate at home, both strategies have ultimately failed to resolve the problem—inevitably so, since each is an attempt to bypass the realm of politics. Whether through seeking some higher moral imperative in humanitarianism and human rights, or through appealing to the lowest common denominator of fear and insecurity, these are fundamentally antipolitical attempts to evade the consequences of the death of politics. As Baudrillard put it in 1991, war "no longer proceeds from a political will to dominate or from a vital impulse or an antagonistic violence." Rather than being a means to realize definite political aims or interests, postmodern war is "the absence of politics pursued by other means."[21]

Searching for Meaning in Iraq

The build-up to the 2003 Iraq war, its conduct and aftermath, provide a striking illustration of the features of postmodern warfare: it lacked any coherent political justification, its conduct was media-friendly but risk-averse, and it ended in chaos. These features all derive from the crisis of purpose and meaning, which the elite has sought to resolve through international action.

The stated justifications for invading Iraq made little sense at the time, and have subsequently been exposed as absurd deceptions. It was a war to avert the danger posed by Iraq's possession of WMD (directly or via weapons falling into terrorist hands), yet there were no WMD and no links between Saddam and Al Qaeda. It was also justified as a war to end the human rights abuses suffered under Saddam's regime and to liberate the Iraqi people. Yet the main human rights violations coalition leaders had in mind were perpetrated while Saddam was their ally, and placing the country under military occupation hardly seems a sure route to liberation. Instead, the coalition kills civilians in its ongoing battle against "insurgents," who it tortures in Saddam's former prisons.

The emptiness of the justifications for war produced an impoverished and bogus public debate as superficial disagreements masked the absence of any more principled clash between supporters and opponents of the war. Blair set the tone soon after 9/11, arguing in his October 2001 Labour Party conference speech that: "Whatever the dangers of the action we take, the dangers of inaction are far, far greater." Explaining his reasons for invading Iraq in another speech to party activists in February 2003 he said,

> I know many of you find it hard to understand why I care so deeply about this. I tell you: it is fear . . . the fear that one day these new threats of weapons of mass destruction, rogue states and international terrorism combine to deliver a catastrophe to our world.

With leaders trying to instill fear instead of making a political argument, it was perhaps not surprising that the debate over whether to go to war often degenerated into a squabble over which course of action would be least scary. Supporting the war, the *Guardian* columnist Martin Woollacott suggested that "action is risky, but turning away could be even riskier" (*The Guardian*, February 7, 2003); while David Aaronovitch parroted Blair's line that "the dangers of inaction are probably greater than the dangers of action" (*Iraq: A Just War?*, Channel Four, February 28); and Johann Hari argued that "this war is going to be terrible—but leaving Saddam in place would be even more terrible. . . . there will be horrible deaths either way we leap" (*Independent*, February 15). Meanwhile, on the antiwar side Timothy Garton

Ash argued that "an American–British 'imperial' invasion of Iraq will increase the chances of Arab terror attacks in Europe and America" (*The Guardian*, February 6); and Jonathan Freedland worried that "a war against Iraq is not just a foolish diversion from fighting terror, it is a sure-fire way to fuel it" (*The Guardian*, January 22). If the advocates of war were motivated by fear, then so were their critics, and nowhere in this unedifying discussion was there any principled opposition to the Western "right to intervene."

In recognition of this underlying consensus, both Blair and Bush increasingly emphasized a humanitarian or human rights justification for war. Bush told the U.S. military that "the peace of a troubled world and the hope of an oppressed people now depend on you"; while Blair told the Iraqis "we will liberate you. The day of your freedom draws near" (*Times*, March 21, 28). In the same spirit, in his February 2003 speech Blair urged people to "remember Kosovo." Yet it seemed everyone already had. Former Women's Minister Joan Ruddock declared that "Taking action over Kosovo was justified" (*Independent on Sunday*, February 2), for example, and former Culture Secretary Chris Smith proclaimed: "I supported the action we took in Kosovo . . . [Blair] was brave, and determined, and right" (*Independent*, March 6). Both, however, were arguing *against* war with Iraq. Indeed, Blair's hawkish Foreign Secretary during the Kosovo crisis, Robin Cook, emerged as the "the standard-bearer of the Labour 'doves' " over Iraq (*Mail*, August 16, 2002). Cook had been a key architect of Labour's "ethical foreign policy," but he resigned from the government on March 17, 2003, the day the United States and United Kingdom abandoned the pursuit of a second UN resolution authorizing force. In the media, Rupert Murdoch supported Blair's pro-war stance as "extraordinarily courageous and strong," praising him for having "shown great guts, as he did, I think, in Kosovo" (*The Guardian*, February 12, 2003). Meanwhile those liberal, left-of-center newspapers that opposed war also emphasized their previous support for the bombing of Yugoslavia. "We supported the war in Kosovo," announced the *Independent* in an antiwar editorial (February 7), and the *Guardian*'s Jonathan Freedland criticized the build-up to war while writing that "US power can sometimes be a force for good in the world: that's why I supported the Kosovo campaign" (February 5). The only question was whether invading Iraq would be "moral" enough.

Even when commentators felt that the war would not meet the supposedly high ethical standards set by the Kosovo bombing, they were likely to support some form of coercive intervention. Garton Ash, for example, though sceptical about an invasion, nevertheless argued for "intrusive and rigorous" weapons inspections backed by "the threat of force," because,

> we need a world in which sovereignty is limited by some basic international norms, in which a Saddam, a Milosevic, a Pinochet or an Idi Amin know: thus

far I may go, but no further, or my country will be bombed and I'll end up in court at the Hague. (*The Guardian*, September 19, 2002)

Similarly, the *Independent* advocated "intrusive inspections backed by the threat of limited force" as an alternative strategy (February 7, 2003); and in the *Guardian* Freedland argued that "the peace camp has to set out its own, alternative method of ridding Iraq of its oppressor," such as "muscular rights inspectors" backed by "a military presence" (February 19). More broadly, this acceptance of the West's right to intervene was reflected in the position adopted by many leading critics of war that invading Iraq was wrong unless sanctioned by a further UN resolution, in which case it was right. Perhaps the most telling illustration of the antipolitical debate over Iraq was the reduction of the issue of going to war to a question of personal conscience. The slogan of the antiwar movement—"Not In My Name"— was less a political demand than an abdication of responsibility. War was seen as inevitable: the aim was not so much to stop it as to absolve oneself of blame. Matching the tone of these sentiments, Blair's response, in July 2004, to the official enquiry into the misuse of intelligence on WMD was to emphasise that he had acted "in good faith." The cry of the protestors that "Blair's not listening" was echoed by the Prime Minister's plea at a February 18, 2003 press conference: "I just ask people to listen to the other side of the argument."

It is the elite's lack of political purpose and vision that gives rise to those phenomena that critics see as typifying the conduct of postmodern war: the use of hi-tech weapons and the emphasis on media spectacle.[22] When war is not "born of an antagonistic, destructive but dual relation between two adversaries," Baudrillard contended, it becomes bloodless: "an asexual surgical war, a matter of war-processing in which the enemy only appears as a computerised target. . . ."[23] The propaganda always emphasizes the West's "humane" approach to killing people, using "smart weapons" to minimize "collateral damage," but the more important aim is to eliminate the risk to Western troops themselves. As Baudrillard noted mockingly in 1991, American soldiers were actually safer in the war zone than at home: the casualties were lower than the rate of deaths from traffic accidents in the United States.[24] In 2003 the combination of "shock and awe" bombing and laying siege to troublespots such as Basra was supposed to bring victory with as little risk as possible.[25]

The fear of "another Vietnam," which surfaces whenever the U.S. military goes into action, is a fear that deaths cannot be justified when the political rationale for war is threadbare. As Colin Powell has argued, referring to the 1994 withdrawal from Somalia following the deaths of 18 U.S. servicemen, the public are "prepared to take casualties," but only "as long as they believe it's for a solid purpose and for a cause that is understandable and for a cause that has something to do with an interest of ours."[26] Conversely, the lack of any such "solid purpose" means that the conduct of war becomes risk-averse. In Iraq, "the US military is fighting desertion, recruitment shortfalls and legal challenges from its own troops," despite the fact that "[at] 10 per cent, the death rate among war casualties is the lowest in history" (*Times*, December 10, 2004).

For similar reasons, the media presentation of war assumes a disproportionate importance, as staging the spectacle of war becomes a substitute for an inspiring cause to rally public support. As Baudrillard put it: "The media mix has become the prerequisite to any orgasmic event. We need it precisely because the event escapes us, because conviction escapes us."[27] Coalition forces encountered more difficulty than anticipated in securing control of towns, claiming to have "taken" Umm Qasr no fewer than nine times before actually gaining control, for example. Far easier, however, was to create the impression of success by rolling tanks and armoured vehicles over shrines to Saddam, painting over his murals, and ripping up his pictures. As Jonathan Glancey noted in the *Guardian* (April 10, 2003), this was "not . . . a knee-jerk reaction by angry soldiers. . . . The photographs are too many, press coverage too knowing for that." It may have proved difficult actually to gain control of the country, but it was possible to simulate victory by defacing the enemy's image and pulling down his statues.

Yet no amount of media management can overcome the political malaise that makes contemporary war so image conscious. Traditional ideological standbys—celebrating a martial, national, or Western identity—now seem to cause disquiet instead of cohering support. This was why news audiences witnessed the Stars and Stripes being proudly hoisted in Iraq one minute, only to see it hauled down in embarrassment the next. There were also worries about appearing too militaristic, as exemplified in Britain by the debate about whether to hold a victory parade, a "cavalcade," or a church service after the Iraq campaign. In the event, a "multi-faith service of remembrance" was held at St. Paul's Cathedral, designed to be "sensitive to other traditions, other experiences and other faiths," including Islam (*Independent*, October 11, 2003). Similar considerations applied beforehand, one journalist revealed:

> We were not allowed to take any pictures or describe British soldiers carrying guns. I was told that there was . . . a decision made by Downing Street that the military minders of the journalists down there were to go to any lengths . . . to not portray . . . the British fighting man and women as fighters.[28]

An inability to celebrate victory or to portray soldiers as soldiers is symptomatic of the elite's lack of confidence.

The attempt to resolve the West's "crisis of meaning" by going to war in Iraq may have failed, but antiwar critics can take little comfort from the elite's incoherence. Baudrillard's critique seems more apt than ever, but only because the postmodern scepticism toward grand narratives now afflicts Western society as a whole. Judging from past attempts to "export democracy" to Afghanistan, the former Yugoslavia, and elsewhere, it seems improbable that the postwar disorder would be resolved by the 2005 elections and it has not been. It is more likely that the West's own lack of purpose and cohesion will be mirrored by empty institutions in Iraq.

Notes

* This chapter is a revised and updated version of: "Postmodernity goes to War," *spiked*, June 1, 2004 <http://www.spiked-online.com/Articles/0000000CA554.htm>

1. J. Baudrillard, *The Gulf War Did Not Take Place* (Bloomington: Indiana University Press, 1995).
2. C. Norris, *Uncritical Theory: Postmodernism, Intellectuals and the Gulf War* (London: Lawrence and Wishart, 1992).
3. See, for example: J. Appleton, "Back to Baudrillard," *Spiked*, April 10, 2003 <http://www.spiked-online.com/Articles/00000006DD41.htm> (accessed April 10, 2003); S. Brown, "From the 'Death of the Real' to the Reality of Death: How Did the Gulf War Take Place?" *Journal for Crime, Conflict and the Media* (2003) <http://www.jc2m.co.uk/Issue1/Brown.pdf> (accessed December 19, 2003); and B. Kampmark, "Wars that Never Take Place: Non-events, 9/11 and Wars on Terrorism," *Australian Humanities Review*, 29 (May–June 2003) <http://www.lib.latrobe.edu.au/AHR/archive/Issue-May-2003/kampmark.html> (accessed January 10, 2005).
4. Baudrillard, *The Gulf War*, 74.
5. Ibid., 62.
6. Ibid., 26.
7. *Newsnight*, BBC2, April 8, 2004.
8. J.-F. Lyotard, *The Postmodern Condition: A Report on Knowledge* (Manchester: Manchester University Press, 1984), xxiv.
9. P. Anderson, *The Origins of Postmodernity* (London: Verso, 1998), 29.
10. Baudrillard, *The Gulf War*, 77.
11. Ibid., 79.
12. Ibid., 85.
13. J. Heartfield, *The "Death of the Subject" Explained* (Sheffield: Sheffield Hallam University Press, 2002), Chapter 6.
14. Baudrillard, *The Gulf War*, 66.
15. Quoted in D. Campbell, *Writing Security* (Minneapolis: University of Minnesota Press, 1992), 3.
16. Quoted in S. Chesterman, "Ordering the New World: Violence and its Re/Presentation in the Gulf War and Beyond," *Postmodern Culture* 8:3 (May 1998) <http://www.iath.virginia.edu/pmc/text-only/issue.598/8.3chesterman.txt> (accessed May 10, 2004).

17. Z. Laïdi, *A World Without Meaning: The Crisis of Meaning in International Politics* (London: Routledge, 1998), 1.
18. Baudrillard, *The Gulf War*, 24.
19. Ibid., 32.
20. Quoted in M. C. Miller, *The Bush Dyslexicon* (London: Bantam Books, 2001), 260–261.
21. Baudrillard, *The Gulf War*, 83.
22. See, for example: S. Best and D. Kellner, *The Postmodern Adventure* (London: Routledge, 2001), Chapter 2; J. Der Derian, *Virtuous War: Mapping the Military-Industrial-Media-Entertainment Network* (Boulder, CO: Westview Press, 2001); and C. H. Gray, *Postmodern War: The New Politics of Conflict* (London: Routledge, 1997).
23. Baudrillard, *The Gulf War*, 62.
24. Ibid., 69.
25. B. O'Neill, "Rewriting Basra," *spiked*, April 9, 2003 <http://www.spiked-online.com/Articles/00000006DD3A.htm> (accessed April 9, 2003).
26. Quoted in S. Livingston, *Clarifying the CNN Effect* (Joan Shorenstein Center on the Press, Politics and Public Policy, Harvard University, 1997) <http://sparky.harvard.edu/presspol/publications/pdfs/70916_R-18.pdf> (accessed June 10, 1999).
27. Baudrillard, *The Gulf War*, 75.
28. *Correspondent*, BBC2, May 18, 2003 <http://news.bbc.co.uk/nol/shared/spl/hi/programmes/correspondent/transcripts/18.5.03.txt> (accessed May 20, 2003).

Chapter Six

Orientalism Revisited: The British Media and the Iraq War

Judith Brown

In 1978 Edward Said's *Orientalism* stirred the academic world to review relationships between East and West. Said argued that during the period of colonialism European Imperialists had established a discourse in which Western culture and societies were essentially and inherently superior to Eastern ones, using examples from the political, academic, and literary world to demonstrate his case.[1] Said called the discourse that he revealed "Orientalism" and he described it as a tool for dominating, restructuring, and having authority over the Orient, but most particularly the Middle East.[2]

Said built on work of the Foucault who saw power not just as a "top-down" mechanism, but existing at all levels. Power could only be exercised with production, accumulation, circulation, and functioning of discourse[3] taking the form of statements that are spoken and written, dispersed, and of frequent occurrence.[4] Said also drew on the work of Gramsci who described the hegemonic power structures within society. Gramsci's theories show that in civil society power works not through domination but by consent, and Said claimed this gave Orientalism its durability.[5]

This chapter examines the relevance of Orientalism in British society 25 years after Said's observations, using the context of the media coverage of the 2003 Iraq War. The United States was established as world hegemon, but when the U.S. Administration made a case for war in 2003 despite its strength it did not dominate the British media. A sharply divided debate emerged between those who wanted to go to war and those who did not and Iraqis featured in this new emerging discourse.

Iraqi viewpoints had had low priority since the first Gulf War. The economic sanctions that followed caused great suffering within Iraqi society, but this did not become a prominent discourse. A letter in the *Lancet* reported that 567,000 Iraqi children died because of sanctions,[6] after which the U.S. Ambassador to the UN claimed: "the price was worth it." Later Iraqi health department and UNICEF figures pointed to total child deaths of between 1.2 and 1.5 million.[7] Two UN oil-for-food coordinators resigned, citing their reason as the effect of sanctions. Despite this a persistent media debate on Iraq suffering did not arise, although from 1998 the media started to show interest.[8]

Many Iraqis were frustrated when trying to publicise Iraqi concerns. Dr. Kamil Madhi said Iraqis had grown out of the habit of engagement with the media. He continued,

> It would be difficult because they would be forced to make a certain choice of words in order to get published. This happened over a long period of time, people have been "pigeon-holed" and if their views weren't in favour they could not get anything published, not even a letter. If you are not saying what is acceptable, you simply have no chance . . . there is a refusal to acknowledge the Iraqi voice if it is a view which is independent of the US position.[9]

Many Iraqis from a range of political backgrounds tried novel ways to bring their concerns to the British public, for example publishing newspapers, arranging visits to Iraq, and exhibitions and meetings in the United Kingdom. They built up media interest although their concerns still did not have a high profile. Some did not make protestations such as Canadian/Iraqi journalist Firas Al-Atraqchi who knew about the effect of sanctions but did nothing about getting it into the public domain. "I didn't write about it because I was part of the media system, I was sucked in, part of it, I didn't step outside how the media works."[10]

Media disinterest demonstrated the insidious nature of hegemonic power as, first, the media were informed of the alarming consequences of sanctions not only by articulate and resourceful Iraqis but also by respected organizations and international experts. Second, even the liberal sections of the British press were silent on Iraqi suffering; although to an extent this taboo was broken after 1998 but it was still insufficient to raise general awareness. And third, this uniformity within all sections of the media occurred without the need for an official censor. Foucault said power could not be established, consolidated, nor implemented without a functioning discourse[11] and a discourse on Iraqi concerns and Iraqi-led solutions to a difficult humanitarian and political situation did not arise. A new discourse arose only when U.S. President George W. Bush raised the idea of another Iraqi war. There was a corresponding large increase in media interest with some journalists strongly opposed to military action. This media debate occurred even though the main U.K. political parties supported the U.S. position.

Discourse is dynamic, and the "never said" can become the "always said" when new power relationships surface.[12] In this new scenario opposing groups questioned the advisability of war. It included politicians on the left and right, and other people with a high media profile.[13] This was a debate between different groups of Western elites rather than a discourse in which Iraqis themselves presented the alternative view. Amongst Iraqis there was a range of opinions, with some wanting a war to free themselves from the Baath regime and others fearing war. The discourse that did not appear in the British media was a search for alternative means of self-determination for Iraqis. The positivity of discourse means that ideas can gain credibility without contributors realizing that debate is in some way controlled[14] and Iraqis and others who were speaking for or against the war were, knowingly or not, confined to Western agendas.

Hidden Iraqi Images

After Bush started discussing war the British media did not immediately present Iraqi images. To demonstrate the early lack of Iraqi input into the debate I examined press coverage from November 15 to November 29, 2002. There were 232 articles about Iraq in nine British national newspapers.[15] Only six articles focused on Iraqi citizens, five on fringe issues, and only the *Mirror* that was taking a strong antiwar line reported the potential war casualties.[16] The remaining articles occasionally gave glimpses of Iraqis, but the majority dealt with the UN, U.S. and British governments' positions. A pro- or antiwar stance was associated with particular papers and correspondents.

One typical day was November 28, 2002, the day after weapons inspections resumed in Iraq. There were 15 articles, and within these articles 14 minor references to Iraqis. This included seven quotations, five descriptions of Iraqis, and two references to Saddam Hussein's war crimes. Iraqis were described as unaffected by events, smiling, and unconcerned.[17] The unspoken impression was that Iraqis were somehow immune to threat of war. Minor descriptions used negative imagery such as "shiny suits" and "Saddam moustaches."[18] There were no photographs of Iraqis and quotations were minimal, for example, "They didn't find anything because we don't have anything illegal."[19]

Emergence of Iraqis

The imagery changed in January 2003 when the pro-war and antiwar groups started using Iraqis to support their case. The antiwar correspondents presented Iraqis as "victims" who would suffer during hostilities, whereas the pro-war correspondents showed Iraqis needing release from a tyrannical regime. There was no indication that the correspondents were listening to Iraqis and Iraqi experts and modifying their views; instead they were using them as evidence for earlier stated positions.

Some interviewees pointed to times when their opinions were being unfairly manipulated. For example Said Aburish an expert on Saddam Hussein said:

> The person who interviews has the advantage, except when it is a live broadcast. They can do as they want and take you out of context . . . I was quoted as saying that Chirac took money from Saddam in order to justify it [Chirac's opposition to the war]. But I did not say that. Yes, people [journalists] do use someone like me to suit their own purposes, they are trying to push you in one direction.[20]

Another example was Maysoon Pachachi an Iraqi filmmaker asked to visit the Prime Minister to talk about the life of Iraqi women under Saddam Hussein. She refused, as she did not want to be limited to a specific agenda. Three days later she saw Blair on television describing how Iraqi women told him of their suffering under the Baath regime.[21]

Said described "Orientalists" not as people who portrayed Arabs and Muslims negatively, but those who used their European ability to "comment on, acquire knowledge of, and possess."[22] Thus being pro-war or antiwar did not safeguard against an "Orientalist" agenda. Both "sides" used images of women and children; whatever the underlying motivation female and child imagery emphasised Iraqi helplessness. For example, the antiwar *Mirror* produced pictures of two dead sisters, killed by British bombs,[23] whereas the pro-war *Telegraph* reported a Kurdish woman who was set afire by Iraqis; the accompanying photograph showed her "whimpering in pain."[24] A *Guardian* article described the damaging effects of the decade of conflict on middle-class Iraqis, and an illustrating photograph was of an Iraqi woman.[25] The pro-war *Sun* showed women and children leaving Baghdad giving the impression that innocent Iraqis would not be in the areas where bombs might fall.[26]

Another recurring theme was tyranny and barbarism. A prowar correspondent wrote "Stop the war? Try telling that to the tyrannised people of Iraq." He described the ethnic cleansing of Marsh Arabs and gassing of Kurds.[27] The *Telegraph* described Saddam Hussein as "a tyrant who matches Stalin."[28] As well as describing a barbaric regime the common theme extended to ordinary Iraqi people as powerless victims who "needed" the West to save them. The writers claimed that they spoke on behalf of Iraqis, thus as "knowing" Westerners they became like earlier Orientalists who considered they were "representing those who cannot represent themselves."[29]

However during this period Iraqis also had acknowledgement of their competency as they were getting letters and articles printed, and were frequently interviewed by broadcasters. Both pro- and antiwar Iraqi activists claimed that they were busy. There were also interviews with representatives of the Iraqi government. In the period leading up to the war there was increased cooperation with the Western media as the Iraqi regime desperately tried to put its case.[30] After the start of the war the volume of published Iraqi opinions and political comments was significantly reduced.

War Stories

Whilst it is easy to understand why political leaders of the Iraqi regime were not featured during hostilities, intelligent Iraqi comment that had become part of the British media in the period before the war was also reduced. Dr. Kamil Mahdi said that before the war he was contacted several times a day for his opinion, but on the day the war started the phone calls stopped.[31] This was also reported by Said Aburish who said, "Arab experts were called in before the war but as soon as the shooting war started it was 'My country has gone to war and I am a supporter of my country.' So the call for Arab opinion ceased."[32]

The journalist Al-Atraqchi said that numerous Iraqi experts stopped providing him with information from the first day of war. He explained "I wasn't getting emails. . . ." for Arabs there was this overwhelming feeling of shock that they had done it, it had happened. . . . [33] Maysoon Pachachi pointed out the stress of making comments during the war. When the bombs were falling on Baghdad she was asked to appear on television to explain her feelings, but she found this insensitive and she did not think that she could contribute meaningfully to the debate at that time.[34] By contrast pro-war Iraqis were being used for interviews on radio and television, one stating "They [the media] were calling us."[35] They were asked to explain terms like "fedayeen" and other times to talk about their reactions. Before the war the emergence of images of competent, articulate Iraqis in the British media had contradicted the Western emphasis on Iraqis who "needed" intervention, thus challenging the U.S. Administration's position.

When compared with subordinate groups the hegemon is more able to regain control because it has more resources.[36] The U.S. Administration used its economic strength and hegemonic influence to try to ensure that the Iraqi images that dominated the worldwide media were those that they preferred, rather than allowing alternative voices to dilute their version of "truth." The United States set up a media facility reputed to have cost 1 million dollars.[37] The system of embedded journalists was streamlined and journalists signed an agreement to abide by the coalition's rules of reporting. Reporters who disobeyed were sent home.[38]

In a highly competitive media, stories with a different perspective have a commercial value, therefore almost all media organizations continued to use non-embedded journalists. The U.S. and U.K. governments discouraged independent methods of collecting information, the United States stating they would offer no protection to journalists working independently.[39] Non-embedded journalists were also criticized by the British government.[40] Negative imagery of Iraqis also had a commercial value during the war. The *Mirror* tried to empathize with Iraqi victims but lost circulation, which was for some time tolerated but the newspaper eventually succumbed to shareholder pressure and sacked the editor.[41]

The real power of hegemony is its ability not to coerce or persuade people to follow the will of the leader but in the way that power infiltrates minds. In the end those who are bound most tightly by hegemonic control feel empowered by it rather than restricted.[42] Many journalists and media elites follow decisions of politicians because they have internalized their position and automatically portray images that meet the needs of the ruling elites. This was explained by New York editor Michael Massing following apologies by a number of journalists in the United States for their lack of rigor before the war:

> It [the press corps] is part of an elite, they are well paid, they attend the same social functions as their sources such as those high up in government. They make an effort to develop close relationships with sources and if you get a scoop you will be patted on the back by your bosses even though your scoop has been manipulated.[43]

It was difficult to find British journalists willing to talk about their work during war, which may be due to lack of time or interest. However one journalist declined saying "It always comes back and is usually not good for the reporter!"[44]

BBC journalist Clive Myrie agreed that embedded journalists were spoon-fed information although he tried to check facts. He added, "I didn't wear a uniform, but I lived in the same way as the marines, looking at the tiny window of life inside combat, in a prison provided by the marines . . ."[45] Another embedded journalist became so close to the troops that he even acted as a lookout for suspicious vehicles.[46] Reporting the war from this angle meant that Iraqi troops were seen from the perspective of "the enemy" and would be difficult for journalists to retain full objectivity.

However, those who operated independently also showed compliance with U.S. wishes. One example occurred when U.S. troops fired on a number of sites used by non-embedded journalists, killing three media workers.[47] The following day U.S. troops assisted Iraqis to pull down a statue of

Saddam Hussein with Iraqis thanking "Mr. Bush." This was reported on every television channel and newspaper, nullifying the debate on the earlier unprovoked U.S. attacks on journalists. On this measure it appeared that the media were pacified to the extent that they reflected the U.S. Administration's preferred imagery even when this overrode a story in the interests of their own employees' security.

The pro-war *Times* and *Telegraph* decided to take their correspondents out of Baghdad during the war for security reasons.[48] *Times* correspondent Janine Digiovanni who specialises in human-interest stories said that although she was disappointed the *Times* had prioritised her safety even though it meant missing "scoops."[49] By comparison, the antiwar *Mirror,* the *Guardian*, and *Independent* retained Baghdad correspondents. Rageh Omaar of the BBC had stayed in Baghdad for several months prior to the war and empathetically stated: "The people of this country did not appear to matter either to the Iraqi government or to the press conferences of the coalition."[50] In the war the propaganda was from the other "side" and reporters were taken to bombed civilian areas and visited injured people in hospital.[51] Omaar's sympathetic accounts provoked Downing Street to ask for his removal, which the BBC refused.[52] Various disagreements between Downing Street and BBC about Iraqi coverage eventually caused senior BBC staff to resign.[53]

Notably media employees who lost their jobs had maintained a viewpoint that differed from the coalition line. Job losses occurred without direct government intervention as a result of perceived reporting inaccuracies, although there was evidence that all offending stories were based in fact.[54] Gramsci described the use of coercive power to "legally" discipline those who do not give consent to the ruling groups' ideas.[55] By comparison, embedded journalists were offered Ministry of Defence medals for their "collective bravery and achievements" even though they too had reported inaccuracies during the war.[56]

Abdulhadi Ayyad a local producer working for the BBC in Kuwait gave insight into journalists' attitudes and story-selection:

> Most British reporters didn't seem to have any understanding of the basic things about the culture and nationality issues . . . we would be told they wanted a story of a British expatriate living in Kuwait, how they were coping and how they were affected . . . I thought they were looking for a story of brave British.[57]

Both Ayyad and Aburish pointed out that there were a few excellent journalists who really understood Middle East issues but that the majority did not.[58] Without understanding the complexity of Middle East politics it is more difficult to write a balanced article when the journalist is writing about "the Other" from a Western perspective for a Western audience.

Iraqi Imagery in the War

To see how far this Western perspective influenced imagery I examined four newspapers on the fourth day of the war, the *Sun* (pro-war tabloid), the *Mirror* (antiwar tabloid), the *Times* (pro-war broadsheet), and the *Guardian* (broadsheet, mixed views, but generally antiwar). There were 21 articles in the *Sun*, 29 in the *Mirror*, 40 in the *Times*, and 42 in the *Guardian*.

The pro-war papers emphasised Iraqi barbarity. They used events such as showing U.S. prisoners and corpses on Arab television as evidence. The *Times* method was to print the relevant Geneva Convention articles inviting readers to compare their reports to international standards.[59] The front page of the *Sun* showed pictures of the prisoners with a caption "At mercy of savages," followed by a double page spread entitled "Gloating bastard." A leader on the subject uses the words "obscene, barbaric, horrific" and "chuckling and rifling through the personal possessions of the victims" adding Iraqis are "fundamentally decent but they have fallen under the spell of a pitiless monster" implying that if Iraqis were properly managed by the West they could improve.[60]

The *Times* described the coalition as using minimal force "confirmed" by its short and infrequent references to Iraqi casualties, such as "Seven Iraqi bodies were lying in the dust."[61] A U.S. bombardment of Baghdad is briefly mentioned, describing Iraqis as "puzzled" by this attack.[62] There was one photograph of an injured child illustrating an article on the incitement of Arabs by the Arab media.[63]

The Iraqi military used surprise tactics against a better-equipped army. The *Times* made this seem "less honourable," especially when combined with high emphasis on reporting Western casualties. Iraqi soldiers were described as "concealed" and attacking American forces "from behind" giving the impression that Iraqi soldiers were not fighting fairly. Iraqi soldiers were described as using Iraqi residents as human shields, and having "little sense of loyalty towards Saddam." The places where they were located were described as "rusty" and "dirty."[64]

The Sun described Iraqi deceit, reporting that Iraqi soldiers were misled by propaganda, believing they would be injected with poison if captured. After wounds of captive soldiers were treated by British medics they "relaxed and thanked us."[65] This conjured pictures of simple people with no capacity for original thought who "appreciated" the West.

The *Times* had no Iraqi viewpoints and only one article described Iraqi citizens. The story line described the soldiers' bravery when approached by a Bedouin man who could have been a suicide bomber. There was no suggestion that an invading force could frighten him, instead he was "unfazed" and "waved." He bartered and bribed soldiers for water and food (described as "in true Arab style"), and the article stated Bedu had a "long history" of disruption to fighting forces. He was "old and crusty" his home was "ramshackle" and his sheep "wool matted with dust and dirt."[66] This painted a picture of Iraqis as primitive, untrustworthy, and only interested in personal gain. *The Sun* did not refer to or show pictures of Iraqi civilians; photographs included one of "tyrant" Saddam Hussein,[67] three of a grinning Iraqi morgue attendant,[68] and one of a cowering Iraqi prisoner.[69]

The biggest difference between the *Guardian* and the *Times* was *the Guardian*'s descriptions of Iraqi victims and civilians, thus demonstrating that when the *Times* removed Digiovanni this had an impact on coverage. Altogether the *Guardian* had three main articles on Iraqi victims covering Kurdish and Shia civilian casualties and a U.S. missile strike in Baghdad.[70]

The *Mirror* emphasized victims from each "side." Iraqis were described as "they cling to life . . . their stomachs bleeding from shrapnel wounds" and personalized: "Omar and Saed, two children aged six and seven, were part of a family of 12."[71] There was a photograph of a burned baby[72] and an Iraqi man carrying an unconscious girl with severe leg trauma.[73] The same man was photographed with a less injured child in the *Times* and the *Guardian*. A mother was pictured with her injured, screaming baby, and two Iraqi soldiers' bodies were in a trench with a white flag clearly visible. There was another photograph of a blood soaked Iraqi victim.[74] There was one angry quotation from an Iraqi whose house was destroyed.[75] The general image was of powerless, suffering people who "needed" the *Mirror* to speak up for them.

The *Guardian*'s innocent victims were less vivid but they were shown in a manner that made it easy for the reader to empathise. Photographs included one of an injured little girl,[76] the same photograph used by the *Times* to illustrate incitement to violence caused by Arab television, but the *Guardian* used it to illustrate a possible massacre of children. The *Guardian* showed dignified, bereaved Kurds,[77] and a picture of a clean Iraqi boy in rubble left by a bomb.[78]

Negative Iraqi actions were reported in the *Guardian* but not dwelled on. For example compared with six "Prisoner of War" articles in the *Times*, the *Guardian* had two and instead of total condemnation there was a range of comments.[79] The impression was not of a barbaric nation but individual Iraqis acting illegally and disrespectfully. The *Mirror* briefly described the

Iraqi morgue attendant "A smiling Iraqi uncovered the dead, several of who [*sic*] had blackened faces."[80] Rather than emphasising Iraqi barbarity, The *Mirror* made such things seem part of the horrors of war, describing Iraqi combatants thus:

> Iraqi army officers had nowhere to run. And probably fearing reprisals . . . they were not prepared to surrender, unlike hundreds of their dishevelled subordinates we had seen in the past 48 hours walk off the battle fields with grubby little flags.[81]

There were brief *Mirror* references to "strong Iraqi resistance," and "we already know some Iraqis are fighting in civilian clothes."[82] However, by describing the war as "senseless" and unjustified the *Mirror* gave the impression that all people including troops caught up in the conflict were worthy of victim status.[83] The impression given of the British army was of its efficiency and bravery, whereas the Iraqi army was shown as disorganized and misguided.

The *Guardian* described Iraqi resistance in neutral tones, for example "US and British military troops were locked in fierce gunfights with Republican Guard soldiers yesterday as they struggled to take control of Umm Qasr." "Some Iraqi soldiers, a few in civilian clothing, seem to have made an apparently independent decision to fight on."[84] It also personalized the Iraqi soldiers who surrendered by briefly quoting their views.[85]

The *Guardian* was the only newspaper that gave Iraqis a credible voice, although this emphasised Iraqi powerlessness, for example a Baghdadi who hears that bombers have left Fairford waits for "shock and awe,"[86] and an Iraqi living in the United Kingdom watches what she calls "a snuff movie."[87] An Iraqi farmer was described trying to get his goods to market. In the four papers studied this was the only account where Iraqis were described as acting in a courageous manner, "embarking on a journey more perilous than any soldier's march."[88]

The *Mirror* and the *Guardian* demonstrated different ways in which a paper that had taken an antiwar line coped with reporting a war it had opposed. The *Mirror* took two themes, one was admiration for British troops, whilst portraying everyone involved in what it considered an illegal war as a potential "victim." The *Guardian* had more stories on the war than the other papers covering a huge breadth of war-related topics, such as the cost of war and peace movement issues. The conflict was reported factually, although with more emphasis on the activities of the coalition forces than Iraqi forces.

Each paper's prewar theme was carried forward in the coverage of the war itself. The pro-war correspondents carried on with images of "barbarism," whereas the antiwar correspondents continued to use the theme of "victims." The *Guardian* that had printed articles written by Iraqis before the war continued to give them a voice, but they could only be portrayed as weak and powerless because of the nature of the war. Whatever the political angle, Iraqis generally were depicted as "needing" Western assistance, either to improve or to survive. Only the *Guardian* showed Iraqis surviving due to their own endeavors, but even then weakness was a dominant theme.

Orientalism Continues

The hegemony of the United States can be shown to work through its political allies and through links with media elites. Commercial pressures and customer expectations put pressure on media workers to provide stories in line with the U.S. Administration's perspective but many media workers willingly complied with the expectations of their employers. Subtle pressures influenced the actions of those who opposed the U.S. line to act in U.S. interests. Iraqis had to be depicted as militarily weak and U.S. troops as strong because it was so, and when Iraqis saw their homeland being attacked it created emotions that caused many to voluntarily withdraw from media interactions. With the United States in control of Iraq many journalists saw Iraqi sources as unnecessary. This created long periods when intelligent Iraqi political comment was uncommon in the British media.

There is a new emerging discourse challenging current U.S. Middle East policies, which gained momentum in the run-up to the Iraq war. Where there is power there is always resistance, sometimes as one massive movement but often many separate foci scattered through the power field, which mobilize groups and individuals to act.[89] The discourse of resistance did not start in one particular location but arose when people from all parts of the world thought war was not in their interests. For example in Britain resistance came from the far right as well as parties on the left, there was no single leader of the opposition to war and the tone was generally to criticize the U.S. policy rather than offer alternatives.

What was omitted was any persistent representation of competent, articulate, and courageous Iraqis suggesting their own solutions; any such representation was inconsistent and irregular. Individually and collectively Iraqis were sometimes referred to in favorable terms but for this to have meaning there has to be a persistent system of representation to support rhetoric or otherwise words have limited impact. Iraqi media appearances were often mirrored, with each "side" simultaneously producing the type of Iraqi that "proved" opposing arguments, or both "sides" ignoring Iraqi images and opinions for similar periods of time.

Said claimed that systems of representations of the Orient are framed in a set of forces that brought the Orient into Western learning and Western consciousness. He argued that the Orient was a construct used to benefit the West.[90] In covering issues surrounding the Iraqi war the British media represented Iraqis using themes of barbarity, incompetence, and weakness. Some of these impressions were achieved as much by what was left out of stories as what was included; the debate often centred on Western figures such as Bush, Blair, Chirac, and Blix[91] and it debated Western issues such as the risk posed to the West by weapons of mass destruction and oil security issues, preferring the opinions of Western experts including ambassadors, politicians, academics, the military, and technicians such as weapons inspectors. The "problem" that entered the British consciousness was essentially shown as Western, the "enemy" was often presented as "Bush and Blair" or the "anti-war liberals," and the emphasis was on what the West should do in answer to a series of situations that arose in Iraq during the build up to the war, the war itself, and the occupation that followed.

Said maintained that the West depicted the Orient in a consistent manner, which defined an unequal relationship of power and domination. He believed Orientalism had much more to do with "our" world than "their" world. In both the pro-war and antiwar discourses that emerged before and during the Iraq war, Western issues predominated and real Iraqi concerns remained a secondary issue. Said's Orientalists are still a force to be reckoned with.

Notes

1. E. Said, *Orientalism* (London: Penguin, 1995), 6–7, 31–36.
2. Ibid., 3.
3. M. Foucault, "Disciplinary power and subjection," in *Power*, ed. S. Lukes, 229–242 (New York: Pantheon Book, 1986). First published in Michel Foucault, *Power/Knowledge: Selected Interviews and Other Writings 1972–1977*, ed. and trans. Colin Gordon (New York: Pantheon Books, 1980), 229–230.
4. M. Foucault, trans. A.M. Sheridan Smith. *The Archaeology of Knowledge* (London: Tavistock Publications, 1972), 26–28.
5. Said, *Orientalism*, 6–7.
6. S. Zaidi and M.F. Fawzi, "Health of Baghdad's children," *Lancet*, 346: 8988 (1995): 1485.
7. C. Rowat, "Sanctions on Iraq: background information" *CASI*, January 6, 1999 <http://www.casi.org.uk/halliday/backg.html>
8. R. Omaar, *Revolution Day* (London: Penguin/Viking, 2004), 35–39.
9. Interview with Dr. Kamil Mahdi, Exeter University lecturer, November 5, 2003.
10. Interview with journalist Faris Al-Atraqchi, June 2, 2004.
11. Foucault, *Disciplinary Power and Subjection*, 229–230.

12. Foucault, *The Archaeology of Knowledge*, 23.
13. J. Vidal, J. Wilson, and T. Branigan, "Threat of war: Strikes, sit-ins and walk outs planned to shut Britain down," *The Guardian*, February 17, 2003, 4.
14. Said, *Orientalism*, 14.
15. The newspapers examined were Daily Telegraph (Telegraph), Financial Times, Guardian, Independent, Times, Daily Express, Daily Mail, Daily Mirror (Mirror), and Sun.
16. O. Blackman, "Exclusive report spells out stark cost of war on Iraq," *Daily Mirror*, November 25, 2002, 8.
17. K. Ghattas, "All smiles for weapons inspectors' first day," *Financial Times*, November 28, 2002, 13.
18. K. Sengupta, "UN teams fan out for first day of inspections," *Independent*, November 28, 2002, 2.
19. M. Ellis, "UN team in Iraq swoop." *Daily Mirror*, November 28, 2002, 15.
20. Interview with author Said Aburish, May 31, 2004.
21. Interview with Iraqi filmmaker Maysoon Pachachi, May 20, 2004.
22. Said, *Orientalism*, 160.
23. J. Pilger, "These sisters were killed by one of our bombers," *Daily Mirror*, March 16, 2003, 6–7.
24. J. Strauss, "Agony of mother set ablaze by Iraqis," *Daily Telegraph*, March 7, 2003, 1.
25. S. Goldenburg, "Iraqis with cash dig deep for survival," *The Guardian*, January 31, 2003, 6.
26. B. Graham, "Women and kids flee Baghdad blitz," *The Sun*, March 18, 2003 <www.thesun.co.uk/article/0,2-2003121754,00.html>
27. J. Hari, "Stop the war? Try telling that to the tyrannised people of Iraq," *Independent*, February 7, 2003, 16.
28. N. Cohen, "The Left betrays the Iraqi people by opposing war," *Daily Telegraph*, January 14, 2003, 20.
29. Karl Marx quotation in E. Said, *Orientalism* (London: Penguin, 1995) prior to page 1.
30. R. Omaar, *Revolution Day*, 72.
31. Interview with Dr. Kamil Mahdi, Exeter University lecturer, November 5, 2003.
32. Interview with author Said Aburish, May 31, 2004.
33. Interview with journalist Faris Al-Atraqchi, June 2, 2004.
34. Interview with Iraqi filmmaker Maysoon Pachachi, May 20, 2004.
35. Interview with Ahmed Shames, Chairman, Iraqi Prospects Organisation, May 3, 2004.
36. A. Gramsci, ed. D. Forgacs, trans. Quinton Hoare and Geoffrey Nowell-Smith, *A Gramsci Reader; Selected Writings 1916–1935.* (London: Lawrence and Wishart, 1988), 217–222.
37. D. Miller, "The Propaganda Machine," in *Tell Me Lies*, ed. D. Miller (London: Pluto Press, 2004), 88–89.
38. J. Tomlin, "Censored in the desert," *Press Gazette*, May 16, 2003, 15.
39. John Simpson, BBC1 Panorama Special *In the Line of Fire*, May 23, 2004.
40. T. Gopsill, "Target the media," in *Tell Me Lies: Propaganda & Media Distortion in the Attack on Iraq*, ed. D. Miller (London: Pluto Press, 2003), 251–261; "Speech row," *Birmingham Post*, April 4, 2003, 2.

41. I. Burrell, " 'Mirror' editor sacked in row over fake photos." *Independent*, May 15, 2004, 1.
42. M. Foucault, "Truth and Power," in *Orientalism, a Reader*, ed. A.L. Macfie (Edinburgh: Edinburgh University Press, 2000), 41–43. First published in Michel Foucault, *Power/Knowledge: Selected Interviews and Other Writings 1972–1977,* ed. and trans. Colin Gordon (New York: Pantheon Books, 1980), 141–143.
43. M. Massing, interviewed by *Broadcasting House*, BBC Radio 4, May 23, 2004.
44. Unnamed journalist, confidential email to author, May 28, 2004.
45. C. Myrie (BBC reporter) Lecture Dubai Media Summit, October 7, 2003.
46. D. Miller, "The propaganda machine," 89–91.
47. T. Gopsill, "Target the media," 253; R. Fisk, "Is there some element in the US military that wants to take out journalists?" *Independent*, April 9, 2003, 4.
48. T. Gopsill, "Target the media," 253; C. Byrne, "Media mull Iraq evacuation." *Media Guardian.* March 18, 2003 <http://media.guardian.co.uk/broadcast/story/0,7493,916727,00.html>
49. J. Digiovanni (Times reporter) Answer to questions after lecture Dubai Media Summit, October 7, 2003.
50. R. Omaar, *Revolution Day*, 82.
51. Ibid., 140–158.
52. S. Hattenstone, "Reluctant warrior," *The Guardian*, February 28, 2004, 32.
53. "Decapitation," *The Guardian*, January 30, 2004, 29; D. Ponsford, "Corporation condemned," *Press Gazette*, February 13, 2004, 13.
54. R. Norton-Taylor and M. Wells, "Dossier findings support Kelly's allegations," *The Guardian*, July 16, 2004, 5; P. Waugh, P. "How a judge's narrow remit allowed Government off hook on vital issues of case for war," *Independent*, January 29, 2004, 4; "Whether or not the 'Mirror' pictures are fake, they exposed some awkward truths," *Independent*, May 14, 2004, 36.
55. A. Gramsci, trans. Quinton Hoare and Geoffrey Nowell-Smith, *Selection from Prison Notebooks* (London: Lawrence and Wishart, 1971), 12–13.
56. W. Azeez, "Embedded media urged to reject war medal," *Press Gazette*, February 27, 2004, 1; A. Lawson, L. O'Carroll, C. Tryhorn, and J. Deans, "War Watch," *Media Guardian*, April 2, 2003 <http://media.guardian.co.uk/iraqandthemedia/story/0,12823,921649,00.html>
57. Interview with Abdulhadi Ayyad, local BBC producer in Kuwait, June 15, 2003.
58. Interview with author Said Aburish, May 31, 2004.
59. "From the Geneva Convention," *Times*, March 24, 2003, 2.
60. "Monstrous," *Sun*, March 24, 2003, 8.
61. D. McGrory, T. Butcher T. "How a walkover turned into a three-day battle," *Times*, March 24, 2003, 5.
62. R. Beeston, "Burning cloud of doom hangs over Baghdad," *Times*, March 24, 2003, 4.
63. N. Blanford, "Al-Jazeera inflames Arab fury with vivid TV reports," *Times*, March 24, 2003, 9.
64. T. Baldwin, "Irregular troops leave a mark on history," *Times*, March 24, 2003: 5; M. Evans, "Pockets of resistance frustrate advancing coalition," *Times*, March 24, 2003, 4; D. McGrory, T. Butcher, *Times*, 5.

65. D. Larcombe, "POW poison lie," *The Sun*, March 24, 2003, 2.
66. C. Ayres, "Marines tackle Beduin [*sic*] goat herders with bribes and gestures," *Times*, March 24, 2003, 5.
67. D. Wooding, "SOS for Saddam surgeon," *The Sun*, March 24, 2003, 12.
68. B. Flynn, G. Pascoe-Watson, *Sun*, 2–3.
69. T. Richards, "Deadly game of cat and mouse," *The Sun*, March 24, 2003, 9.
70. O. Burkeman, "Battle for key city leads to 'massacre of children' claim," *The Guardian*, March 24, 2003, 4; L. Harding, "This makes us love Saddam, not America," *The Guardian*, March 24, 2003, 7; S. Goldenburg, "Rogue missile wrecks home," *The Guardian*, March 24, 2003, 10.
71. A. Antonowicz, "Not so smart," *Daily Mirror*, March 24, 2003, 10–11.
72. "Still anti-war? Yes, bloody right we are," *Daily Mirror*, March 24, 2003, 1.
73. "In your name," *Daily Mirror*, March 24, 2003, 12.
74. B. Reade, "Images to explode the myths of war," *Daily Mirror*, March 24, 2003, 18–19.
75. A. Antonowicz, "Not so smart," 10–11.
76. O. Burkeman, "Battle for key city leads to 'massacre of children' claim," 4.
77. L. Harding, "This makes us love Saddam, not America," 7.
78. S. Goldenburg, "Rogue missile wrecks home," 10.
79. S. Goldenburg, "The band plays for Baghdad's new mood," *The Guardian*, March 24, 2003, 1; E. MacAskill, O. Burkeman, "American prisoners paraded by Iraqis," *Guardian*, March 24, 2003, 1.
80. R. Wallace, America'a nightmare. *Daily Mirror*, March 24, 2003, 2.
81. T. Dunn, "Sniper on the roof, keep your f***ing heads down," *Daily Mirror*, March 24, 2003, 12–13.
82. B. Roberts, "Deadly fightback," *Daily Mirror*, March 24, 2003, 8–9.
83. "Terrible day, terrible war," *Daily Mirror*, March 24, 2003, 8.
84. J. Borger and R. Norton-Taylor, "Resistance raises fears for the endgame," *The Guardian*, March 24, 2003, 4; N. Parker and R. McCarthy, "Fierce battle around port," 5.
85. N. Parker, R. McCarthy, "Fierce battle around port," 5.
86. L. Hickman, "Baghdad calling," *The Guardian G2 Supplement*, March 24, 2003, 2–3.
87. A. Kaisy, "It's my family they're bombing," *The Guardian*, March 24, 2003, 19.
88. J. Meek, "Dodging between two hostile armies, desperate to reach the market of Baghdad," *The Guardian*, March 24, 2003, 3.
89. M. Foucault, trans. Robert Hurley, *The Will to Knowledge. The History of Sexuality* (England: Penguin, 1998), 95–96.
90. Said, *Orientalism*, 201–203.
91. UN Weapons Inspector Hans Blix.

AUSTRALIA

CHAPTER SEVEN
THE WAR IN IRAQ: A VIEW FROM AUSTRALIA

Daniela V. Dimitrova

Mass media are important institutions in any society and exert influence on public opinion as well as on public policy makers. The media provide a critical connection between politicians and voters. They also have a mission to inform citizen in a democratic society about events taking place at home and abroad. The focus of this chapter is a global news event—the 2003 Iraq war. The coverage of the war is examined and analyzed in one of the leading Australian newspapers, focusing on the images of war, tone of coverage, and framing of the war.

Australia and Its Role in the War

The 2003 Iraq war started on March 19, 2003, long after the president of the United States announced military action in Iraq. The war did not receive equal support around the globe. First, the United Nations declared they were not going to be involved, in contrast to the 1991 Persian Gulf War. Second, some European nations such as France and Germany clearly stated their opposition to unilateral military intervention in Iraq. Yet other European countries decided to support the war effort and join the so-called Coalition of the Willing. The two big allies of the United States in the 2003 Iraq war were Great Britain and Australia.

Australia joined the Coalition of the Willing in March 2003.[1] Around 2,000 Australian troops were sent to Iraq, with 900 remaining in the country as of mid-2004.[2] The opposition to the 2003 Iraq war in Australia was strong, in particular before the official start of the war. A poll conducted in January, 2003, showed that 27 percent of Australians opposed any military action against Iraq, about 56 percent supported military action only with UN backing, and just 12 percent favored unilateral action by the

United States. and its allies.[3] Australians showed their opposition by organizing protests. On February 16, 2003, for example, an estimated 500,000 people took part in one of the biggest peace marches in Australian history.[4]

In mid-March, when war was still only a possibility, a poll asked Australians whether they would support sending troops to Iraq if the United Nations was not involved. Only 25 percent of the respondents said they would be in favor and 68 percent said they would be against such actions. A few days later, after Prime Minister John Howard indicated Australia would join the U.S.-led war, Newspoll reported that public opinion was split: 47 percent opposed sending Australian troops to be involved in a military action against Iraq whereas 45 percent were in favor.[5]

As a result, the popularity of the prime minister began to drop. Opinion polls showed Howard's popularity reaching an eight-month low, indicating declining voter satisfaction.[6] Fortunately, no Australian troops had been reported killed in Iraq as of May 3, 2003. However, an Australian journalist was killed by a car bomb in the northern Iraq early in the war.[7]

Australia's role in the war and the reaction on the home front is expected to have influenced the way the national media covered the 2003 Iraq war. The next section reviews literature that positions the mass media within the boundaries of their political, cultural, and economic environment.

Media in the Age of Globalization

Technological advancement and interconnectedness have made the world a smaller place. We live in the age of globalization when information, goods, and services cross national borders more easily than ever before. This process of globalization has lead some to believe that we will have truly global media—media that cover international events in very similar ways. But is this really the case?

Media institutions have indeed become more global in reach thanks to the Internet and to global media conglomerates. Yet anecdotal evidence will show you that CNN reporting in Europe, for instance, differs from CNN reporting in the United States. Similarly, Murdoch's News Corporation owns TV stations in many different countries around the globe. The news coverage broadcast between those stations differs even more. A recent documentary titled "Control Room" illustrates this point well by showing the vastly different war coverage by *Al Jazeera* compared with other television networks such as BBC or CNN. The main reason for such local differences lies in the roots of the national media system. Just like other national institutions, media institutions are born and exist within the context of the sociopolitical environment of the country.[8] They are limited and influenced by the power structures that exist around them. De Beer and Merrill agree that context is all important and note that in order to understand media developments scholars "must look at the political and economic philosophy and current conditions in that country."[9] If we subscribe to the notion that national news media differ based on the unique environment to which they belong, then we would expect to see differences in the coverage of news events, and particularly events in which the country of origin is involved politically or otherwise. Clausen, for example, examined television news coverage of the September 11 attacks in six different countries, including Japan, Qatar, and the United States. She concluded that "all national broadcasters are found to be biased in favour of their own national political and organizational interests."[10] This argument was also made by Topoushian who examined the coverage of the 1991 Gulf War in two Arab and two North American newspapers published in four different countries. She found that the coverage of the same global event differed in many ways, "all in relation to the newspapers' distinctive roles in articulating their local, historical, cultural, and political interests and foreign policy in the Gulf War."[11]

Precisely because the mass media are situated in unique sociocultural environment, they have to report the same event differently, targeting their particular local audience. In other words, they need to frame the news event in such a way as to appeal to and resonate with their local readers, viewers, or listeners. For instance, some Arab audiences expect the media to use the word "shahid" (martyr) instead of "suicide bombers" in the news.[12] As Clausen argues, localization does not exclude or exist in opposition to globalization. On the contrary: today both processes of globalization and localization are exhibited by national media simultaneously. Clausen uses the term *domestication* to refer to this phenomenon and defines it in the realm of media reporting as "the process of selecting particular elements and adapting global information to suit a local framework."[13]

One way in which *domestication* is achieved is by using different frames in the media text. According to Entman's definition, to frame is "to select some aspects of a perceived reality and make them more salient in a communicating text, in such a way as to promote a particular problem definition, causal interpretation, moral evaluation, and/or recommendation."[14] This definition of framing will be used in this study. In the following pages of this chapter, we examine which aspects of the 2003 Iraq war were made more salient in the Australian media and what kind of interpretation(s) and evaluation(s) they invited in the audience. We examine not only what was made salient, but also look at which aspects of the event were missing from the news coverage. Finally, we try to link the framing of the war to Australia's domestic and foreign policy. We focus in particular on the war coverage of the *Australian*, one of Australia's most popular newspapers.

Characteristics of the Coverage in
The Australian

Today, the *Australian* is among Australia's most popular newspapers, along with the *Sydney Morning Herald* and the *Daily Telegraph*. These three newspapers dominate the newspaper market. The *Australian* is the only national broadsheet newspaper. Their Web sites states that their "editorial values focus on leading and shaping public opinion on the issues that affect Australia." The *Australian* is a national daily with total readership of 423,000 as of March 2004.[15] In this chapter, we analyze the coverage of the online edition of *The Australian* located at <http://www.theaustralian.news.com.au/>

The home page of the *Australian* was downloaded from March 20, 2003 to May 1, 2003, the official war period. The online version of the newspaper was chosen because it has global reach, allowing for the influence of globalization. The online version also allows the researcher to easily determine what is considered most "newsworthy" since only the top news are presented on the home page of the newspaper. As such, the home page allows us to capture the news hierarchy selected by the gatekeepers—the newspaper editors. The home page with the top stories also contains the news information that most people are likely to read/access. Based on these criteria, the home page of the *Australian* was downloaded daily. The *Australian* does not publish on Sunday so a total of 34 home pages were archived for the official war period and used in our content analysis.

Amount of Coverage

First, we examined how much coverage about the 2003 Iraq war was offered on the home page of the *Australian*. Despite the challenges of war journalism, this War became major news story in the paper for most of the official war period. In fact, 23 out of 34 home pages contained stories about the Iraq war. All 34 homepages contained links, images, or other war-related information, even if there was no major story about Iraq. In 12 cases, the war was not the lead story. The SARS scare took the spotlight during that time. Considering the geographic proximity of Australia to Southeast Asia, this should not be a surprise. This finding also supports arguments that "all news is local" or at least localized by the news media.

Images of War

Images were often used in the online coverage of the *Australian*: 23 (67.6 percent) of the home pages had at least one photo about the war. The photo source was the Associated Press (AP) in eight cases and Agence

France Presse (AFP) in one case. One photo was unattributed. The remaining 13 photos were provided by staff. Thus, 39 percent of the photos used in the *Australian* came from the leading international news agencies. This finding indicates that the news flow today is still dominated by Western news agencies. The one-way news flow has been discussed in previous research.[16] While the domination of major news providers was found for photos sources, it was the case for story sources. All the Iraq stories in the *Australian* online were attributed to staff reporters. In this case, the newspaper did not need to rely on major news agencies since they had coalition media reporters deployed in Iraq to cover the war.

What were the most common photographs of the 2003 Iraq war? The *Australian* incorporated many images of military equipment (30 percent), fewer photos of Iraqi civilians (13 percent), and, notably, only two pictures of antiwar protesters (9 percent). The most common photographs were those of military tanks, aircraft, etc. Photos featuring the protestors showed students opposing the war, but those images were rare, despite the antiwar sentiments that existed among many Australians.

It is important to note that the *Australian* also ran the infamous picture of the U.S. solider putting the American flag over Saddam's statue in Baghdad as well as a picture of the toppled Saddam statue on April 10, 2003. American news media have been criticized for covering this "staged" event and also utilizing the draped statue in their coverage. It seems that coalition media were trying to demonstrate the victory, symbolized by the American flag and the fallen statue, and convey to their readers the idea that the troops were successful on their mission in Iraq.

Another noteworthy characteristic of the images used in the online edition of the *Australian* was the selection of photos that showed Iraqi prisoners of war (POWs). Those were usually featured along with coalition soldier guards: for example, U.S. troops carrying POWs or American soldiers giving a prisoner a drink of water. Such photographs indicated an attempt to personalize the war, by featuring human beings from both sides of the conflict. It also seemed to provoke sense of caring for the prisoners on the part of their captors framing the coalition forces as helpful and responsible. At the same time, some pictures showed coalition soldiers as "dominating" over the situation by pointing guns at POWs who were in turn kneeling or lying on the ground. Another interpretation of such photos then may lead to the idea that the American soldiers were powerful and potent while the Iraqis were powerless, defeated, and at their mercy. A good example of this double meaning was an AP photo featured on the front page on March 23, 2003. While visual frames were open to interpretation, they remained a useful device for audience impact.

Web-Specific Features in *The Australian*

Only two videos about the war were present on the Web site, but there were eight audio links offered. One of the audio links was to a speech by George W. Bush about captured POWs. Another common audio link frequently featured in the *Australian* online was a daily battle update. Even more popular were custom-made graphics such as maps of Iraq and trajectories of military activities. Two home pages had as many as seven interactive graphic features related to the war.

On March 28, 2003, a memorable multimedia collage was built for the Web; it featured a coalition soldier with an Iraqi woman and her child; the collage was entitled "Bloody Business." As images of prisoners and civilians changed on the screen, the voice of Tony Blair was heard giving a statement about the war. He explained that "war is a bloody business." The juxtaposition of his words about the war and the images of everyday Iraqis was quite powerful.

Perhaps more impressive than the audio features and interactive multimedia was the addition of audience feedback features. Links such as "Email our troops" and "Share your views" were often provided on the home page. the *Australian* regularly took advantage of interactive Web features and invited their online readers to send comments about the war to the editors.

Tone of War Coverage

One of the ways in which subtle cues are given in news coverage—often to suggest a causal interpretation or moral evaluation—is by selecting certain terms to describe the news event. In cases of military conflict, journalists can refer to the event as aggression or occupation versus an operation to free the country, for example. The most common reference was to the 2003 Iraq war in the *Australian* was simply "war" (this reference was present in 88 percent of the home pages), "attack" or "strike" (29 percent), and "military action" (29 percent). The *Australian* referred to the Iraq war as "Operation Iraqi Freedom" only two times. Interestingly, it also labeled it an "invasion" two times during the official war period. The term invasion was almost never used at that time by mainstream U.S. media.

We also examined whether strong moral terms were used in the Iraq war reporting, provoking an emotional response or interpretation in the audience. In the total war coverage, six positive moral terms and eight negative moral terms were used. The positive terms included words such as "justice," "freedom," and "victory." Negative moral terms included "horror," "anti-God," and "monstrous." One negative term stood out—the word "bloody" used in reference to the war.

The most obvious indication of bias in media content is the tone of the media coverage. Our study included three categories for tone: (1) pro-war tone; (2) antiwar tone; and (3) neutral or mixed-tone coverage. The content analysis of the *Australian* indicated that the majority of the war reporting was balanced: 28 home pages were coded as neutral or mixed-tone—in other words, neither side of the war was clearly favored in 88 percent of the cases. We also found two examples of coverage against the war and two cases of pro-war coverage. To summarize, most of the coverage of *The Australian* was neutral and balanced.

Framing of the 2003 Iraq War

One of the ways that *domestication* was achieved in the Australian national media was by including Australian politicians in the war coverage. Such a self-focus in the war coverage was evident in the multitude of quotes from local political leaders and military personnel. For example, the March 30, 2003, online edition quoted Australian Prime Minister Howard as saying that the war was going "remarkably well" so far. In all, 24 out of 34 home pages mentioned Australia in relationship to the war. This may be expected because Australia was involved militarily in the conflict. The coalition of the Willing was mentioned in 10 home pages. It is important to note that the United Nations was mentioned in 6 cases and the European Union in 2 cases. This international focus in the war reporting reveals a push of globalization.

The Australian: Dominant Frames

The war coverage included several different frames. Naturally, the most common episodic frame in their war reporting was the military conflict frame. It was present in 62 percent of the coverage materials. This is also a common episodic frame in the coverage of conflict as shown in the TV coverage of the Israeli–Palestine conflict.[17] Episodic frames in general present the readers with isolated episodes and by so doing prevent them from constructing a complete picture of the entire event.[18] Considering the presence of Australian troops in Iraq, the dominance of this frame should not come as a surprise. In localizing this global event, the journalists brought home coverage about the progress of the war, military successes, and captured POWs. The focus on separate military developments, however, provided little context to understand the whole complexity of war—that is why this frame was qualified as episodic.

While the dominant frame was episodic in nature, the second most prominent frame in the newspaper was thematic. Thematic frames typically provide broader context out and allow readers to see relationships and causality of events.[19] The prognostic frame emerged as the second most common frame in the war reporting—it was present in 56 percent of the coverage. This frame deals with the outcomes of the war in general. It is to the editors' credit that they included such prognostic themes in the *Australian* war stories. Topics of postwar Iraq ranged from discussions about future government structure to humanitarian aid to rebuilding of the country's infrastructure.

The victims of the war frame ranked third: 44 percent of the Web coverage contained that frame. It may be surprising that less than half of the coverage incorporated this element. Any war results in victims on both sides. Yet this consequence of military action was not featured perhaps as often as expected. Including explicit pictures of civilian casualties may have been too graphic or could undermine the legitimacy of the war among the Australian public. While casualties were mentioned in the text, they were rarely shown in the photographs.

In sum, three frames dominated the coverage in the online edition of the *Australian*: the military conflict frame (episodic), the prognostic frame (thematic), and the victims of the war frame (episodic). Even though there was substantial coverage of the victims, it was not as prominent as the other two frames.

The Australian: Missing Frames

Framing is achieved not only by what is highlighted by journalists, but also by what is absent from the media coverage.[20] Therefore, it is important to examine which frames were excluded from the coverage. Our analysis shows that two particular frames were missing in the war coverage by the *Australian*: the responsibility frame and the diagnostic frame.

Indeed, there was very little discussion about the reasons for war—the so-called diagnostic frame—in the online coverage of the paper. In fact, this frame was mentioned only once during the entire war period. It is possible that the diagnostic coverage was more common before the beginning of the war— in the prewar period. It is also plausible that most readers already knew about the war buildup.

The *Australian* also offered very little reporting about responsibility for the 2003 Iraq war and its consequences. As a participant in the war, Australia like any other ally carries some responsibility. Yet responsibility issues were discussed in only two cases.

Another frame that was rarely included in the coverage was the antiwar protest frame. Antiwar protesters were rarely mentioned. That is worth noting in light of the fact that marches against the war took place around the country. Yet, only 7 out of 34 pages covered this topic. Reporting on the antiwar sentiments was infrequent despite vocal opposition, particularly among student population.

Conclusion

The analysis of the *Australian* shows that it covered the war in such ways as to *domesticate* this global news event for their local Australian audience. Responsibility issues as well as reasons for the war were rarely discussed in the newspaper at that time. The military conflict frame, the prognostic frame, and the victims of the war frame were most common. Military conflict is a common frame in news coverage of wars. While discussing the consequences of war can show the long-term effects of such an event, the military conflict frame may distance the reality of war from the reader. It will be interesting to examine what were the common elements between Australian reporting and other coalition media coverage.

There was some tension in the war coverage in the *Australian*. The reporting remained mostly balanced in tone throughout the war. Yet, several times, the coverage was openly critical of the war and the "bloody business" of war. At other times, however, the reporting was in sync with the national foreign policy, celebrating victory and praising the success of allied troops on their mission in Iraq. These two perspectives reflect, on the one hand, the official Australian involvement in the conflict, and on the other hand the national resistance against the war.

Finally, the *Australian* skillfully used Web-specific features to complement their traditional newspaper reporting. The online edition of the paper incorporated email links, audio features as well as interactive elements, thus empowering the readers to add their views about the war to the traditional coverage. The most likely reason for this was to encourage two-way communication between the newspaper and the Australian people.

Notes

1. Geography IQ, "Australia—Foreign Relations" (2003) <http://www.geographyiq.com/countries/as/Australia_relations_summary.htm> (accessed July 29, 2004).
2. BBC News, "Australia's Iraq war case damned" (2004) <http://news.bbc.co.uk/2/hi/asia-pacific/3915759.stm> (accessed July 29, 2004).
3. Eriposte, "Gallup International Poll" (January 2003) <http://www.eriposte.com/war_peace/iraq/world_support/gallup_intl_2003_by_country.gif> (accessed July 29, 2004).
4. Keith Suter, "Australia's involvement in the Iraq War," *Contemporary Review* (November 2003) <http://www.findarticles.com/p/articles/mi_m2242/is_1654_283/ai_111858199> (accessed July 29, 2004).

5. The Sydney Morning Herald, "Polls apart on whether this is a conflict worth waging" (April 1, 2003) <http://www.smh.com.au/articles/2003/03/31/1048962700473.html> (accessed July 29, 2004).
6. Eriposte, "Gallup International poll."
7. The World Messenger, "British, Scottish, Irish, Welsh Casualties In Iraq" (2003) <http://www.worldmessenger.20m.com/brits.html> (accessed July 29, 2004).
8. Denis McQuail, *Communication Theory: An Introduction*, 3rd ed. (London: Sage, 1994).
9. Arnold S. de Beer and John C. Merrill, *Global Journalism: Topical Issues and Media Systems*, 4th ed. (Dallas, TX: Allyn & Bacon, 2004).
10. Lisbeth Clausen, "Global news communication strategies—9.11.2002 around the world," *Nordicom Review* 3 (Göteborg: Nordicom, 2003) <http://www.nordicom.gu.se/reviewcontents/ncomreview/ncomreview203/105–116.pdf> (accessed August 1, 2004).
11. Mayda Topoushian, "Interpreting the constructed realities of the 1991 Gulf War: A comparative textual analysis of two Arab and two North American newspapers" (Ph.D. diss., Canada: Concordia University, 2002).
12. Samantha M. Shapiro, "The War Inside the Arab Newsroom," *The New York Times*, January 2, 2005 <http://www.nytimes.com/2005/01/02/magazine/02ARAB.html?ex=1106570919&ei=1&en=746d59b9793559b4> (accessed January 17, 2005).
13. Clausen, "Global News."
14. Robert Entman, "Framing: Towards clarification of a fractured paradigm," *Journal of Communication* 43: 4 (1993): 51–58.
15. The Australian, "Demographics" (2004) <http://newsmedianet.com.au/home/titles/title/Demographics.jsp?titleid=5> (accessed July 22, 2004).
16. Daya Kishan Thussu, "Managing the media in an era of round-the-clock news: Notes from India's first tele-war," *Journalism Studies* 3: 2 (2002): 203–212.
17. Rasha Kamhawi, "Television news and the Palestinian Israeli conflict: An analysis of visual and verbal framing" (Paper presented at the Visual Communication division at the Association for Education in Journalism and Mass Communication (AEJMC), Miami Beach, Florida, 2002).
18. Shanto Iyengar, *Is Anyone Responsible?* (Chicago: University of Chicago Press, 1991).
19. Ibid.
20. Shapiro, "War Inside."

PART II
THE GLOBAL DEBATE

EUROPE

CHAPTER EIGHT
LE MONDE ON A "LIKELY" IRAQ WAR

Anne-Marie Obajtek-Kirkwood

Of Current Events, History, and a French Newspaper

Musing on the relationship between current events, history and the acceleration of time, Marc Augé writes:

> History—I am referring primarily to what is called contemporary history—is not protected from the profound mutations our world is undergoing. On the one hand, national and regional histories are more caught up in planetary development. On the other hand, we are experiencing an "acceleration of history"—another expression for shrinking of the planet—that involves both objective interactions within the "world system" and the instantaneity of information and image dissemination. Each month, each day, we experience "historical" events; each day the border between history and current events becomes a bit more blurred. The parameters of time, like those of space, are changing, and this is an unprecedented revolution. Just as our modernity uncontrolledly creates otherness, so it is uncontrolledly creating the immediate past-history—even as it claims to stabilize history and unify the world.[1]

His statement rings particularly true in conjunction with the events preceding the Iraq war, resounding throughout the planet through satellite dishes, the internet, the audio–visual, and written press. Faced with the abundance of daily news and developments ever-changing, one experiences difficulty absorbing this impact of ongoing news that soon make history or rather are history in the making. This complexity is further magnified when events go on unfurling into the present and do not seem to reach a conclusion as is the case with the Iraq war so far.

Years have passed since the end of military actions in Iraq was officially declared and so much has happened since in Iraq, the United States, Europe, and the world that needs to be forgotten if one is to go back to

2003, namely February and March—the weeks and days preceding the armed conflict—and give an accurate account of the French press coverage of events with then current data.

Reflecting the population's attitude and the government stance, The French press at large was not in favor of another Iraq war but could feel it coming inexorably. Apart from some (and really quite few) dissenting intellectuals and politicians, there were in France, before the war, not many attempts at finding justifications or reasons *for* the conflict, but on the contrary—resignation prevailed at what was coming, when not resentment and criticism. Articles were questioning motives and rationale of this "likely" war, pointing out that war should be the last resort when all other channels of communication and constraints would have been exhausted. Others, were imagining scenarios and consequences that could/would unfold out of that war, for the United States, Iraq, the Middle East, the rest of the world, as well as for the French–American relationship.

This chapter investigates how the French daily *Le Monde* focused on the "likely" war—in what terms, with what arguments. Politically speaking, *Le Monde* is center left but in the instance of the Iraq war, the political left held the same opinion as the right. since objectivity is a high ideal but does not really exist in any newspaper, the choices *Le Monde* made in its Iraq coverage were mainly motivated by its high intellectual standards and the tradition of the best and deepest coverage it offers usually to the French public. When needed in this chapter, contributions from *Libération* (left wing daily) or some weeklies such as *Le Nouvel Observateur* (left wing), or *Le Point* (right wing) will be added.

January 1, 2003 and the Franco-French Debate on the "Likely" Iraq War

War was on the horizon on the dawn of 2003. In his article "2003: Will the Iraq War happen?"[2] Serguei summed up French worries: "The year 2002 is ending up on big international uncertainties. Is the military offensive, wished for by the United States to topple Saddam Hussein's regime, inescapable?" and assessment of the situation: "2002 had started with American president Bush's declaration placing Iraq at the head of the list of the 'axis of evil.' It finishes with still Saddam Hussein's regime is at the heart of international issues at stake." France's position and the role it could play was delineated:

> France is to take the United Nations Security Council presidency this January 1st. It believes that only this body is qualified to decide the Iraq case, and that no armed intervention can be started without a new resolution of

the UN. In the military dimension, it is holding minimum preparations. Will the war against Iraq, that a major part of the American Administration seems to have backed, take place? Is it inescapable? What will the UN inspectors say in their final report, the delivery of which is set for January 27, 2003? What will France's position be if the United States maintain their determination?[3]

Serguei's January 1 article was followed by an analysis of the international situation and a parallel drawn between the possible intervention in Iraq and that of Kosovo in July 1999.[4] Special representative of the secretary-general of the United Nations and head of the UN Mission in Kosovo Bernard Kouchner,[5] philosophers Alain Finkielkraut and Bernard-Henri Lévy, director of *Esprit* Olivier Mongin, European parliament member Daniel Cohn-Bendit, and researcher emeritus at l'Institut d'Etudes politiques Pierre Hassner were faced with three questions: Can Kosovo be equated with Iraq, Milosevic with Saddam Hussein, and thus armed conflict against Iraq be justified. There was general consensus on the similarities between the two heads of state and their brutal regimes. If Kouchner spoke of Saddam's "criminal productivity" and the barbaric nature of his regime, Mongin and Cohn-Bendit asserted that it was nothing new, nor was it a new development, and that nothing has fundamentally changed since September 11, 2001. Proofs of the monstrous character of the Iraqi regime already existed when the United States backed and even guided Iraq in its war against Iran from 1981 to 1988, while France armed Baghdad just as the United States did, and neither Washington nor Paris felt morally tormented when Iraqi armed forces used gas against Iran.

The urgency of an armed conflict with Iraq was questioned on several fronts, namely, the danger that Iraq represented. American aims were also questioned. The reasons put forward by the White House to justify an armed intervention, namely, Iraqi WMDs that Iraq might avail to Al Qaeda terrorists who might then use them against the United States, seemed fragile for lack of substantial proof. Differences between Kosovo and Iraq were stressed: "We were in favor of an intervention in Kosovo in the name of regional stability. With Iraq, we are afraid of de-stabilization" Kouchner said, and Mongin added: "Iraq lies in the midst of a troubled region where a war may reinforce repressive regimes." For Pierre Hassner, the Israeli-Palestinian conflict could not be subtracted from the equation and was related to the entire situation. Doubts existed about what Americans had in store for Iraq after Saddam's removal. According to Mongin, "one of the principles of a 'just war' is to foster an after-war environment, which is likely to be better. In the present case, one may question this outcome." Washington's intentions prompted Kouchner to formulate the following apprehensions: "After Saddam is removed UN mandate is needed. If it is all just about U.S. business feeling the smell of oil and about American home politics, it won't be good. This is the reason why everything is perverted, distorted in this case." Pierre Hassner also questioned the democratization goal put forward by the Americans and the credibility of the entire battle against the "axis of evil," which was conducted involving some allies who, have committed crimes equivalent to those of Saddam Hussein.

This January 1, 2003 article stressed that September 11 had upset the paradigm of international relations that had been working since the end of the cold war. The 1990s were marked by efforts at creating a kind of international order of law where the United Nations were to play a pivotal role. Both vulnerable and all powerful, the United States were perceived as holding the monopoly of power as well as the monopoly on moral values; they were, according to Pierre Hassner, "both the emperor and the pope." As in the situation with Kosovo, but in a different way, the whole concept of the international order was at stake with Iraq.

More Franco-French Debate from Various Personalities

The two articles from *Le Monde* discussed in the previous section were published one month before the period under consideration in this chapter but already were emblematic of the major worries of the New Year. The issues mentioned in those articles constituted the Franco-French debate on the "likely" Iraq war among French citizens—from different walks of life and intellectual status. The analysis of positions of French politicians from the entire political spectrum, and the position of the French government will also be considered here.

Exploring the points of view of intellectuals, in February 2003, *Le Monde* asked twenty-seven personalities, key questions. Artists, writers, architects, lawyers, sportsmen, filmmakers, and more,[6] all very well known by the French in their various disciplines, were asked the following questions: (1) Is the new war against Iraq justified?; (2) Do you approve of the French position? Only one, Arno Klarsfeld,[7] was resolutely in favor of the war, because of the Saddam regime and the atrocities, and also because of some historical parallels with 1936 and 1938. Klarsfeld also deemed it France's duty to line up behind the United States, their liberator in World War I and II. Kiejman in turn had this ambiguous answer: "No to war. Yes to the possibility of it happening."[8] He thought that the United States, in spite of their errors, remained the sole safeguard of an imperfect but perfectible world fit to live in. The rest of the panel approved of the French position of "no war" while some feared though that it would bring a rift in the French–American relationship and that France would suffer economic sanctions and retaliation for its opposition to the U.S. views. Others still applauded France's courage (and also Germany's) since "few nations dare oppose the Americans"[9]; they praised its determination, encouraged its duty as an old country to utter its own point of view and say no to "the arrogance of a badly brought up person like Bush or the shameful lies of Mr. Blair"[10] while deploring American sarcasms, "like those of Peter King's, a Republican congressman who described France as 'a second-rate country' and the French as 'yesterday's people.' "[11]

Though it was recognized across the board that Saddam Hussein was a frightful tyrant, nobody found war against Iraq justified at that stage; although if any, out of all the existing tyrants—Saddam Hussein was the only one to be pursued. Was it because other tyrants did not possess strategic production capabilities interesting enough for the United States like those in Iraq? The American war plan was a caricature: in 1991 Saddam Hussein was spared and his tyrannical power kept intact against all logic while the Iraqi people had to put up with an unfair embargo and suffered from it. If there were to be a war, it would all be about oil again and not about the Iraqi people.

The Iraqi menace seemed greatly exaggerated: no real link could be established between international terrorism and Saddam Hussein; on the contrary, Saddam was said to have no links with Muslim extremism. After ten years of embargo, the country was not economically sound. How could it therefore have the resources to hide the military arsenal that the Bush administration attributed to it? The population was suffering, Iraq since the 1990 Kuwait affair did not commit any aggressions, so why attack it? Saddam Hussein was contained and should be contained still, but only through peaceful means.

War is justified if one is attacked or on the verge of being so, which did not seem to be the case. There were musings on what a "just" war was and how violence was really not the solution, all the more in this context as forces deployed were so disproportionate, so heavily in favor of the West. Any war is horrible and a preemptive war is worse yet. It was strongly condemned: "The world is not an American protectorate. Preemptive war is the law of the jungle."[12] Henri de France was against it: "No preemptive war can be justified. It would mean opening the gates to chaos. In this case, no serious proof has been provided by the UN inspectors of the existence of weapons of mass destruction in Iraq. An old saying expresses quite well, it seems to me, the present will of the American power: 'Who wants to kill his dog shows it rage.' "[13]

The consequences for the world of a possible war were widely discussed. For Soulages: "Starting a second war nowadays is a remedy worse than the evil; it would, by enhancing fanaticism, provide the best pretext to all those who aspire to oppose the Muslim world with the European–American

West. It is the best turn that could be given to bin Laden and terrorists."[14] Desmarest further agreed: "A war in Iraq may have de-stabilizing consequences in lots of Middle-Eastern countries already shaken by the fact that lots of the attackers of September 11, 2001 originated from there and more yet by the deadlock of the Israeli–Palestinian conflict. One may also fear the repercussions on the Muslim world at large, in South-East Asia, in North-Africa and in Western countries."[15]

Since there was no established link between international anti-American terrorism and Saddam Hussein, Nourissier painted a very bleak picture of what war might mean:

> The Americans' determined bellicosity expresses this apocalyptic acknowledgment that big religious, ideological, economic blocks are doomed to a fatal death struggle. . . .
> No "progress" is to be hoped for from history. Comparing forces in presence? The "Western" military power is overwhelming; but the anti-American, anti-Christian fury, etc., with its paroxystic discourse, its anachronism, its kamikaze, is no less spectacular. Justifying war—which would be an American counter-attack—by all means would boil down to proclaiming/deploring that big human societies are promised to collective suicide.[16]

Finally the rationale for war advocacy was questioned: "I have no certainty, no proof backing up the arguments given by the Americans to launch war,"[17] "I can't believe the proofs that the Bush Administration pains to gather,"[18] "War is not justified as long as the United States attempt to convince us with false proofs and fake photos,"[19] "None of the advanced arguments is convincing, there only appears the Bush administration determination which, in its way, is as fundamentalist as those it denounces."[20] The reasons recognized behind the American pro-war position are acknowledged again and again as electoral and economic, boosting the faltering American economy through vested interest in Iraqi oil, as Ernaux summed it up: "The war that the United States want has not much to do with the proclaimed democratic ideal but all with their interests: to hold economic and political sway on the Middle-East, restart the home economic machine, etc."[21]

George Bush was "not an idiot, but he is convinced of being inspired by God and he is dangerous."[22] "His warmongering and religiousness were no solution: Opposing the fundamentalism of the 'axis of Good' with the terrorism of 'the axis of Evil' won't push the world progress in the right direction, when there is so much to do: reduction of inequalities between rich and poor countries, tolerance and comprehension of others, improvement of living conditions of the planet and its inhabitants . . . "[23] The underlying condemnation of American aims was as strong as was the condemnation of hypocrisy Bush and others were accused of: "I find it extremely shocking to receive moral and political lessons from politicians who did their best at arming a dictator whom they denounce today as dangerous. [A] people is [are] asked to destroy [those very] weapons that [not only] the American but also the English and the French governments provided! I'll believe in the democratic intentions of the Americans and in their will to fight terrorism the day they deal with financial support to [*sic*] Islamist terrorist networks [get]."[24]

A total loss of credibility of American arguments and deep criticism of the way in which they were presented to the American citizens and the world ensued. The administration was bluntly accused of having manipulated data and shaped their presentation accordingly. Writer Rufin analyzed the administration procedure very sternly:

> The United States have built up justification, in an artificial manner, using methods of manipulation of public opinion. The subject first emerged in Bush's declarations on the axis of Evil. It was worked on by reports, formal demands, rhetorical dramatization. Finally the "failure" of the inspections came about. A perverse dialectic then transformed this negative assessment into guilt: "If there is nothing, it is because nothing has been shown to us. . . ."
>
> Those who are against the war, are "against the disarming of Saddam," therefore pro war! The honor of democracies during the Cold War had been to utter the truth as opposed to totalitarian lying. It is shocking to see nowadays bad faith pass into the camp of the country that symbolizes freedom.[25]

Ernaux deconstructed the administration rhetoric too:

> What differs from the first Gulf War is that the wrong reasons for killing thousands of Iraqis have been made manifest and prevail over the "right" ones in most opinions. . . .
>
> Like any hegemonic nation, the United States make the error of thinking that their most obvious lies won't be caught by citizens from other countries. In a way, they overdid it, and allowed to emerge to consciousness the fact that "means are part of truth as well as results"—Marx, of course, but is this not the foundation of any morals and science and the foundation of not wanting this notoriously imperialistic war?[26]

This collection of opinions by *Le Monde* concluded with a critique[27] by its very readers who reproached the paper for airing mainly antiwar statements and the "mediator" tried to balance opinions by showcasing those of two by strongly pro-war readers. And thus one Parisian wrote: "I am pro-war, as it can be a just war like in Serbia or Afghanistan, and because I remember September 11, 2001 and so many numerous murders which demand condemnation, reparation and memory," while another added: "How lucky Europe is to have statesmen like Blair, Aznar and Berlusconi, who having to face head winds at times, manage to direct it in the direction of honor. How lucky for Europe that the countries which have just joined it remind old France that it is more than high time for it to wake up from its wintery torpor."

In spite of his trying to balance opinions, Solé had to confess that *Le Monde* had difficulty in finding pro-war opinions, that some solicited people refused to answer so that it finally had to close this series of articles on February 21 for the lack of participants. He concluded that "the French in general and *Le Monde* readers in particular are in their vast majority opposed to the preemptive war wanted by Bush."

By March 20, there appeared again in *Le Monde* two articles in favor of the war as the paper still tried to balance different views. Kendal Nezan, director of the Kurdish Institute in Paris, really wished for a war to oust Saddam but with the UN sanction, not led unilaterally by the United States. The other pro-war article featured writer Pascal Bruckner, philosopher André Glucksmann, and filmmaker Romain Goupil. On March 10, they had launched in *Le Monde* a petition to be signed, the title of which was: "Saddam must go, by choice or by force." That petition started with recalling Milosevic's ethnic cleansing atrocities in Croatia and NATO intervention, it then focused on the atrocities and ethnic cleansing that were going on in Iraq similarly, for lack of concrete action. The petition ended with the following paragraphs:

> It would be regrettable so reduce the present crisis to a Franco-American conflict when the two countries' points of view could have been complementary. . . .
>
> It would be catastrophic if, out of vainglory and stubbornness, Paris resorted to the veto, at the risk of shattering Western solidarity and leaving Europe somewhat shaken (which, let's remember, cannot be reduced to the Paris–Berlin axis alone). . . .
>
> Saddam must go, by choice or by force ! The Iraqis, the Kurds, Shi'ites, but also Sunnis will breathe freer and the peoples of the region will be relieved. . . .
>
> After Milosevic, the Balkans are no heaven but there is more peace and less dictatorship. The post-Saddam era will not be rosy, but less black than 30 years of tyranny, summary executions and war.[28]

Glucksmann's criticism of France's independence from the United States and fear of its persistence, the possible repercussions, and political and economic isolation (particularly from future Iraqi deals) were shared by all pro-war intellectuals and politicians as was their stressing of the terrible nature of Saddam and his regime.

Yves Roucaute[29] thus deemed that moral demand alone would justify the removal of Saddam. Generally speaking, in the pro-war articles or petitions, there was no criticism whatsoever of American actual or ulterior motives and no doubt that a military intervention could only benefit Iraq and the whole Middle East. Roucaute expressed forcefully the views of that camp.

> As the war is just because of its political and humanitarian ends, it is also just by its means.[. . .]The war will soon appear as a wise decision to the world. In spite of the doomwatchers, there will be no resistance from a population waiting for the tyrant's removal. And just a few cameras will be needed to reverse international opinion which is fooled today. . . .
>
> Thus this region powder keg will be reorganized, Saudi Arabia and the Emirates security comforted, Israel existence assured and Palestinian authority democratized while the war started against the hooligan states of Afghanistan, carried on in Iraq will continue imposing on the globe this perpetual peace treaty that universal conscience demands. . . .
>
> Right without a sword is just a word, and morals without will a hollow dream.[30]

Two days before the pro-war petition was published, four well-known Europeans, Spanish filmmaker Pedro Almodovar, German literature Nobel prize-winner Günter Grass, Swedish writer Per Olof Enquist, and Finnish political editor Helle Klein signed a kind of tribute entitled "Continue, Jacques Chirac" in which they underlined the consequences that a war with Iraq would entail: great loss of human lives, increased spread of terrorism, worsening of relations with the Southern part of the world, especially Muslim countries, weakening of international law and the UN, marginaliziation of Europe currently engaged in a major constructing phase of its political identity. They thanked Chirac for the course and the actions he had taken so far and begged him to steer the same course all the way to a UN veto to stop the war, if need be. They also stressed the long-standing ties between France and the United States throughout history and pointed to the fact that France's position demonstrates authentic solidarity with the American people and institutions. They also emphasized that France in its continued action would thus follow its destiny of independence and responsibility, serving Europe and the whole world.[31]

Analyzing the pros and cons of war, trying to make sense of the entire situation, Jean Daniel[32] stated that the more countries rallied directly or indirectly around the American position, the less there were public opinions in favor of the war, that there were already two winners in this story— bin Laden whose aim was not war for the sake of war but vengeance for centuries of Arab humiliation and George Bush not altogether correctly elected but who managed to get his whole country to support him after September 11, and following an indecisive and botched operation in Afghanistan, financial scandals, and an economic crisis at home, took the Iraq operation where his father left off, assimilating in the process Saddam Hussein to bin Laden because he couldn't support his actions by Hussein's annexing another country anymore as his father did. Pierre Hassner blamed both the United States and France for having greatly undermined the European Union, NATO, and the UN and the United States for having managed, after two years of aggressive unilateralism and Manichean rhetoric, to have Saddam Hussein appear as the first victim of an adventurous enterprise, both region- and worldwide.[33]

The Debate among French Government and Politicians

The Franco-French debate on the Iraq war gave voice to public opinion expressed by thoughtful, enlightened people, on the basis of what Michaux[34] wrote: "The democracies in which we live are public opinion and media regimes, which means that in principle public affairs are treated in a transparent manner with the media operating as the fourth power. . . . " In turn, media are used by governments to convince or shape public opinions at times as Augé states: "Every government today—given that it governs at least in part through word and image—must convince a majority of citizens."[35] Yet, on the subject of a likely Iraq war, the French government did not need do much convincing as the lack of pro-war opinions[36] also noticeable among politicians echoed in the citizenry.

On January 31, 2003, Lionel Jospin[37] breached the subject of Iraq and expressed himself in terms very similar to those previously encountered. He agreed to a military intervention in case of a proven link between Iraq and Al Qaeda. He did not believe Iraq was able to strike without risking its own destruction. Though he recognized the Iraqi dictatorship, he wondered if the UN were going to make a list of all dictatorships and act militarily against them all. He declared that "it is not true that only principles are at stake in this conflict." Musing on a possible war, he reminded France of its role:

> This war would be led exclusively by the United States forces, the other participating countries being there only as political caution. It is not France's calling to be reduced to back-up troops, even less so when the outcome is uncertain. If this war takes place, France should not participate in it. I wish that together with Germany, we may convince our European partners to adopt this position. If not, let us decide for France.[38]

As for the traditional left/right divide which dominates French politics, there was consensus across the board—albeit with some nuances—with the policy conducted by Chirac and Dominique de Villepin, then French Foreign Affairs minister. Actually, differences lay within some members of the UMP (Union for the Presidential Majority, Chirac's party) since some, but very few, did support a military intervention, a few individuals from Chirac's party and the Démocratie Libérale party[39] (those people were sometimes referred to as "Atlantists"[40]). A part of the UMP feared that a veto from France at the UN Security Council would antagonize France and the United States even more, entail political and economic isolation on the world arena, and that France should finally choose to side with the United States. There was a faction of the right, the extreme right, who were openly supporting a possible veto from France (they feared that France might back out of it at the last minute[41]). All of the left (Socialists,[42] Communists, and extreme-left) were strongly in favor of France's veto. One Socialist deputy said: "One can't reason only in terms of repercussion which, of course, might be considerable for the European Union, NATO, the UN. One has to accept this stage of tension with the United States and rebuild afterwards. There will be an after-Bush."

By mid-February, there was talk that the National Assembly and Senate would vote on the issue of Iraq to confirm France's position by showing how the country was behind its President. Then this movement weakened as some did doubt what the voting issue would really be about with the uncertainty of international politics. Finally Chirac upheld the Gaullist view that foreign policy really was exclusively his turf that is it was only up to him to decide in the final analysis. Nevertheless, a debate about Iraq did take place in both chambers of the French parliament and summary was given in *Le Monde*, notably abundant in extracts from Prime Minister Jean-Pierre Raffarin's speech to the National Assembly. It entailed meaningful and concerned passages on the prewar situation as Raffarin redefined France's position in regard to the conflict, the UN or the United States, and assessed the nature of a possible conflict, plus its consequences:

Today's crisis may be tomorrow's war. This perspective mobilizes public opinions. [. . .] Beyond the current crisis what is at stake is people's confidence in the future of international law. Such is the deep meaning of France's engagement and its diplomacy in this crisis. [. . .] Nobody can assert that the path to war might be shorter than the path to inspections. Nobody can assert either that it could open up on a safer, fairer and stabler world. [. . .] War is always the outcome of failure. [. . .] France relies on the United Nations. [. . .] Our differences on Iraq should not challenge the strength of our relationship with the United States [. . .] We are old allies, we cooperate on many vital dossiers, starting with the fight against terrorism. [. . .] We share on Iraq the same objectives, those of Resolution 1441. We diverge on the means of achieving them. We have a duty of truth towards Allies who respect each other.

[. . .] Today, a military intervention, when all the avenues of a pacific solution have not been explored, would divide the international community.

[. . .] It would emphasize fractures and tensions in a complex country and region.[43]

[. . .] War would weaken the coalition formed against terrorism after September 11. It would cause an increase of this phenomenon whereas this scourge which threatens us all, in that part of the world as here, needs to be fought against.[44]

Alain Juppé[45] declared that the disarming of Iraq was first on the agenda, and contemplated pessimistically that instead of "democratic contagion" in Ryad, Damascus, and Teheran, after the end of Saddam's dictatorship, there might be on the contrary "a prolonged occupation of Iraq under American administration" which "might end up causing rejection reactions and even maybe an increase in terrorism."

Noël Mamère,[46] fully approved of France's position "against a war decided unilaterally by a hyper power," criticizing "the new doctrine of 'preemptive action,' according to which the Unites States take upon themselves the right to invade countries and topple governments hostile to their interests." This doctrine reflected "the methodical organization of imperial globalization, on the basis of preeminence of the American order in every domain." Its danger was underlined: "As it feeds upon the consequences of North–South inequalities, tied to liberal globalization, and the alibi of the fight against terrorism, it is a global war without time or space limits."

Alain Bocquet[47] added that "the war policy of the American Administration is not accepted but rejected by public opinion throughout the world, mobilized more by anti-hegemony than by anti-Americanism." He then envisioned the consequences not only for the Middle East but also for the French suburbs: "The whole of the Middle-East and the Muslim world would live through an American war as a provocation, an extra humiliation, an injustice adding to others, noticeably the one endured so harshly by the Palestinian people. We are not immune in our popular suburbs to the difficult consequences of such a hypothesis."

After that debate, Le Monde in its analysis account of it,[48] stressed another factor not so forcefully nor openly expressed before by politicians: the fact that, while backing France's antiwar position and wanting the UN as arbiter, quite a few leaders were already then (i.e., about a month before the outbreak of the war itself) strongly foreseeing the likelihood of war. Pessimistic about the overruling of the UN, Raffarin said: "We do not discard war." Balladur,[49] inviting the government "to prepare for the future, reflect on the consequences on the world balance of this conflict which seems unavoidable." uttered: "Will France manage or not to avoid war and have its conception of law respected? It is far from being certain."[50] Alain Juppé bluntly affirmed: "I won't beat around the bush. Of course, we all want to hope still that there remains a chance to avoid war. But rumors of mobilization are starting to cover voices that still call for reason. Nevertheless it won't be said that we did not express our worries loud and clear."

On March 6, a UMP member accompanying Chirac and Villepin on a visit to Algeria confided to *Le Monde*[51] that the president was convinced that Americans wouldn't back out but go to war against Iraq, come what may. On the same page of *Le Monde*, Guy Tessier, president of the Defense Commission at the National Assembly commented that Americans have been in a war logic since September 11, and seen evil everywhere, that they would not change course for fear of losing face, unless Saddam Hussein were to go in exile. He doubted the presence of WMDs, convinced that "the Iraqis have accepted all conditions. What remains is only conventional weapons."

On March 15, fears of war approaching inexorably were even more confirmed as Blair and Bush renounced the bringing to the UN Security Council vote the United States, United Kingdom, and Spain resolution asking Iraq to disarm before March 17 and blamed France heavily for what in their eyes was a diplomatic failure, which France did not recognize as such. This last step was illustrative of what had been developing throughout 2002 and even more during 2003, that is, a rift among pro- and antiwar European Union members. This divide between its members was at times forcefully promoted by Donald Rumsfeld or, in turn, initiated by Jacques Chirac's position against new pro-war European Union members like Poland. This was also another episode of the widening of the gap between the United States and France in their appraisal of the situation and decisions about Iraq, which engendered francophobia in the Unites States on a scale never witnessed before. Finally, it highlighted the failure of the UN as an international body: it jeopardized the supremacy of international law; it confirmed the worst fears as to "might against right" as Kagan had promoted it.[52] No wonder then that *Le Monde* on its front page of March 21, 2003 had this big title above a picture of the first explosions in Baghdad: "The American War Has Started."

Last Points of View before the Outbreak of the War

Finally on March 20, there appeared two articles underlining the lack of logic and rationality, the madness and the absurdity of the whole situation. Martin Amis's article bore in French a more provoking title than in the original English: "Bush against Saddam: delirium shock."[53] At the start, Amis stressed the confounding proofs backing the American and British decisions: "We accept that there are legitimate casus belli: acts or situations 'provoking or justifying war.' The present debate feels off-centre, and faintly unreal, because the US and the UK are going to war for a new set of reasons (partly undisclosed) while continuing to adduce the old set of reasons (which in this case do not cohere or even overlap)." He then expanded on the change of terms from "the axis of hatred" "the axis of evil"(reminiscent of Reagan's evil empire) to underline Bush's religiousness and the heady mix of religion and politics that are his, Bush "being intellectually null," with these scathing remarks:

> [W]e are obliged to accept the fact that Bush is more religious than Saddam: of the two presidents, he is, in this respect, the more psychologically primitive. We hear about the successful "Texanisation" of the Republican party. And doesn't Texas sometimes seem to resemble a country like Saudi Arabia, with its great heat, its oil wealth, its brimming houses of worship, and its weekly executions?

Amis questioned the attack of Iraq on the basis of WMDs, as there were two countries in his view that would deserve such an attack more: Iran and North Korea (but then South Korea would have suffered too which therefore could not be envisioned). He doubted the validity of the whole enterprise:

> There are two rules of war that have not yet been invalidated by the new world order. The first rule is that the belligerent nation must be fairly sure that its actions will make things better; the second rule is that the belligerent nation must be more or less certain that its actions won't make things worse. America could perhaps claim to be satisfying the first rule (while admitting that the improvement may be only local and short term). It cannot begin to satisfy the second.

In the order of comparisons, Bush versus Saddam or Bush versus bin Laden as "his opposite extreme twin,"[54] another opposition was made between war and peace served by faltering rhetoric. Morin and Saussure based their analysis on the fact that European and world opinions were not as receptive as American public opinion to the Administration theses, presented as expert and competent. Recalling the means through which totalitarianisms used to convince the masses, they inferred that Bush has had resort to similar methods where the individual is to adhere to the position of the power in place, not thanks to rational arguments illustrated by facts but simply because the power in place rests on an unconditional demand of allegiance to the State, that fights a dangerous enemy, sometimes real, but often imagined. They added that the big conflicts led by the United States in the last decades "have regularly distinguished themselves by the absence of ethical and rational justification." Jean-François Kahn held the same view, finding it strange that after the cold war, the United States pick up Marxist dialectics, and "like the Communists," are "ready to resort to their methods, photos, montages, arbitrary imprisonments . . . to put forward their point of view."[55]

Of Newspapers and War and Consequences

What to conclude from this selection of mainly *Le Monde* articles on the "likely" Iraq War? In our "paradoxically intimate relation to the world, a relation which is both image-charged and abstract [. . .], though we are informed of all that is happening, we generally only know what we are told about it" Augé writes.[56] This is obvious and particularly well illustrated by the people from various walks of life who expressed themselves in *Le Monde*. They all reacted to the looming event with data then known to them and also their own analysis according to their psychological, political, or professional characteristics. One must acknowledge that the positive outcomes of the war, so forcefully put forward by the pro-war camp have so far not materialized and admit with sadness that lots of the misgivings or dire predictions about the war have materialized to a lesser or greater degree,[57] causing Michel Barnier (the French Foreign Affairs minister in 2005), beg the world to come out of "this black hole which is in the process of absorbing the Middle-East and beyond it, the world."[58]

What also stands out is the sense of utter helplessness engendered by such a situation. As Augé has it again, we live in a world that gives us the illusion that we know everything but we are also helpless to do anything about what we know. Ours is "an anxiety-producing world,"[59] our new century its most brilliant illustration as "after a fanfare start, the third millennium crashed at take-off!"[60] People of good will or wisdom seem powerless to counteract what was mainly one country's decision. Baudrillard rightly points out that in this Iraq war there was "an absolute schism between power on one side and the will of populations on the other, mobilized everywhere against this incomprehensible war, and still not bringing about even a slightest change whatsoever."[61] Since international institutions and treaties are not respected by the United States, other people, governments, or nations are all powerless to influence the course of events. September 11, has allowed the Bush administration to lay the bases of "the new American century."[62] Using "might against right" controversy has undermined the previously existing world order by creating a "new world disorder," as it is often termed. Michel Barnier says, "All the principles we hold dear—respect of human dignity and international law, force as ultimate resort, solidarity in striving for dialogue between cultures and civilizations—all these principles have been shaken."

In the final analysis, we can agree with Augé, that history is "dirty," "mad," "with desires and delirium running through it."[63] September 11, by the shock and phenomenal magnitude, has set the United States on a "gigantic task of retrospective contraception"[64] striving to erase that fall cataclysm by attacking terrorism and therefore Iraq as a target of choice. Baudrillard perceives it as a humiliation that the Unites States want to see vanish but that is always there—traumatic, the reverse of the positive American Myth, the myth of American destruction. It results in an asymmetrical confrontation of a world power, which attacks who it wishes when it wishes and an underground adversary, which keeps on reproducing all the more as it is being exterminated. Are we then living "in a safer world" as President Bush claimed it in 2004? Will we? Won't we anymore? The answers to these questions are still not clear.

Notes

1. Marc Augé, *An Anthropology for Contemporaneous Worlds* (Stanford, CA: Stanford University Press, 1999), 14.
2. Serguei, "La guerre d'Irak aura-t-elle lieu," *Le Monde*, January 1, 2003.
3. For most of *Le Monde* articles, the source is the online version of the newspaper and since *Le Monde* <http://www.lemonde.fr> has its policy of making articles older than one week available to online subscribers only, their URL will not be given as they won't be available to the common reader. For other sources URLs will be given or newspaper pages will be provided when available.
4. Alain Frachon and Daniel Vernet, "Guerre en Irak: Chirac entend affirmer sa différence. Pour les intellectuels français partisans de l'intervention armée dans les Balkans, 'l'Irak n'est pas le Kosovo,' " *Le Monde*, January 1, 2003.
5. Also gastroenterologist, cofounder of Doctors without Borders, and former Minister of State.
6. Their profession is listed after their names in the series of articles starting with "Irak le débat français."
7. Son of Serge Klarsfeld, author and attorney who has published a dozen books on the fate of French Jewry during World War II.
8. Georges Kiejman. Avocat, ancien ministre, "Irak le débat français," *Le Monde*, February 13, 2003.
9. Thomas Castaignède, international de rugby, "Irak le débat français," *Le Monde*, February 21, 2003.
10. Jacques Vergès, avocat, "Irak le débat français," *Le Monde*, February 18, 2003.
11. Bertrand Tavernier, cinéaste, "Irak le débat français," *Le Monde*, February 15, 2003.
12. Viviane Forrester écrivain, "Irak le débat français," *Le Monde*, February 18, 2003.
13. Henri de France, comte de Paris, "Irak le débat français," *Le Monde*, February 21, 2003.
14. Pierre Soulages, peintre, "Irak le débat français," *Le Monde*, February 15, 2003.

15. Thierry Desmarest, PDG de TotalFinaElf, "Irak le débat français," *Le Monde*, February 13, 2003.

16. François Nourissier, écrivain, "Irak le débat français," *Le Monde*, February 19, 2003.

17. Juliette Gréco, chanteuse, "Irak le débat français," *Le Monde*, February 12, 2003.

18. Patrice Chéreau metteur en scène et cinéaste, "Irak le débat français," *Le Monde*, February 18, 2003.

19. Bertrand Tavernier, cinéaste, "Irak le débat français," *Le Monde*, February 15, 2003.

20. Jérôme Clément, président d'Arte, "Irak le débat français," *Le Monde*, February 19, 2003.

21. Annie Ernaux, écrivain, "Irak le débat français," *Le Monde*, February 21, 2003.

22. Christian Boltanski, artiste plasticien, "Irak le débat français," *Le Monde*, February 20, 2003.

23. Jérôme Clément, président d'Arte, "Irak le débat français," *Le Monde*, February 19, 2003.

24. Bertrand Tavernier, cinéaste, "Irak le débat français," *Le Monde*, February 15, 2003.

25. Jean-Christophe Rufin écrivain, "Irak le débat français," *Le Monde*, February 18, 2003.

26. Annie Ernaux, écrivain," *Le Monde*, February 21, 2003.

27. Robert Solé, "Chronique du médiateur. Tous en chœur." *Le Monde*, February 23, 2003.

28. The English translation is to be found at <http://watch.windsofchange.net/themes_46.htm> (accessed February 10, 2005). Curiously enough, people who signed this petition could not be found, though the petition itself appeared on several Internet sites in French or translated.

29. A law professor at Nanterre University.

30. Yves Roucaute, "Une guerre juste," *Le Monde*, March 8, 2003.

31. Pedro Almodovar, Per Olof Enquist, Günter Grass, and Helle Klein, "Continuez, Jacques Chirac," *Le Monde*, March 8, 2003.

32. Jean Daniel, "Editorial. Le bel avenir de la guerre," *Le Nouvel Observateur*, February 6–12, 2003, 21.

33. Pierre Hassner, "Point de vue. Guerre: qui fait le jeu de qui," *Le Monde*, February 25, 2003.

34. A philosopher and professor at Paris I University. Michaux, Yves, "Le cauchemar de la démagogie . . . ," *Libération*, April 2, 2003.

35. Augé, *An Anthropology*, 77.

36. On March 7–8, 2003 an IPSOS survey by 1,000 French about the war gave 25% of pro-war opinions, but more were among right-wing voters than left.

37. Former Socialist party Prime Minister and unsuccessful candidate during the first round of the 2002 presidential elections.

38. Lionel Jospin, "Etre utile," *Le Monde*, January 31, 2003.

39. Such were Pierre Lelouche, J-J Descamps, Axel Poniatowski, H. Mariton, and H. Novelli.

40. A term found in *Le Point* article (March 14, 2003) entitled "France- Le camp des faucons (The Hawks' Camp)."

41. As did Philippe de Villiers, head of the MPF (Movement for France, close in quite a few of its theses to the extreme-right of Le Pen).

42. Bernard Kouchner, who in January was against the war, evolved to a pro-war position and made his colleagues from the Socialist Party very uneasy as did Pierre Moscovici, former minister in Jospin's government, "an honest representative of the American left of the Socialist party" according to Claude Askolovith, a journalist at the *Nouvel Observateur* who commented with irony on this pro-war camp that chooses war "in spite of Bush" and longs for a Kennedy or a Clinton, turned off as they are by the "arrogant ideology and saving imperialism" of the present United States, reminiscent of the one portrayed in Sinclair Lewis's *Babbitt*.

43. A Paris I and VII Universities professor, Vallet, published an article in *Le Monde* just on that subject. After quoting De Gaulle in his introduction: "I was flying towards the complicated Orient with simple ideas," he underlined several factors that added to this Middle Eastern complexity: "The current American project of war in Iraq does not take into account the complexity of this country which is a tower of Babel of languages, peoples and Churches: war may act as a cluster bomb between enemy groups and worsen ancient rifts between rival regions." "Point de vue. Du haut de ces ziggourats . . . ," *Le Monde*, February 17, 2003.

44. Jean-Pierre Raffarin, "La crise aujourd'hui, c'est peut-être la guerre demain." *Le Monde*, February 28, 2003.

45. Former Foreign Affaigrs and later Prime Minister, leader of the UMP until 2004.

46. A leader of the Green Party, belonging to the left of the political spectrum.

47. Member of the Communist Party and of the Defense Commission at the National Assembly.

48. P. Le Cœur, "La crise irakienne. Les chefs de la droite jugent inévitable le conflit armé en Irak," *Le Monde*, February 28, 2003.

49. Former finance and later prime minister under Mitterand's Presidency, now head of the commission on foreign affairs at the National Assembly.

50. This was in the immediate context of the United States, United Kingdom, and Spain submitting a new resolution to the UN stating that Iraq had not seized the opportunity given to it to destroy its WMDs by UN Resolution 1441, deliberately couched in vague terms so that it really meant a war declaration without being expressed so bluntly, "La Crise irakienne. Irak: résolution pour la guerre," *Le Monde*, February 26, 2003, 8.

51. P. Le Cœur, "Face à une guerre certaine, la droite en manque de certitudes," *Le Monde*, March 6, 2003, 8.

52. Especially in *Of Paradise and Power*: "It is time to stop pretending that Europeans and Americans share a common view of the world, or even that they occupy the same world. On the all-important questions of power—the efficacy of power, the morality of power, the desirability of power—American and European perspectives are diverging. Europe is turning away from power, or to put it a little differently, it is moving beyond power into a self-contained world of laws and rules and transnational negotiations and cooperation. [. . .] Meanwhile, the United States remains mired in history, exercising power in an anarchic Hobbesian world where international laws and rules are unreliable,

and where true security and the defense and promotion of a liberal order depend on the possession and use of military might. [. . .] When it comes to settling national priorities, determining threats, defining challenges, and fashioning and implementing foreign and defense policies, the United States and Europe have parted ways." (New York: Alfred A. Knopf, 2003), 3–4.

53. The very same article title in English was "The Palace of the End," in *The Guardian* on March 4 and in *The New Yorker* on March 15.

54. The expression comes from Paul Virilio, "Clausewitz aux invalides," *Le Nouvel Observateur*, April 3–9, 2003, 12–13.

55. Jean-François Kahn, "La guerre en Irak: un an après," Librairie Gaïa <http://www.librarie-gaia.com/CML/KahnJF/Kahn.htm#Conférence> (accessed July 28, 2004).

56. Augé, *An Anthropology*, 65.

57. "Failure in Iraq," *Le Monde*, April 15, 2004, cites some negative outcomes. In a year's time, the United States has been unable to stabilize the region and have multiplied political and military errors. They have wasted the sympathy capital they had from the Iraqis, now torn between hostility toward them and fear of their leaving. Part of the country is still at war, insecurity is rampant elsewhere. Hijackings have made investors and humanitarians flee, and there is a revival of nationalism and Islamism in the region.

58. *Le Monde*, May 13, 2004.

59. Augé, *An Anthropology*, 66.

60. Former Socialist Foreign Affairs minister Hubert Védrine's phrase, "Point de vue. Inquiétudes et divergences occidentales," *Le Monde*, December 23, 2003.

61. Baudrillard in A. Lancelin, "Le nouvel essai de Baudrillard. 'La guerre américaine est un exorcisme.' " *Le Nouvel Observateur*, July 1–7, 2004, 56–58.

62. Cambadélis (Socialist Party deputy), *Le Monde*, February 18, 2003.

63. Augé, *Journal de Guerre* (Paris: Editions Galilée, 2002), 62.

64. Baudrillard, "Le Nouvel," 58.

CHAPTER NINE

THE GERMANS PROTEST: STILL A
COUNTRY OF PACIFISTS?

Simone Schlichting-Artur

During the months preceding the war in Iraq, American as well as German press coverage overwhelmingly demonstrated support of the politics of their respective governments concerning the looming war. The American press seemed to unabashedly (almost shamelessly) back the Bush administration and its desire to go to war, while the German press applauded Chancelor Schröder's adamant stance of not involving Germany in a war against Iraq.[1] American journalism offered little coverage of antiwar protests within the country or abroad, whereas the majority of German reports in both print and television focused on the antiwar movement and raised the question whether the peace movement in Germany was still alive or in fact a relic of times passed.[2] The question that many journalists were asking during the postwar days was whether the higher ideology of the peace movement had given way to the reality of politics or whether it was a different cultural and social understanding that drove Germans to protest the war. In Germany, journalists from the political left were keenly interested in renewing the debate on German national identity and in reminding Germany's population of the role it had played in the peace movement. There seemed to be a lot of contention regarding the current state of the German peace movement and the role that various population groups played, or did not play, within the movement. Some journalists from the left were applauding the German government, the people and its intellectual elite, whereas others were much more critical of the state of affairs and the complacency into which Germans had fallen.

As the historian Jörg Friedrich put it: "The attitude of the Germans and their mental place is under the bombs rather than in bombers."[3] This lofty sentiment could be found in various dailies and magazines during the post–World War II era, clearly attempting to remind Germans of their notorious past and their duty to contribute to world peace. In the preceding months to the war in Iraq, not all journalists seemed to be in agreement with what pacifism meant and what role it played in German public life, or whether it even played a role. Some authors celebrated the renaissance of the German peace movement and tried to remind their readers of Germany's post–World War II role as a peacemaker rather than an aggressor in world politics. Others took a more pragmatic approach and reasoned that the antiwar movement was driven as much by internal politics, elections, and economic self-interest.

Analysis

On February 15, *Spiegel Online* published an article with the title "Largest peace demonstration in the history of Germany."[4] The author detailed how more than half a million people participated in the demonstration in order to protest the impending war in Iraq. Demonstrators carried banners with slogans such as "no Bush-fire, otherwise large-scale fire" or "work and education instead of war and armament." Participants were members of churches, unions, human rights and peace groups, and even three federal ministers, who participated despite Chancellor Schröder's wishes to the contrary. This demonstration was part of a worldwide protest under the motto "no war in Iraq—no blood for oil."[5] The article also mentioned that similar demonstrations took place all over the world, even in the United States. This article seemed to praise the efforts of millions and left the impression that the German peace movement had united and was as convincing and effective as never before. It truly had found a common ground. However, not all voices were harmonious in their attitude toward the German peace movement and many vented their discontent in various ways.

In an issue of the weekly newspaper *Die Zeit* in January 2003, author Jan Ross caught the reader's attention with the rather lengthy title: "There is only one thing: never again! War against Saddam? Without us! German pacifism, born out of guilt and fear, made its stamp on the bourgeois middleclass. At the same time the German leftist movement is getting used to the fight for human rights. A journey through the emotional world of Germany."[6] In this article, Ross posited that the German peace movement has become a movement of the middle class. In surveying public opinion on war, Ross explained, "There is nothing left, nothing alternative and nothing radical any longer, to be against bombs, rockets, tanks and especially against Americans, it is a German and a majority opinion." According to Ross, it was the slogan "War? Without us!" that won Chancellor Schröder the 2002 elections. He claimed that this mantra alone brought defeat to the opposition, which did not completely reject the war option and Germany's possible

participation. But why do Germans reject war? Is it truly pacifism?[7] There
is no general resistance against a "militarization of foreign policy" but rather
a deep, guilt- and fear-filled aversion to war. Military actions, such as in the
Balkans, are regarded as police actions. "The policeman needs a weapon to
fight evil. War, real war, between states and for naked interests, for energy
sources or power—that is completely different." Ross concedes that this
widespread differentiation between "police military intervention," which is
accepted, and "real war between states," which causes fear and rejection, has
merit; but he warns that this attitude gives rise to a new rejection of reality.
He states that there is consensus that ethnic war and the proliferation of
weapons of mass destruction have to be countered with resistance but the
main message is "The way the Pentagon is imagining, is not the way to deal
with it." There is a flood of documents that confirm that the use of military
force against terrorists and their networks is ineffective. According to Ross,
we live in a world of warlords, drug gangs, and religious partisan groups.
States have been very successful in ignoring the fact that they have played an
important role in laying the ground work for the existence of what Ross
calls "privatized violence." He claims that they have facilitated the existence
of privatized violence either through being failing *states*, in which the
collapse of public order allows the existence of crime, or through *state sponsorship*, which provides an infrastructure for violence.[8] This is where the
"tabooized" zone of the war begins, writes Ross. Germans want to be
"ahead" of others, they no longer see themselves as the avant-garde of
nonviolence but as a people who understand the essence of the challenges
of the twenty-first century that cannot be confronted with "recipes à la
Rumsfeld."[9] According to Ross, a certain tendency of being "smart alecks"
and a selective understanding of reality has remained with many Germans.

In the 1980s, during the time of tactical nuclear proliferation in Europe,
Germans had enormous moral standing and demonstrated idealism that
deserved respect, writes Ross, but with the years they have become compla-
cent and have not shown in their actions the moral substance of pacifism.
They accepted the occupation of Kuwait, were not much bothered by
events in Middle East, and allowed the development of a "progressive
Bellizism, which is the justification of the extension of politics by different
means (usually military force),"[10] when faced with the genocide of the
Balkans. Today things are changing. In Germany, there is no "intellectual
war party" and no one claims justification for intervention in Iraq. Ross
states that even German Balkan Bellizists completely reject a preemptive
strike toward Iraq because it cannot be justified on the basis of preventing
acute genocide and claim that the legal ground for invasion to be "wavering."[11]
The peace movement today is stronger than in a long time, Ross judges, but
he cannot help feeling that the peace movement in Germany is not only a

result of moral idealism but also of hopeless cynicism at times because Germans for the most part are convinced that all motivation for going to war rests in pure self-naked interests, such as in the Iraq model—the quest for oil.

"As seldom before in German history, government, intellectuals and the people seem to be in agreement: American war against Iraq is wrong, even catastrophic. But slowly discomfort with the new peace-culture is voiced; critics are warning against reality-blindness and demand support for a fast win."[12] Thus begins an article in *Der Spiegel*, a liberal newsmagazine, in which its author Reinhard Mohr presents his views on the German peace culture.

Mohr points out that many articles in the German media praise the "surprising renaissance of the German peace movement." The media reports thousands of demonstrations in the country, countless actions, and ubiquitous peace avowals. The protest against the Iraq war of this Bush administration seems to have united government, intellectuals, and the people as never before in German post–World War II history. Germans are willing to demonstrate their independence and seek their own "spiritual place": always victim, never perpetrator.

"It seems that everyone is of one opinion,"[13] writes Mohr. People from different intellectual and ideological camps, parties and generations have come together in the peace movement to protest the impending war in Iraq. Not even during the atomic retro-fitting of the early 1980s, could one find such a common all-encompassing consensus among Germans. The clearly deprecatory attitude of the red–green government coalition[14] has added to this development and, ironically, no one other than George "Diabolo" Bush and his closest political advisors deserve credit for the "emotional reunifica-tion of Germans" on the matter of world peace. In Mohr's words "their self-opinionated, inconsiderate actions with the special effects of the Rumsfeld rhetoric and their fast forward-strategy of old-Europe-bashing has irritated even the most hardened friends of America, the red-wine-loving defendants of the French raw-milk cheese and experienced Bellizists of the German Feuilletons." Mohr continues that in Germany, "from the grandchild in Oldenburg to the grandma at the Starnberger Lake it is widely held the con-viction that there is a dry alcoholic in the White House, who has barely seen anything besides Texas and the military airport in the Azores, celebrates his high-noon event with his learned cowboy walk and his fundamental-Christian conviction, with which he also wants to revenge his father's disgrace and do a favor for the oil industry."

Mohr quotes the German director Wim Wenders, who states that "War is the most horrible thing that human beings can do to each other. Even the modern, computer-geared war creates victims, even if war correspondents prefer to ignore that fact. The first victim of war has always been the truth." Mohr agrees, but believes these words sound like a mantra, a collection of well-used clichés. Only hesitantly people are voicing their discomfort with the German peace movement and those—when they dare to—are accused of cynicism. Mohr refers to Jan Ross' article and his claim that it is morally "taboo" to even consider resolving conflicts with force and that we can observe "an especially disagreeable good human, the bad taste of political kitsch." He is in agreement with his colleague that the fight between "good human and war monger" denies any serious discussion before it has even begun. It seems to Mohr that intellectuals have not noticed that their traditional role as lonely "warners" is suffering with the popular peace-chic. Mohr raises the question as to whether we still need the antiwar statements of the thinking class, if their statements are nothing more than mainstream comment at every gathering. Many intellectuals these days foresee a "world fire" or at least a "destabilization of the Arab world." However, Mohr asserts, intellectuals never ask the important question that remains as to whether the events might proceed differently from the way they have predicted them, whether there was a third way between "reality-blind morality and moral-forgotten Realpolitik." The author reminds us at the end of his article that historical memory is short lived and that history has proven different in many cases, whether it was in Kosovo or Afghanistan. The direst of predictions did not realize themselves; however, reality up to this point has been bad enough.

In another article "Spiritual Politics of Protective Duties," published in *Frankfurter Allegemeine Zeitung* (*FAZ*) in February 2002, Thomas Schmid declares that the message seems to be clear and can be summarized in one sentence: "under no circumstances can there be a war against Iraq."[15] All over the world thousands of people have taken to the street to express this conviction. In the 1980s, and here he seems in complete agreement with Jan Ross, the peace and antiwar movement was "a thing of radicals, more or less anti-capitalist and anti-west minorities." Today, the antiwar stance has united the majority of people claiming an "unconditional no to Iraq." Schmid points out though that not all humanity has been excited and overwhelmed by this communal feeling of the new peace movement. He quotes Amo Naziz, a Kurd from northern Iraq living in Germany, who says "The demonstrations, which take place world wide today for peace, only frighten the people in Iraq. For the Iraqis, they are nothing other than help for a dictator and his Gestapo." Schmid grants that this might be a single opinion but it focuses on the misery of a people, which could possibly be the reason for war.

The supporters of the peace movement seem to think of a lot of issues, writes Schmid, but not of the misery of the Iraqi population. Speakers at rallies have concentrated on venting their anger against the United States, for which they have received a lot of applause, but have spoken little about the crimes of Saddam Hussein, a topic that for the most part has gained little recognition from their audience. According to Schmid, "The new peace movement suffers on one eye from reduced vision, if not from blindness." The new peace movement is characterized by a unique contradiction that remains hidden from most of its supporters. The movement's supporters talk about the interests of humanity, claims Schmid, and of being part of a global community that wants "the good." However, they overlook the dark corners of the world. If one would look at them in more detail, it would become clear that it is not only the will for peace that counts.[16] Schmid continues that in order to prevent the "grander vision" from being destroyed, the new peace friends allow that dictators are ennobled through nothing other than a declared contradiction to the United States and that their "misdeeds can remain in the scurrile light of the half-so-bad." Those marching through the streets, writes Schmid, are probably completely enraptured with an antiwar feeling and the need for reconciliation. The author declares that "In a strange way an idealistic, all-encompassing universalism connects itself with a frighteningly provincial, hard particularism: emotion and toughness go hand in hand."[17] Schmid thinks that the credo "war is always an evil and never creates anything good" is still unfounded because it was the very means of war that brought many dictators down. Today's friends of peace render homage to a new isolationism and believe that it is sufficient, in order to prevent war, to just not want it. Schmid accuses the "peace-mongers" of a weird blindness in overlooking that the events of 9/11 show that "war did not care at all about the Western desire for peace but rather descended onto the Western world."[18] Schmid opines that the tragedy of 9/11 was just the beginning of more violent times to come. It is the goal of Washington to prevent the unification of rogue states, terrorist cells, and weapons of mass destruction. Schmid warns that those who want to counteract Washington need to provide more than "a will for peace, the wish for a timely unpractical unlimited work order for weapon inspectors of this world and an unlimited belief in the merciless tender power of negotiations." With his final words, Schmid raises the question as to whether the Western way of life has a future in those regions where Islam has so much power that it does not allow for the creation of a laizistic[19] understanding of state, which rejects the influence of the clergy in matters of state, educations, and culture. The fundamental lack of the new peace movement lies in the fact that these regions of Islamic fundamentalism, in spite of their one-world-rhetoric, have stayed "white spots on their world map." Schmid continues that "The friends of peace are not interested in the world but rather in themselves . . . and are in an old fashioned way Eurocentric: they believe, the desire for peace in the metropolises of wealth was able to steer the course of the world. That is spiritual politics of protective duties, which is a pacifism of affluence."

Robert Misik starts his article in *Die Tageszeitung* (*TAZ*) on March 20, 2003 with the request "Save the pacifism!"[20] The arguments against a war in Iraq are thin, he claims, and a look at the history of the peace movement in the 1990s proves that a great tradition of intellectual history has been ruined. Misik thinks that the new movement lacks a realistic pacifism, an antimilitarism, which has been unenlightened about its own difficulties.

According to Misik, we see today that positions on war, which had majority support in the 1980s, no longer have validity. There is not only a reason for dark skepticism but also good arguments against a war in Iraq. Many hold the opinion that risks for the Middle East region (human, economic, etc.) cannot be calculated, and a majority of the European public is in agreement with this opinion. Nevertheless, the antiwar position remains strangely powerless. Misik believes that the problem does not stem from the arguments presented by the peace movement alone. It has become clear how much the radical split in traditional left-wing antiwar camps has discredited every critical position. At the same time, the "remainder of the classic pacifist movement" has added to this development by undermining its own position. To support his idea, Misik takes us back in time to the debates of the 1990s when left-liberal elites around the world supported a new "humanitarian interventionism" against the background of Somalia, Rwanda, and Bosnia. French intellectuals expressed the conviction that universal human rights had to be implemented if need be with force. "Appeasement led to tragedy," they argued. The German debate narrowed down symbolically to the word "Auschwitz," writes Misik, and none other than Germany's foreign minister Joschka Fischer took the left away from the old pacifist beliefs. "I not only learned from war: never again war" articulated the foreign minister "but also never again Auschwitz." This change of attitude not only resulted in the creation of the glamorous word "Bellizism" (which evokes the Latin word for war as well as the Italian word for beauty) but also in military action. For the first time since 1945, German soldiers moved into war in Kosovo five months after the Social Democratic / Green coalition came into power for the first time. This change of opinion of an essential part of the global leftist intelligentsia would not have led to such a disaster, if the rest of the pacifist movement had not sunk into "complete infantilism." Misik states that the friends of peace had nothing to complain about when Iraq annexed Kuwait but regarded the intervention in Bosnia and Kosovo as "wars of aggression" against the sovereign Yugoslavia. The author complains that this particular pacifism gives in "stubbornly and heroically" to its own powerlessness without trying to confront intellectually the dilemma that in some situations aggressive action was needed to bring about peace. Misik suggests that a "modernized pacifism" should formulate restrictively the conditions, under which one can react militarily to horrors in a case of emergency. The goal of this new pacifist movement should be to speak out for intervention that is operatively more policing rather than a military action. He proposes that the movement also has to recognize that there are situations in which the ending of human tragedies can only be achieved through a forceful intervention. The current situation is difficult, Misik concedes, because we still exist in a global world order, in which international actors still do not operate in one world where all states pursue the same internal politics, but also no longer operate in the old world of naked state power-politics. According to Misik, all wars of the last ten years (from the Gulf War 1991 to Bosnia to Kosovo to Afghanistan) have had, although in different ways, the character of international police action with military means. However, at the same time the sphere of "the power-politics of Hyper-powers" such as the United States continues to exist. The situation is complicated when we need to not only legitimize the interventions against ongoing human tragedies as police actions but also legitimize those that pose a potential danger, which can only be countered with preventive means.

Misik admits that it is very difficult to formulate a satisfying position and he quotes the well-known American social philosopher Michael Walzer " . . . never could I support a peace movement, whose aims or mere effect is to appease Saddam Hussein."

The previous articles from various papers clearly demonstrate that not all is "well and harmonic" in the current peace movement in Germany and there is a consensus that the movement's old agenda and rhetoric can no longer satisfy the demands of the world whose political order has changed. There is proof of the existence of a rift in the movement and a strong doubt of the validity of pacifism in its old form. The majority of the authors indicate that pacifism in its current form has to be rethought and revised in order for activists to become more credible, although they do not always agree on the way to achieve a more effective course of action and deliberation. They have not placed blame as much on outside forces, although Mohr sometimes uses colorful and forceful language to criticize the American government as well the German peace movement,[21] but rather have taken a close look at internal actions and placed responsibility on Germans themselves to analyze their pacifist stance. The message seems to be that the peace movement is riding on its old agenda, which is no longer compelling in this new world order. It may be that international relationships cannot be as clearly defined as they once were during the cold war era. The authors also seem to indicate that the German peace movement has to define clear principles stating when and how intervention through military action becomes permissible. Bashing the United States does not seem to be an effective means of resistance and the debate about peace and the justification for war should not become an emotional battle between bellizists and pacifists but rather a peace movement grounded in the realities of our times.

Not all articles published on German pacifism and the Iraq war challenged the current status quo in the peace movement, some analyzed whether government and political parties used the peace movement for their own opportunistic reasons or whether there was a more genuine belief at work to reject or support any war in Iraq. The daily *FAZ* and two of Germany's most popular weeklies, the newspaper *Die Zeit* and the magazine *Der Spiegel*, reported extensively and often critically on the Chancellor's stance, the government's official rhetoric, and the opposition's defection to the U.S. position in support of a military action against Iraq.

At the beginning of February 2003, *Die Zeit* published an article by Gunter Hoffman called "The long way to a loud 'no'."[22] In this article, the author analyzes the German government's probable reasons for opposing the pending war in Iraq and the way in which the government's resistance played out. Hoffman claims that the process of resistance was a lengthy and "not well-thought-through" one and that the German government's actions smacked of opportunism at times when opposing the war in Iraq. Although there seemed to have been some debate within the government and among the various German parties, in the end the "no to war" remained. Hoffman cites Chancellor Schröder saying "The idea that 'wars are not normal, not even as an extension of politics by different means, but are rather adventures' has been ingrained into the collective consciousness in this country, maybe even in Europe," to indicate that the German government believes that the stance of Germany against any war cannot be anything other than resistance.

Hoffmann's focus of investigation seems to be on two questions, first, on whether the German government has maneuvered itself with its declarative "no" into an outside position and, second, on whether the "no" was just an election campaign strategy. Hoffmann believes that the German government demonstrated its approval of military actions, such as in Afghanistan, shortly after 9/11 but connected this approval of a constantly repeated promise to listen to civil society and take its hesitancy seriously. This has become Chancellor Schröder's "ceterum censeo."[23] Hoffmann believes that the relationship between Berlin and Washington, characterized by misunderstandings, things left unsaid, the internal development of relationships in Europe, German elections and the need to find "a German way" have contributed to Germany's "no-approach." In addition, the Chancellor has sharpened his "no" to distinguish himself from the opposition and its political rhetoric. Even, when faced with enormous pressure from within the country and Washington, Hoffmann predicts, Germany will not "roll over" or isolate itself, it will rather look for closer alliances with Blair and Chirac.

There were some articles that did not seem to talk about more than typical internal political polemics. At the end of January 2003, *FAZ* published an article tracing the "patriotism debate" that had ensued among the governing Social Democratic Party (SDP) and the opposition parties Christian Democratic Union (CDU) and Free Democratic Party (FDP).[24] *FAZ* offered a whole pallet of quotes from all political spectra. Many of these quotes were reactions to comments made by the general secretary of the SPD, Olaf Scholz, reproaching the opposition for demonstrating a lack of patriotism. The opposition reacted vehemently and the CDU's general secretary was quoted from the "BZ" saying "Especially when one is a patriot, it hurts to see, how Gerhard Schröder has maneuvered Germany into political meaninglessness in foreign affairs because of tactical reasons to win the elections."[25] The article offered more answers to Scholz' comment and highlighted statements using phrases such as "national toadyism" or "divisionary tactics" and "internal failure of Red–Green." The use of language and intonation clearly seemed to demonstrate that government and opposition were caught up in the political game of "pointing the finger."

On February 11, 2003, the title of an Spiegel Online article declared "The Union places itself on the side of the Americans."[26] The article started by quoting Angela Merkel, the head of the conservative CDU, by saying that the Chancellor was a danger for Germany because of his attitude toward the Iraq war. Hence, the Merkel's party aligned itself demonstratively to eight European countries, which supported the Bush course. It reported that the CDU brought forward a motion to support the declaration of eight European states with the title "Europe and America have to stand together." This declaration demanded that Iraq had to fulfill without conditions and immediately all resolutions of the UN. If Iraq would not accept this opportunity of peaceful disarmament, it would have to bear the responsibility for the consequences. Furthermore, the article reported that party members were of the opinion that one had to clarify the danger of Saddam Hussein to the German population and Bavaria's minister president stated that he did not exclude war as the last resort.

The article clearly gave the impression that the opposition was not in agreement with the government's stance on war but it also seemed to indicate that the opposition had no more to offer in order to resolve the Iraq problem than lame rhetoric.

Two days later *Spiegel Online* presented two more articles on the internal German debate on Iraq. It seemed as if the press relished following the ongoing exchange between the parties and considered the internal conflict just as newsworthy as the external one. The first article reported on Schröder's government statement in the Bundestag, in which he declared that "there is a peaceful alternative."[27] In his speech, the author writes, the chancellor confirmed the idea of continuation and the expansion of weapons inspections in Iraq and emphasized Germany's sovereignty in its decision on whether to send German troops to Iraq. At the same time, the chancellor sharply attacked the opposition claiming that the CDU/CSU (Christian Social Union) belonged to "a coalition of the willing for the war with Iraq" thereby endangering the "German–French collaboration, which is indispensable and cannot come apart." Two hours later Spiegel Online published an article with the celebratory title "Hurrah, Germany."[28] The title seemed rather misleading because the true agenda of the author, Markus Deggerich, was the "German Bundestag in times of crisis." Deggerich begins his article with the statement that "government and opposition misuse the threatening war in Iraq for an internal political skirmish." He explained that the chancellor regards the opposition as "a warmonger," whereas the opposition sees him as "an overly ambitious amateur." Deggerich declares, with a good portion of irony, that the chancellor "wore the banner with the white dove last Thursday into the Bundestag and used his government statement to place himself at the top of the peace movement." The author believes that both the government and the opposition clearly demonstrated in their debate that day what ails German foreign policy, namely, that both treat foreign policy the same as internal politics and misuse the debate accordingly. Deggerich is as critical of the government's party line in general, which does not seem to be anything more than an appeal for peace and a diversion from internal problems. He also criticizes the oppositions for its "plan of lack of plan." According to Deggerich, the opposition has nothing new to contribute but presents its arguments merely "newly wrapped."

Conclusion

It is quite open to debate, whether Germans have anything new or novel to add to this discussion on the peace movement and war. After reading these various articles, it seems remarkable that many German authors dedicated as much attention to the internal debate as to the external conflicts as opposed to their colleagues in other countries. In Germany, the discussion on Iraq challenged Germans to grapple with their changing role as participants in major global conflicts. It is obvious that German politicians engaged in the "usual political combat" to promote self-interest but many Germans also debated a serious underlying issue. The potential war in Iraq made Germans face their own demons and engage in a discussion that revolved around Germany's past, present, and future identity and its role in the international political arena. The discussion in the media showed that Germans are still very much shaped by their past and struggling with their responsibility as to how to confront the problems of war.

Some of the authors were more critical than others of the peace movement but no one doubted that the debate had become once again relevant and that Germans, and their intellectual elite, needed to reflect more on the issue of how to become more credible nationally and internationally in the discussion on wars and on other foreign policy issues. Most authors indicated that it was not sufficient to spout slogans such as "responsibility for peace,"[29] but politicians and activists needed to articulate precise directives on "peace and war" in order for Germany to become an important player. There was an underlying notion in many articles that Germans are and will continue to be a unique people in the twenty-first century. Germans are scarred, bruised, and guilt-ridden by the events of the last century and their experience potentially offers much to Americans and other Western nations in finding peaceful rather than forceful solutions to international conflicts if they move from a passive to a more active role.

By the end of February 2003, as the likelihood of war became stark reality, there was a clear shift of concentration in news reporting and many of the aforementioned papers were publishing articles on Iraq analyzing primarily American interests and reasons for engaging in the war. The language of many articles became more and more aggressive and the titles were often eye-catching by using phrases such as "the PR-machine of the Bush-warrior"[30] or "the War that came from the Think Tank."[31] The German debate of the peace movement and Germany's stance on the war had moved to the background. It seemed that attempts at peace were no longer an option internationally and that situation had muted Germany's debate for the time being.

Notes

1. T. Szymankski, "The German Press on the War with Iraq," *Front Line Berlin*, Friday, March 21, 2003 <http://www.tekla-szymanski.com/engl9germanpress.html> (accessed May 5, 2004).
2. Mohr, R, "Kritik an Friedenskultur: Die Alten sagen 'Dresden,' die Jungen sagen 'Oel.'" *Spiegel Online*, Saturday, March 29, 2003 <http://www.spiegel.de/kultur/gesellschaft/0,1518,242484,00.html> (accessed June 6, 2004).
3. R. Friedrich, *Der Brand: Deutschland im Bombenkrieg 1940–1945*. (Berlin: Prpyläen Verlag, 2003).
4. "Anti-Kriegs-Kundgebungen: Grösste Friedenskundgebung in der Geschichte der Bundesrepublik." *Spiegel Online,* Saturday, February 15, 2003 <http://www.spiegel.de/panorama/0,1518,235314,00.html> (accessed July 5, 2004).

5. Ibid.

6. J. Ross, "Dann gibt es nur eins: nie wieder!" *Die Zeit*, Saturday, March 1, 2003 <http://zeus.zeit.de/text/2003/01/03_Pazifismus> (accessed June 2, 2004).

7. Ibid.

8. Ibid.

9. Ibid.

10. Bellizismus is a German term for a political attitude that allows the use of military force as a means to reach certain goals.

11. Ibid.

12. Mohr, R, "Kritik an Friedenskultur: Die Alten sagen 'Dresden,' die Jungen sagen 'Oel.' " *Spiegel Online*, Saturday, March 29, 2003 <http://www.spiegel.de/kultur/gesellschaft/0,1518,242484,00.html> (accessed June 6, 2004).

13. Ibid.

14. Since 1998 the Social Democratic Party and the Green Party have formed a government in Germany. Hence, Germans use the term "red–green coalition."

15. T. Schmid, "Geistige Schutzpolitik," *Frankfurter Allgemeine Zeitung*, Friday, February 2, 2003 <http://fazarchiv.faz.net/webcgi?WID=96053378095461202_16&START=_0&PFEIFE> (accessed June 5, 2004).

16. Ibid.

17. Ibid.

18. Ibid.

19. "Laizistic" derives from the word "laizism," a term used since the French Revolution for a movement, which is against the influence of the clergy in matters of state, culture, and education. Furthermore, it demands the separation of state and church and the removal of churches into the sacral area.

20. R. Misik, "Rettet den Pazifismus!" *TAZ*, Monday, January 20, 2003 <http://www.taz.de/pt/.archiv/suche?mode=erw&tid=2003%2F01%F02%Fa0158.red&List> (accessed July 8, 2004).

21. Ibid.

22. G. Hoffman, "Der lange Weg zum lauten Nein." *Die Zeit*, February 2003 <http://zeus.de/text/2003/05/Hofmann> (accessed July 28, 2004).

23. Ibid.

24. "Union kontert Scholz aus." *Spiegel Online*, Monday, January 27, 2003 <http://premiumlink.net/$61643$1687232693$/RubA24ECD630CAE40E483841DB7D16> (accessed April 29, 2004).

25. Ibid.

26. "Union stellt sich an die Seite der Amerikaner." *Spiegel Online*, February 11, 2003 <http://premium-link.net?$62535$916587175$/0,1518,234698_eza_00050-druck-234698,00> (accessed July 13, 2003).

27. "Es gibt eine friedliche Alternative."*Spiegel Online*, Thursday, February 13, 2003 <http://premium-link.net/$62535$916587175$/0,1518,234876_eza00050-druck-234876,00> (accessed July 13, 2004).

28. M. Deggerich, M, "Hurra, Deutschland". *Spiegel Online*, Thursday, February 13, 2003 <http://premium-link.net/&62535$916587175$/0,1518,234950_eza_00030-druck-234950,00> (accessed July, 13, 2004).

29. REGIERUNGonline, "Unsere Verantwortung für den Frieden" Regierungserklärung von Bundeskanzler Schröder vor dem deutschen Bundestag zur aktuellen Lage am 13. Februar 2003, Thursday, February 13, 2003

<http://www.bundesregierung.de/servlet/init.cms.layout.LayoutServlet?global.
naviknoten=41> (accessed July 4, 2004).

30. J. Bölsche, "Die PR-Maschine der Busch-Krieger," *Spiegel Online*,
Tuesday, March 12, 2003 <http://premium-link.net/$62535$916587175$/
0,1518,239721_eza_00050-druck-239721,00> (accessed July 5, 2004).

31. J. Bölsche, "Der Krieg, der aus dem Think Tank kam." *Spiegel Online*,
Tuesday, March 4, 2003 <http://premium-ink.net/$62535$916587175$/
0,1518,238643_eza_00050-druck-238643,00> (accessed July 5, 2004).

THE MIDDLE EAST

CHAPTER TEN

SHEER AND OPAQUE SCREENS:
THE MEDICAL ETHNOGRAPHY OF ARABIC
TELEVISION, A PHENOMENOLOGICAL
QUANDARY OF COMMUNAL MEMORY,
SUFFERING, AND RESISTANCE

Iman Roushdy-Hammady

They came to this country years ago, escaping injustice, disparities, and the fear of seeing their children turning into numbers lumped uncomfortably under what is called human casualty; they came—like many others—to seek the American dream. They put all their hopes in their two sons, who on September 11, 2001 were both in their offices in the World Trade Center, the Twin Towers, the meaning of success. But the dreams soon ended, as two weeks later their home was full of guests. Their faces were frozen, and the black mourning dresses of the women brought back memories of many other funerals. I did not know why this one felt different, but soon the answer came through the TV screen. On *Fox*, an analyst from the *Economist* was hosted. Commenting on the Arab American communities in the context of the disaster, she said that they only appeared to display feelings of sadness but, running into each other in the streets, they exchanged hidden smiles, and many exchanged congratulation messages via e-mail!

These unjustified comments not only marked the end of this interview but also of painful silence in that house. . . . To appease grieving cries, some of the men soon put on the Arabic satellite channels. I felt that they were browsing to find a forum where their suffering is expressed and believed.

Through satellite dishes, many Arabs, Arab Americans, and Arabic speakers have access to a wide variety of channels that air from different countries of the Arab world. The dish network provides a number of packages for Arabic TV, most popular of which is the "deluxe package." This includes 10 channels: Arabic Radio and Television (ART), including (1) *al-Zikr* channel, a religious programming radio channel; (2) ART music radio channel (ARTMS);

(3) ART TV channel; and (4) ART movie channel (ARTMV). In addition, the package includes (1) The Future; (2) Dubai TV; (3) The Lebanese Broadcasting Corporation Channel (LBC); The Egyptian Satellite Channels (ESC) including; (4) Nile TV (drama); (5) Nile TV (news); and (6) Al-Jazirah. These channels entertain audiences with a wide variety of programs, ranging from arts, drama, religious programs, children's programs, programs for women, sports, culture, politics, and local, regional, and world news, including live programs, allowing participation of audiences globally.

Dealing with one of the most effective media of communication in the context of the 2003 war against Iraq, it is indispensable to explore Arabic news coverage within this larger framework of Arabic television. Also, it is of vital importance to analyze news items interactively with other agencies, such as American and Western media, as well as the audience involvement, perception, and reaction to events.

This chapter provides a journey in time focusing on Arabic satellite channels since September 11, 2001 until the fall of Baghdad on April 9, 2003. Tangled within a complex political web involving Arab/Israeli relations, local democracy issues, economic dependency, U.S. politico-economic hegemony, religious movements, the stigmatization of Arabs and Muslims, as well as the challenged Arab League, Arab cities witnessed a panorama of conferences about and protests aganist the war. This article provides an ethnography of Arab visual media during the build up to this war. Using approaches rooted in phenomenology, suffering, and resistance, this article provides a cultural analysis of Arabic satellite programs, and highlights the profile of the Arab voice as it interacted with TV news, live programs, films, and songs during these uncertain and turbulent times.

Arabic TV after 9/11

It benefits Al-Jazirah to play to Arab nationalism because that's their audience, just like Fox plays to American patriotism, for the exact same reason . . . because that's their audience . . . The big thing for my generation is for these two perspectives— my perspective, the Western perspective, and the Arab perspective—to understand each other better . . . because, truly, the two worlds are colliding at a rapid rate.
—Lt. Josh Rushing, Central Command Press Officer, U.S. Army.[1]

American TV made memorable the expressions of President George W. Bush, which turned to represent his slogans for a global war: "either with us, or against us," "Crusader's fight against Islamic Terrorism," "I want to fight those who want to take away our freedom." These expressions had threatening effect on Arabs, Arab Americans, and Muslims everywhere. Amidst this turbulence, American media reiterated G. W. Bush's continuous emphasis on the need to fight terrorism by attacking Iraq, claiming its possession of weapons of mass destruction. The turning of attention from Afghanistan and bin Laden to Iraq and Saddam was discussed in Arab media in the context of increased risk of an American blind retaliation targeting Arabs. Egyptian Amr Musa, the current secretary general of the Arab League, commented to Al-Jazirah on the threats made by the White House following the events of September 11, 2001 as follows:

> America is now like an injured giant. It always thought it was beyond reach! But it was hit in its very heart, its very symbols of power! So, this giant is now agonizing in pain, hitting anything that comes in its way; it needs its time to cool down.[2]

Nevertheless, with increased intentions to declare war against Iraq, the identity and loyalty of Arab Americans and Muslims was questioned ruthlessly in the United States. In New York City, for example, a number of Arab small businesses were closed with no obvious reasons; numerous Arab immigrants were deported; Arabs and Muslims were held in American airports for nearly 24 hours, and some were sent back home, despite their legal documents; even Arab green-card holders were not let in easily. There was fear in the community, and in vain, people tried to protect themselves behind an outburst of American flags displayed on cars and even in the smallest store windows.

E-mail networks of big academic institutions circulated messages to induce effective action, when American policies were noticed to negatively affect campus life: Arab students and scholars were delayed from entering the United States for months; libraries were instructed to monitor the borrowing of books, especially in nuclear sciences, and to report any borrowers with Arabic or Muslim names. Faculty and staff attempted to protest these policies, as they were in deep conflict with their institutions' philosophy to promote knowledge—the only path to intellectual freedom. However, librarians who showed any reluctance to cooperate were subject to FBI questioning under the existing emergency laws.

During those times, Arab media, sharing global sentiments, repudiated the attacks of September 11. The news announced the cooperation of Arab countries with the American administration to "fight terrorism." Egypt and Israel were given grants to target what came to be labeled *al-harb did al-irháb,* a direct transnation from the American media's "the war against terrorism." Even Saudi Arabia allocated resources to follow the American lead in this respect.

Between programs on many Arabic channels appeared an ad with a message. It showed an Arab family hosting guests of Western appearance.

From the fashion worn by the Arab family and the beautiful Arabic decoration and floor seating, it conveyed the culture of the Arabian Gulf. The family and their guests are shown eating, sipping tea, while socializing joyously. At the end of the ad a caption appeared citing verses form the Holy *Qur'án*, emphasizing peaceful living between Muslims and *Ahl al-Kitáb* (People of the Book) that include Christians and Jews.

The timing of this ad is rather interesting. The majority of Arab countries have local Christian minorities, which were certainly not meant in this ad. The piece was an invitation to, and/or manifestation of, cultural pluralism in a religious garb. The ad showed Western blond guests—foreigners—but had a verbal, written message targeting Christians. Identifying Westerners as Christians and Arabs as Muslims gave the visual component a meaning different from the literal meaning of the *Qur'anic* verses, making it a defensive reaction to G. W. Bush's slightly threat to launch a "Crusaders' fight against [Islam]," where he identified Americans (and Europeans) with crusaders.

The Shadows of War and Shifting Scenes on Arabic TV

Before the invasion of Iraq on March 19/20, 2003, Arab media reflected a transition from showing complete cooperation with the American administration (to fight global terrorism), to showing resentment against participating in the Iraq war. In contrast, American TV emphasized the volunteering of Arab Americans in the U.S. Army to engage in the war against Iraq, which was smoothed out by its assigned military name: Operation Iraqi Freedom. It is not clear whether the intention of such footage was to make mainstream America accept Arab–American coexistence, or to entice more military cooperation between Arab Americans and Arab countries. Whatever the case may be, Arab media could not be in tune with these messages.

In a program, which weekly aired on ART in 2003 entitled "*Lá ará, lá asma', lá atakallam*" (I don't see, don't hear, don't talk) an Egyptian commentator Mona Zaki surprised audiences with a serious statement by the *Mufti* (casuist) of Egypt: "If any Muslim stays in America and supports the war, then he is a *káfir* (infidel)." This statement had serious effect on the Muslims of America, who found themselves in a confounding situation, as for many of them America is the only homeland they know. Ms. Zaki arranged for a meeting with the *Mufti* on her program, which aired in early March of 2003,[3] asking him to explain what he meant by his statement:

> *Mufti*: Provided that America starts the war against Iraq, as threatened, then
> if Muslims stay in America, a country that defined its war as a crusaders'

war against Islam, and if they support this war, then they are *kuffár* [pl. of
káfir] because they would be partaking in an attack against fellow
Muslims. . . .

Zaki: So, if the war takes place, what should these people do? Where should
they go? . . .

Mufti: They should come back to their countries of origin! . . . If America is
their only homeland, then they should emigrate! God's earth is spacious!
They should go somewhere where they feel safer. They would not be safe
as Muslims if America launches a war against Muslims.

Challenged Countries

Amidst this local resentment to the war, *"Lá ará, lá asma', lá atakallam"*[4]
presented an item of news that shed some light on the delicate situation of
Egypt and its dilemma. Egypt had to face the challenge of having a public
opinion protesting the American war against Iraq on the one hand, and
having its over political and economic interests on the other, contextually
rendering Egypt dependent on various forms of American aid. This challenge
was crystallized in an incident portrayed by Ms. Zaki's program.

Footage was shown of an international conference, which was organized
in Egypt in an attempt to discuss global strategies of how to resist the
American and British decision to launch the war. Meanwhile, Ms. Zaki was
giving an account of the sequence of conference events. The conference was
difficult to organize. The organizers, including academicians and profes-
sionals, faced problems of, first, obtaining all the necessary permits from
local authorities, and, second, of finding a hotel to hold the conference. The
title of the conference was changed several times during the course of its
organization, in order to be able to overcome these two hurdles. Though the
final title could not be clearly identified from the footage presented on that
Egyptian TV Program, it seems from the coverage that the title's final word-
ings reflected a special consideration given by the Arabs to the issue of the
appropriate portrayal of the United States.

At the closing session of the conference, a member of Saddam's administration spoke. At the podium he repeated slogans of nationalism, of supporting Saddam, condemning America and Great Britain for their unjust
brutality, and for their "barbarian war" against Iraq. While some showed
their support by clapping, a participant from Germany made his way to the
podium, took the microphone, and expressed his discontent:

Who invited this man? I am not here to support the autocratic regime of
Saddam! Had I known that he would be speaking, I would not have come to
this conference! We are not here to support Saddam! And unless Arabs get rid
of their autocratic regimes, they will remain under the mercy of America!
What is happening to Iraq [may happen to any of you].

His upset tone and loud voice alerted the organizers of the conference, who rushed to salvage the situation. The organizers were shown frantically going through the list of participants under the watchful eyes of the German participant. It seemed that the Iraqi official came uninvited to the conference. But the whole situation turned into a chaotic scene, and was left without further comments, by the TV program so that spectators could make their own inferences and interpretations.

The Image and Colonial Memory

The first three months of 2003 particularly witnessed antiwar protests on a global scale. Arabic satellite channels reflected some memories and interpretations of the war within the Arab community. The war was initiated by two strong colonial powers, Great Britain and the United States. Iraq itself, until recently (October 3, 1932) was under British occupation, and few decades later suffered from years of American political and economic sanctions that began in 1991.

To express their resentment against a neocolonial rule, the Arab street personified their resistance to the amalgamation of the two—ancient and contemporary—superpowers in two corresponding heroes. The first heroic image was that of Nasser, the ex-president of Egypt, the first country in the Arab world to gain its independence from British colonialism. His idealistic project to unify Arabs made him a symbol of nationalism in modern Arab history. The second image was that of Saddam. He symbolized resistance against the American attack. However, both images presented a complex sociopolitical and cultural *problematique*, which should not be overlooked in order to understand the Arab opinions and attitudes during these turbulent times.

In the streets of Morocco, Syria, Egypt, and Palestine, America was usually identified as an "occupying terrorist" and "invading force." For some Arab viewers this only revealed a lack of Arab leadership and an impoverished shaky ideology. Nasser was a symbol of a past Arab dream while Saddam symbolized power in Iraq. By no means did the appearance of Saddam's pictures during Arab protests reflect any kind of support for his regime. Rather his image was a personification of Iraq because there was no other leadership to take the place of this image.

Yet symbols of such volatile nature are not static. In the heap of events, the invasion of Iraq became an extension of the Arab/Israeli conflict for the street protesters. The suffering of Iraqis was intertwined with that of Palestinians. Philanthropic associations, such as "Kind Hearts," which placed advertisements on LBC, The Future, Al-Jazirah, and ART to collect money and aid for needy Arabs, especially in Palestine, focused on Palestinians and Iraqis in their appeals. Pictures of heavily wounded women and children after the first days of the American and British invasion in March 2003, accompanied by captions indicating the scarcity of medical supplies and nutrition, filled their advertisements (ads). These appeals were particularly influential after the American forces hit two big Red Cross storage locations in Iraq in March and April of 2003. Images of wounded and dead Palestinians and destroyed homes during Israeli attacks in the news were followed by identical images from Iraq.

To provide a forum for its disempowered audiences, Arabic news showed footage of young Arab citizens volunteering to serve in Palestine and Iraq. Al-Jazirah and Nile TV news repeatedly showed footage of young Egyptians from the Law School of Cairo University who volunteered to fight in Iraq or Israel. While this was an emotionally moving scene, it was questioned by some of the Arab audience members in America:

> This is fake! How are they going to transport them to Israel? By air? Of course not, as they will have to land in the airport of Tel Aviv. By land? Neither the Egyptian, nor Israeli, nor Jordanian authorities will permit it. . . .
>   How are they going to get to Iraq? By air? Impossible! By land? Tell me how? Via Saudi Arabia or Kuwait? Or via Israel and Jordan? No way!

Nobody had answers to these questions. But the footage fit well in the general scheme of images that were shown on the Arabic movie channel of ARTMV.

The Hidden Wish: Film and Song as Expressions of the Arab Dream

Philadelphia, March 15, 2003. I am flipping through the Arabic channels late at night while sipping my tea and doing paperwork. I caught myself by surprise humming tunes from the 1950s and 1960s, tunes that had disappeared from Egyptian radio and television since the death of ex-president Nasser in 1970. I knew the tunes from recordings and people who had witnessed the glory of an ideology of Arab nationalism, the pride of which rapidly shattered after the Israeli victory in 1967. I lifted up my head, and here were the songs, image, and sound. I was so happy to have finally seen them, all the famous participating singers, so young, repeating the compositions of legendry 'Abd-al-Wahhab: Al-gíl al-sá'id (the Rising Generation), Al-Watan al-Akbar (the Greater Homeland). The songs are so full of enthusiasm, pride, and hope, that I think people were and are in love with the songs, regardless of the political regime or ideology they glorify.

There was an intensive focus in Arab media on two genres of movies, emphasizing images of resistance and martyrdom respectively. The first of these genres developed in the 1940s and 1950s in Egypt, where the time frame was purposefully unidentified, but the entire setting—with palaces, markets, wealth, costumes, harem-like-dressed-women—looked like a mixture of A Thousand and One Night Baghdad, and Egypt under Memluk rule.[5] The most common theme is a battle between powerful men—good and bad—to rule a particular land. The woman in this genre is the trophy, as she also symbolizes the land.

Though simple in plot, these movies implicate autocratic and unjust rulers. The distinction is made between a helpless nominal king and the actual evil sub-rulers. When these movies were first made, this scenario alluded to contemporary local politics.

In the 1950s, the king's authority became more and more marginal toward the end of the British rule in Egypt. Among the sub-rulers, there were those in favor of the status quo and those who opposed it and sought freedom. Set in an elusive space and timeframe, this movie genre provided a safe way to express opposition to the existing sociopolitical regime.

On Arabic satellite channels this genre was showed during the time when the Arab League failed to stop the American war against Iraq. In all live programs presented by *Al-Jazirah*, especially between January and April of 2003, Arabs globally shunned the Arab League, highlighting its powerlessness, blaming its failure on economic interests, and on the dependency of its member countries on the United States:

> Every Arab country has a Saddam in it, so, why are [America and Britain] picking on Iraq's Saddam? Why now? Isn't this the same Saddam whom they supported in the 1970s and 1980s to hit Iran? . . .
> Nobody can save Iraq, [Arab countries] all need America! . . .
> There is no need for the Arab League! Whom are they representing anyway? Only themselves; not their people.

The movies of the second genre were played intensively after the invasion of Iraq started. This genre developed in the 1950s and 1960s under Nasser's regime in Egypt, some of which highlight the vital role of the "Free Officers" in ending Egypt's colonial rule and monarchy, while others glorify martyrdom for the Palestinian cause. Interestingly, the presentation of these movies on ARTMV was padded with songs praising pan-Arabism and Arab nationalism—such songs as Abd-al-Wahhab's famous composition *Al-Watan al-Akbar* (The Greater Homeland).[6] The main refrain of this song can be translated as follows:

> My beloved homeland, the greater homeland
> Its glories increase, day after day
> And its victories fill its life

> My homeland is growing independent
> Oh homeland! Oh homeland!

After the choir repeats this refrain, six famous singers of the time rise one by one and sing a stanza about resistance and struggle in Arab countries, ending with the phrase "May the Arab people live long and be victorious." On the background there were corresponding folkloric dances of the glorified countries. The message, spirited with Nasserist socialism, is that all Arab countries are one people, sharing one history of struggle for its freedom and independence. These lyrics found resonance in Mohammed Saeed Al-Sahhaf's (ex-foreign minister of Iraq) statements on all Arabic channels as American and British forces destroyed various targets in Baghdad, which included historical monuments and architectures:

> They want to destroy our national and cultural heritage! None of their targets are military! . . .
> But Iraq will resist! Every stone will turn into embers to fight those invading terrorists! . . .
> Our men are resisting. [American troops] will never reach Baghdad. Baghdad is a quiver that will throw back [arrows] at all those taking part in this coercion, in this usurpation!

Televised Religion and Emotional Memory: Al-Ummah

Religious programs were also used to encourage resistance and promote among Arabs and Muslims the concept of a united (Islamic) *ummah* (nation). All this was considered important to provide support for the Iraqis in their resistance. One such program was aired weekly on ART and carried the title *"Wa-Nalqá al-Ahibbah"* (Knowing the Beloved Ones).[7] The program was created and anchored by 'Amr Khálid.

Originally, this program was designed to introduce *Al-Sahábah* (the companions of Prophet Muhammad), their sayings, and to discuss their importance in providing life models for Muslims. The program also emphasized through the concept of *ummah* the importance of unity among Muslims, as well as of righteous and powerful leadership. The ads accompanying this program featured the following quotes of Mr. Khalid:

> If you want to know your history and be proud of it, let's imitate those Beloveds, let's imitate those *Sahábah*. . . .
> Company of friends [addressing the audience]! If we want out progress, we need to be one *ummah*, one connected *ummah*, so, let's look at those *Sahábah*, and see how they were able to realize this. . . .
> Look at the importance of women in the first epoch of Islam!

By the end of March 2003 there were increasing reports of military victories in the American media, the images showing destroyed villages and buildings in Baghdad, the cheering of some Iraqis in small villages and towns upon the arrival of the American forces. At that time, Mr. Khalid's program was broadcast daily. The tone and purpose of the program changed. While initially it had an educational overtone, the program later assumed the role of restoring hope and providing moral and spiritual support for the Iraqis in particular and Arabs in general:

> Don't give up; don't lose hope!
> God promised victory for believers!
> Look at the Quranic stories! Look at our history!
> This religion [Islam] was saved before! We will survive if we keep believing, we will be empowered to resist, so never give up!
> Let's all tell our brothers in Iraq: don't give up, don't lose hope, we are behind you with our hearts and prayers.
> If you saw some Iraqi people cheering on TV at the arrival of foreign military forces, it does not mean you should give up; it does not mean that they do not care about their own country. [Iraq] is a country under attack, unexpected reactions are not surprising. Don't let these images discourage you; Iraqis need your support!

By then, the ad about multicultural coexistence analyzed earlier in the chapter had totally disappeared. Emphasis fell on other types of messages. In one ad, three women intend to go shopping. The call of prayer accompanied by strong sunshine starts just as they open the house-door. They pray together, keep their head covers on, and go shopping for a wedding gown. The background music gradually switches from the solemn call to prayer to vibrantly syncopated rhythm associated with weddings in many Arab countries. The eyes of the young women are full of tears of joy. This ad alternated with another one showing a group of young men playing handball. They take a break as the call for prayer starts. They pray together, and then are shown playing another round and this time the team that prayed wins. Both pieces end with the following verbal message: *Aqim salátak, tan'am bihayátik* (If you hold your prayer, you will enjoy your life). The frequency of these ads' appearence increased as the war deadline of March 19–20, 2003 approached. The shadows of the war left little doubt that it was going to happen, and these messages attempted to create hope spiritually.

In the last two days before the fall of Baghdad on April 9, 2003, the general feeling from the Arabic satellite news channels, movies, songs, as well as 'Amr Khálid's *"Wa-Nalqa al-Ahibbah,"* brought to mind stories from the painful memories of many Arabs about the 1967 war,[8] when Arabs lost both war and land to Israel. This war is known as The Six Day War, and as *al-Nakbah* (disaster) and *al-Naksah* (relapse) in Arab political and historic discourse:

> On Egyptian radio (sarcastic laughter) they were telling us: "Our forces are progressing! Our forces hit the enemies' airplanes! Then they told us we lost the war and the land! We were shocked! . . .
>
> They told us we were victorious. But then we found out that we lost our sons, our land, and more so, we lost our dignity. . . .

This feeling of the loss of dignity and shame rematerialized with the fall of Baghdad on April 9, 2003, when American forces and tanks were shown live on Arabic channels breaking into the heart of the city, amidst a strange-looking crowd of exclusively young Arabic men who looked suspiciously uniformed for their age and appearance. They all marched in the company of American tanks into the empty square. Arab spectators were wondering about those young men: who were they? Where did they come from? Why was the square empty? Where were the women and children?[9] But the high-light came when the statue of Saddam was torn down and the American flag was raised. Only then indeed for Arab spectators did Baghdad fall into a core of emptiness, without resistance; and Iraq as a whole fell under American occupation. Arabs since have been wondering, "Who is next?"

Reality, Cultural Redefinitions, and Hegemony

In the same vein, I expected Arabic channels to play movies and songs that would express the sorrows of *Al-Naksah*, as the fall of Baghdad might have evoked similar memories of loss. After the 1967 Arab defeat, Nasser's image was everywhere—lamenting with the Arab people, sharing their agony, and trying to restore their self-esteem. The songs and movies that appeared in that period, songs such as *Fidā'ī* (Martyr) and feature films like *Awdat al-Ibn al-Dal* (Return of the Erring Son)[10] expressed the pain of the loss as part of the experience, but also as an impetus to keep struggling and looking forward to a brighter future.

But in the case of Iraq, the previous government disappeared with the fall of Baghdad, including Mr. Al-Sahhaf and his threatening feverish state-ments. All Arabic satellite channels showed deserted governmental infra-structure in a chaotic state. At that moment, Arabic satellite programming took an unexpected turn following these events. Movies about colonialism and martyrs, songs about Arab nationalism, as well as *Lá ará, lá asma', lá atakallam* and *Wa-Nalqá al-Ahibbah* programs all but disappeared. News about events in Iraq, discussions, and analysis of local and global politics surrounding the issue remained covered by Arab TV and other relevant programs such as Al-Jazirah's weekly *Al-'Ittijah al-Mu'akis* (Adverse Direction) also stayed on air. Pictures of the wounded and the dead, hungry and terrified children, screaming women, mothers lamenting their beloved have all these images come to characterize news items about Iraqis. And soon after the fall of Baghdad, coverage of pain and suffering in Iraq became equally routinized.[11]

> Arabic satellites mediate weeping, mourning, and lamentation. They specialize in scenes of death and sorrow and now we got used to it! (Arab American professor)
> Al-Jazirah opiates people! It reminds me of songs on Arab nationalism. (Arab-Israeli musician)

While some spectators may think of Arabic news as expressed above, others appreciate Al-Jazirah for allowing criticism of Arab and related global politics. Al-Jazirah—a network branded "Osama Bin Ladin's mouthpiece" "and subject to intense criticism from US administration officials for showing images of Iraqi casualties and American POW's that American viewers never saw,"[12] gained more recognition form Arabs and Westerners alike. Its footage showing American casualties and the infamous incidence of torture of Iraqi captives at Abu-Ghraib prison on March 20, 2004, among others, have been used by Western networks, for example, the French TV5. This "suggests that its views on news reportage might actually be more in tune with democratic ideals than those of its Western counterparts."[13]

Yet while Arabic media may have their own independent profile, the American hegemony was manifested in a number of ways, the most obvious of which was the domination of American coined terminology on Arabic satellite channels, resulting in rather interesting proliferation of synonyms. For example, the American military presence in Iraq was referred to as: "the American military interference," "the presence of American forces in Iraq," which were almost interchangeably used with "the American military invasion" and "the American military occupation of Iraq."

Another manifestation of American hegemony on Arabic TV screens can by found in changes of certain cultural values. For many years Arab media acknowledged being *fidá'i* (commando, self-sacrifice) and *shahíd* (martyr) as values associated with courage, self-denial and readiness to sacrifice one's life for one's own people and nation. On Arabic screens, the term *fidá'i* was extensively used in post 1956 and 1967 war periods in the news as well as in artistic repertoires. One of these artistic works is the *fidá'i* song,[14] which was performed in the context of the 1967 Arab defeat. The following are select verses of the lyrics portraying bitterness of defeat, as well as Arab nationalism:

> *Fidá'i, Fidá'i, Fidá'i,*
> I'd sacrifice my blood for the [Arab nation] . . .
> It only suffices to see the survival of the flag of the [Arab nation] . . .
> Mother, if I die, don't cry
> I would die, so my country lives . . .
> And on the day of victory, remember me!

The concept of *fidá'i* mostly characterized the Nasserist period and associated with it Arab nationalism and the Arab/Israeli struggle. Yet it hid in the shades of history during the following regimes of Sadat and Mubarak. These regimes brought a new emphasis on *siyásit al-'uhúd* (Treaty Politics), a term interchangeably referred to as "peace treaties" in different types of discourses. The word *shahíd* remains associated with the images of Arabs lamenting their victims, who are carried in coffins wrapped in their countries' flags with the written words *Allahu Akbar* (God is Greatest) and the name of the victim preceded by the word *shahíd*. On Arab satellite channels, mostly Palestinians, and lately Iraqis fall into this category of people, whose death is attributed to Israeli and American attacks respectively. When Tariq Ayyub, a correspondent of *Al-Jazirah*, died from an American missile targeting *Al-Jazirah*'s office in Baghdad on April 8, 2003, his death ignited anger among journalists and news organizations globally. In Arabic news coverage, Tariq Ayyub's death while fulfilling his professional duties turned him into a *shahíd*. The showing of his corpse wrapped in Palestinian flag and carried away and followed by mourners immediately reminded everybody of his Palestinian background. His death was sadly dramatic and moving for Arab audiences and was indirectly associated with similar tragedies in Israel.

The disappearing term *fidá'i* from Arabic TV news was replaced by *amaliyyát intiháríyah* (suicidal operations), which parallels the American-coined term of "suicide bombers." Nevertheless, in the laments, those so-called suicide bombers tend to be considered *shuhadá'* (plural of *shahíd*) by local people, as their engagement in such operations is considered to be an act of resistance. By changing the labels, probably, to be in tune with global media, while keeping these images, Arabic media is sending messages that carry more than one meaning. The change in Arab media terminology in the context of the current world hegemonies reflects an unavoidable manipulation of the cultural meaning of death. The persistence of struggling people in the Middle East to use their own labels and definitions of death not only marks their tension with hegemonic structures, but also their very resistance.[15]

The Phenomenology of a Hidden Threat: Who's Next?

Who is next is the question that has been on the minds of people for a long time. In modern history, and especially after the colonial era was over, this question kept haunting Arabs decade after decade—since the 1950s in the context of the Arab/Israeli conflict and now in the context of the new American hegemony.

In *khutbat al-Jum'ah* (Friday's sermon) or broadcast Muslim Friday prayer, some sheikhs have used a common metaphor of *ummat al-Islam* (the Islamic nation). This metaphor equates the nation with the [human] body; if any of its members complains—the rest of the body would be threatened with collapse while staying up in feverish ailment. During the war against Iraq this metaphor was repeated by Arabic television to acknowledge the suffering of Iraqis and to express emotional support of Arabs in Iraq.

In my work exploring genetic cancer, I looked at how the embodiment of disease, pain, and suffering moves from the confinement of the patient's body to the entire kinship. In this context, every member in the community is at risk by virtue of the existing kin relations to the patient or the deceased.[16] This new approach toward the phenomenology of genetic disease finds its parallel in the treatment of the war against Iraq in the context of the Arab world on concentric levels. The question "Who is next?" arises every time an individual is wounded, dies, or fears a war or an attack, and every time war is declared against a country in the region. There is no guaranty that what happened in Iraq would not happen to other Arab countries under the current hegemonic world order. The suffering and pain—in this case of fear—is not confined to the individual, as is commonly argued.[17] Rather their embodiment is diffused and made abstract in a region whose different populations are referred to as one entity called "Arabs," based on its shared language, religions, Semitic background, and history.[18]

Yet there is awareness of the potential global extension of a diffused phenomenology of suffering under new hegemonies. In February 2003, all Arabic cameras showed the viewer the protest organized by the syndicate of artists in Egypt. Among them was Salah al-Sa'dani, an actor, who expressed his views against the war saying "These nations have to wake up before they become another image of the Red Indians." By that he clearly meant the Arab countries and the necessity for them to take effective action so that they would not become another Iraq, other occupied territory, or simply almost extinct as American Indians.

After the fall of Baghdad, the prevailing turbulence brought the Arab viewer from a state of protest to acceptance to analytical thinking. The films, which accompanied this stage of the war focused on controversial elements in the Arab society. The feature film *muwátin wa-mukhbir*

wa-harámí (a citizen, a detective, and a thief)[19] is a case in point. The film
is richly symbolic on multiple levels. It philosophically examines the human
condition under different circumstances and in response to power pressure.
By so doing, it talks about class structure and its change in the Egyptian
society as a result of the corresponding changes in political regimes. On a
different level, each class symbolically represents a nation; and among those
nations the film shows which one will have ultimate hegemony and will be
able to manipulate others to follow it either by force or by "Treaty Politics."

Notes

Identities of individuals are concealed to insure anonymity and confidentiality.
    Most of the programs were repeated and the date of original premier is unknown.
When this is the case, the date on which the author viewed the program is provided.
    I would like to express my deepest gratitude for Dr. Shawqi Kassis for sharing his
valuable insight at early stages of this work.
    Many thanks to David Sternman for his generous help in editing this article.

1. *Control Room.* Film. English and Arabic with English subtitles. Middle East and
   U.S. production. Directed by Jehane Noujaim, 2004.
2. Al-Jazirah. Satellite Network. News, programs, ads, 2/22/2003.
3. *Lá ará, lá asma', lá atakallam* (I don't see, don't hear, don't talk.) Arabic program.
   Presented by Mona Zaki. ART. Arab Radio & Television, March 3, 2003.
4. Ibid., March 10, 2003.
5. Examples of this genre are *Al*-Saqr (The Eagle). Film. Arabic. Directed by Salah
   Abu Sayf, 1950; *Amír Al-Intiqám* (The Prince of Revenge, adapted from
   Don Quixote). Film. Arabic. Directed by Shády Abd-al-Salám. Egypt, 1950;
   and Danánír. Film. Arabic. Directed by Ahmad Badrakhán. Egypt, 1940, in
   which the main female character was the famous Egyptian singer Umm
   Kulthum (died in 1975).
6. *Al-Watan al-Akbar* (The Greater Homeland). Song. Composed by Mohammad
   Abd-al-Wahhab. Egypt, 1964.
7. *Wa-nalqá al-ahibbah* (Knowing the Beloveds). Arabic program on ART, presented
   by 'Amr Khálid, 2003.
8. On memory and trauma see Byron Good, "*The Heart of What's the Matter:
   The Semantics of Illness in Iran,*" *Culture, Illness, and Psychiatry* 1 (1977): 25–58,
   Laurence J. Kirmayer, *Landscapes of memory: trauma, narrative, dissociation,*"
   In Tense Past: cultural essays in trauma and memory, ed. Paul Antze and Michael
   Lambek (New York: Routledge, 1996), 173–197.
9. See also *Control Room*, 2004.
10. *Fidá'í.* Song. Performed by Egyptian Abd-al-Halim Hafiz (died 1978).
    Arabic,1968; *'Awdat al-Ibn al-Dál* (Return of the stray son). Film. Arabic, with
    French subtitles. Directed by Youssef Chahine. Egypt, 1970.
11. See Arthur Kleinman, "Pain and Resistance: the delegitimation and relegitima-
    tion of local worlds," *Pain as a Human Experience: an anthropological perspective,*
    ed. M.-J. DelVecchio Good et al. (Berkley, Los Angeles, and Oxford: University
    of California Press, 1991); Nancy Scheper-Hughes, *Death without weeping: the*

violence of everyday life in Brazil. (Berkeley, CA: University of California Press, 1992).

12. *Control Room*, 2004.
13. Ibid.
14. On *fidā'ī* see note [9].
15. See Kleinman, "Pain and Resistance," 1991.
16. Roushdy-Hammady Iman, "Recombination and Forensics: Cancer risk among two Cappadocian communities in Turkey, Sweden and Germany." Committee on Middle Eastern Studies, Ph.D. thesis, Department of Anthropology, (Cambridge, MA: Harvard University, September 2001), 54.
17. See Kleinman, "Pain and Resistance," 1991.
18. See Roushdy-Hammady, "Recombination and Forensics," 230; I. Roushdy-Hammady, "Introduction. Contested Etiology and Fragile Castles: An Ethnography of Cancer Risk and Cancer Research in Two Parts," *Culture, Medicine, and Psychiatry*, in press (a); I. Roushdy-Hammady, "Contested Etiology: Cancer Risk Among Two Anatolian Populations in Turkey and Europe," *Culture, Medicine, and Psychiatry*, in press (b).
19. *Muwātin wa-mukhbir wa-harāmī* (A citizen, a detective, and a thief). Film. Arabic. Directed by Dawud Abd-al-Sayyid. Egypt, 2001.

CHAPTER ELEVEN

AMERICAN CRISIS–ISRAELI NARRATIVE: THE ROLE OF MEDIA DISCOURSE IN THE PROMOTION OF A WAR AGENDA

Lea Mandelzis and Chanan Naveh

In many ways, the events of September 11, 2002 marked the beginning of new relations between the Western and Muslim worlds. Al Qaida's terrorist attack on the United States caused the loss of more than 3000 lives and ignited debates relating to the democratic world's security. In addition to the U.S. war in Afghanistan, UN Security Council resolutions called for Iraq to cease involvement in terror, wars, and human rights violations. The Bush administration offered three reasons for the need to wage war: Iraq's development of nuclear and biological weapons of mass destruction and sponsorship of international terrorism; the need to replace the "ruthless Iraqi dictatorship" regime with a democratic successor; and enforcement of international law due to Iraq's violation of UN Security Council Resolution 1441 (passed on November 8, 2002).[1]

Many of the debates that took place in most Western countries focused on the question of whether or not to join the U.S. coalition in the war on Iraq? These debates focused on issues such as: Does Iraq produce and possess weapons of mass destruction (WMD)? Is it possible to impose a democratic regime on Iraq by force? Could Iraq become a center of regional instability? Is there a need to accept the claim that war is needed? Conjectures about these issues set the political agenda and were discussed daily in the world's media.

However, the "Iraqi threat" was not just a conjecture for the Israeli collective memory. Due to the experiences of the 1991 Gulf War, alarming and longstanding anxieties of being targeted by Iraqi missiles were aroused. The traumatic effect of 9/11 led to an assumption that there might be an alliance between Saddam Hussein and Al Qaida terrorism. These political and security uncertainties provided a basis for fear and mobilized public opinion in support of what appeared to be an inevitable war on Iraq.

Consequently, there was no real public debate in Israel relating to the "Iraqi threat." A majority of Israeli politicians followed public consensus and solidarity in support of the American claim that a war on Iraq was just. The authors of this research argue that a uniform attitude in favor of the U.S. policy toward the war on Iraq was reflected by the Israeli news media and almost no other voice was expressed in the Israeli news discourse.

Applying agenda setting and discourse theories, this study focused on the media as a social collective experience involving language, beliefs, and social practices. In particular, the study examined the media frames used in Israeli news discourse regarding U.S. preparations for war. We found that the news media primarily emphasized identification with U.S. administration arguments and policies as well as possible Israeli benefits from a war.[2] Furthermore, the media faithfully reported defense authorities' appeal for public preparation for possible missile strikes aimed at population centers as well as their recommendations to purchase means of domestic protection and to recondition gas masks.

The Israeli Context

In order to understand the functioning of the Israeli media and the agenda it created, it is particularly important to note that since the outbreak of the Palestinian Al-Aqsa Intifada (September 2000) the media have supported Israeli government policy. This can be seen clearly in adoption of a dichotomous language with references that assume or state directly that there are "good guys and bad guys," "aggressors and victims," "them" and "us."[3] Furthermore, the "Eastern Front" has constituted a central threat that has preoccupied Israel's security forces for many years. Thus, given this context, Saddam Hussein was portrayed as representing the side of the "bad guys," symbolizing those in the Arab world who support Palestinian terrorism and who seek to eradicate Israel. In contrast, President George W. Bush was portrayed as representing the democratic, enlightened, and sane Western world to which Israel belongs and with which it is faithfully allied.

Public discourse included discussion of several classic issues that have formed the foundation for Israeli thinking in the contexts of military power, political interests, and deterrence. The State of Israel felt that it was an integral part of the international coalition involved in the war on terrorism declared by President Bush. The Israeli public accepted Coalition claims that Saddam Hussein possessed (Weapons of Mass Destructions) WMDs, due to two precedents: Iraq launched missiles against Israel in the 1991 Gulf War and Iraq's nuclear reactor was destroyed by the Israeli military two decades prior to the 2003 crisis. Furthermore, Saddam was seen as a supporter of terrorism since Iraq financed suicide bombers and their families during the second Intifada.[4]

Prime Minister Ariel Sharon and Defense Minister Shaul Mofaz hinted that Israel would be obliged to respond if attacked by nonconventional warheads. The United States responded with a clear message to Israel: do not become involved in this war. This was accompanied by a promise to protect Israel in case Iraq launched a missile attack on the state. An intelligence-sharing system was established between the United States and Israel, and *Patriot* air defense systems were deployed in Israel. Israeli deterrence strategy was based on these missile, systems as well as on the Israeli-built *Arrow* missiles, Israeli Air Force, and other measures that were taken to protect the civilian population, such as anti-chemical shelters and gas masks.

Prepared for the eventuality of missile strikes at population centers, the Israeli public heeded the appeals of defense authorities to purchase domestic protection devices and to recondition their personal gas masks. The guidelines issued by the defense agencies held that although probability of war was low, precautions should be taken. Kurtz and Maltz[5] note that the routines of everyday life were maintained by Israelis despite these overt apprehensions. They argue that this is due to the national consensus and public support for the aims of the United States in engaging in a just war against Iraq. Surveys conducted during the year preceding the war found strong support among Israeli public for a U.S. attack on Iraq. The Jaffe Center poll reported that 58 percent of respondents encouraged such an attack, while the Peace Index of the Tami Steinmetz Center showed such support at over 77 percent.[6]

The Case Study of the Israeli Media

This study explored the implicit ideological construction of meanings reflected by the Israeli newspapers from passage of UN Security Council Resolution 1441 through two weeks after the United States declared war on Iraq (i.e., November 10, 2002–March 31, 2003). We found that the aforementioned narrative was adopted by the country's leading newspapers—the quality daily *Ha'aretz* and the popular *Yedioth Aharonot*, which together constitute 65 percent of daily readership in Israel.

The choice of these two newspapers allows for comparison of the "quality" *Ha'aretz* newspaper with the "popular" *Yedioth Aharonot* newspaper. *Ha'aretz* maintains liberal and dovish attitudes, and supports the peace process.[7] It enjoys wide circulation within political, intellectual, and business circles, and serves as a mediator among political, economic, and social elites. The second paper, *Yedioth Aharonot*, is the most widely distributed newspaper in Israel. It enjoys a very high degree of popularity and was designed as a pluralistic newspaper. Thus, while it has adopted many features of the popular press, it publishes a wide variety of commentaries across the entire political spectrum.

The researchers found that the news discourse on the front pages of these newspapers reflected the attitudes of Israeli politicians who supported American preparations to invade Iraq. There was no real debate or discussion in Israeli news before the war, as the media were unanimously mobilized in favor of the U.S. attitudes. Moreover, the coverage of the war on Iraq was linked to national concerns regarding its impact on the Israeli–Palestinian conflict.

Research Methodologies

This study combines conventional quantitative and qualitative forms of content analysis with textual analysis of news discourse. Thus, statistical analysis of frequencies of the manifest content of messages was applied by identifying and counting key units of headlines and contents.[8] This was followed by analysis of the textual thematic structure of news discourse in which topics are a property of the text's meaning.[9]

The *agenda setting* role of the media was analyzed and then followed by an examination of the discourse of the news in order to deal with the properties of the text and the "context" used to communicate information and ideas. This revealed the meanings with which people identified.[10] Further, we found that *agenda setting* was applied in the informative and interpretive roles of the media, as well as, in setting the mood. In this case study, an "imagined" foreign policy environment was created that constructed the reality.[11] As B. Cohen stated, "For the most of the foreign policy audience, the really effective political map of the world—that is to say, their operational map of the world—is drawn by the reporter or the editor. . . . The press may not be successful much of the time in telling its readers what to think, but it is stunningly successful in telling its readers what to think about."[12] In short, the investigation of headlines revealed that everyday interactions were structured by the social and political relations experienced through various discourses that established the familiar routine of "reality" through language.[13]

Results: The Representation of the Crisis in the News

The prominence of preparations for war in the media was examined in several areas. First, the degree to which reporting on the crisis occurred over

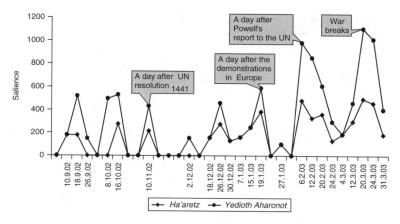

Graph 11.1   Development of front-page crisis coverage.

the entire period of study. This produced an understanding of the dynamics of the subject's appearance over time. Second, the prominence of the issue of possible involvement in the crisis was examined vis-à-vis Israel's involvement in the U.S. war, exclusive U.S. involvement in its own war, or the possibility of Israeli participation in the war alongside the United States.

Graph 11.1 presents the status of the crisis coverage on the front pages of both newspapers throughout the six months preceding the outbreak of the war on Iraq. During this period, three main phases can be distinguished, as is detailed below.

First Period: The Escalation

The first phase—Escalation—began in September 2002 and continued until passage of Security Council Resolution 1441 on November 8, 2002. In this phase, media reference to the developing crisis was in direct correlation with the events evolving in the international arena. However, the frequency and prominence of coverage of the crisis was relatively low. What stood out particularly in this phase was the distribution of reports on the crisis. In addition, the pattern of coverage on the front pages of both newspapers indicates that the time when most reports of the war were most prominent was still only 30 percent of the level recorded later. The graph reveals that the spread of coverage is similar in both newspapers, with four to five reports appearing during the two months preceding the passage of Security Council Resolution 1441.

Even though the media agenda hardly focused on the Iraqi crisis, an analysis of the qualitative content over the course of these two months provides us with a clear trend in preparation of public opinion for the expected war and definition of the major actors and partners for this war.

In September 2002, a *Ha'aretz* headline proclaimed "Disagreement in Security Council: Powell Demands Anti-Iraqi Resolution." The paper also reported: "Jerusalem Estimate: US to Try Saddam Assassination." Characteristic of a popular tabloid, *Yedioth Aharonot* applied emotional rhetoric in its headlines to express U.S. preparedness for war and mistrust of Saddam: "US Rejects Saddam Ploys" and "Gearing up for War."

The U.S. Congress endorsed the administration's decision to attack Iraq on October 11. *Ha'aretz* reported the appointment of an American liaison officer between Israel and the U.S. army: "Liaison Officers for the Iraq War: An Admiral and a General," emphasizing the military relations between the two states. Another headline in the paper heralded "Bush To Ask Sharon Tonight for Israel To Show Maximum Restraint in Case of Iraqi Attack." At the same time, *Yedioth Aharonot* declared "Tel Aviv Unready for War" in a story that exposed deficiencies and waste in preparations for the war. A week later, under the headline "Dramatic Meeting," the newspaper reported about discussions between Sharon and Bush to coordinate positions and moves in preparation for the war in Iraq, developing of a plan to block the launch of Iraqi missiles, and the U.S. administration demand that Israel refrain from involvement in the war, in return for a U.S. commitment to defend Israel.

Second Period: A Transitional Phase

The second phase started following the passage of Security Council Resolution 1441 when the Council supported Bush's offer to give Saddam Hussein one last chance, and concluded on January 19, 2003. Accordingly, there was a lull in news stories for about a month. Indeed, the frequency of reports and coverage was sporadic, though this was more noticeable in *Ha'aretz* than in *Yedioth Aharonot*. Here, too, the analysis conducted in this study found almost a full correspondence between the news coverage of the Iraqi crisis in the Israeli press and the events evolving in the international arena. Overall, then, this was a transitional phase, featuring reduced frequency of coverage and relatively low prominence.

The most prominent coverage of events connected with the crisis reported on the wave of mass demonstrations in Europe and the United States against the intended war on Iraq. A picture featured in *Ha'aretz* featured a sign held by demonstrators proclaiming—"War Is Not the Answer," against the backdrop of the White House. Here, it is important to note that the newspapers of January 19, 2003 were included in the sample because of these mass events. It can be assumed that if it were not for this specific choice, no exception at all would have been found to the low-intensity coverage pattern. Further, it is noteworthy that the coverage of the subject by *Ha'aretz* was found to have been more than double the coverage it received in *Yedioth Aharonot*.

While the coverage level for the months between November 2002 and January 2003 was low in quantity, it was identical to the number of reports in the previous two months (September to November 2002). Further, the contents exemplify the trend in the press to inform the public of U.S. policies and demands for international legitimacy and to support their "just war" against the sources and dispatchers of terrorism. From even a cursory reading of headlines in both newspapers, one must conclude that it is absolutely clear that—there will be a war, Saddam possesses WMD, and he intended to use them against Israel.

During this phase, the United Nations Security Council unanimously adopted Resolution 1441 imposing rigid inspections on laboratories and Iraqi weapons' stockpiles.[14] *Ha'aretz* reported: "Bush After UN Resolution: This Is the Last Test"; and *Yedioth Aharonot* declared that same day: "Countdown: UN Requires Saddam To Accept Disarmament by Friday," followed by a report of the decision that United Nations inspectors would return to Iraq for the first time in four years on Frdiay, November 18. Simultanously, in Israel, official spokesmen began discussing a scenario for war on Iraq and explained how it planned to deal with legions of foreign journalists expected to arrive in Israel during this war.[15]

About a month later, on December 11, 2002, a U.S. presidential warning was issued stating in effect that the United States reserved the right to respond with force and would use all means at its disposal against any use of nonconventional weapons, even beyond the physical boundaries of the United States.[16]

Details from talks held between Israel and the United States about plans for the day after the U.S. offensive were leaked to *Ha'aretz* and reported continuously starting from December 18. The U.S. administration was greatly displeased with this action and Israel's General Security Services interrogated senior military, security, and political figures in an attempt to detect those responsible for the leaks.

In contrast, *Yedioth Aharonot* continued to foster intimidation by reporting, for example, that "Saddam's Death Scientists Smuggled out with Chemical Weapons." The news report went on to elaborate that the Iraqi scientists smuggled out weapons to Syria before the arrival of the UN inspectors in Iraq. Thus, apprehension was created that given an eventual U.S. attack on Iraq, Syria would transfer nerve gas to Hizbullah for the use against Israel. Here, most of the headlines were conjectures, rather than factual reports. For example, it was reported that a call up of army reserves was imminent. Further reports added to the frustrations and fears of Israelis. The government announced it was opening stations for reconditioning gas masks and a decision made at the Ministry of Health not to inoculate citizens against smallpox for the time being.

In January 2003, the United States continued its preparations for a military offensive on Iraq. At that same time, a *Ha'aretz* headline stated— "Saddam Attacks Israel and Inspectors; Calls for Martyrdom"—referring to threats reported in the media calling for Arabs and Muslims to serve as suicide bombers against U.S. forces and civilians worldwide. Therefore, the removal of Saddam's regime was presented as supremely important for the local and international security. The threat of terrorist use of nonconventional weapons, too, started to be prominent in the news.

Toward the end of January 2003, there were definitive reports in *Ha'aretz* that "Iraqi Shipments to Syria Include Rockets for Hizbullah," and on the 27th of the month, it was reported: "Powell: We Are Prepared to Attack Iraq on Our Own." *Yedioth Aharonot* reported at length on Saddam's tyranny and cruelty in a long headline—"Saddam Will Force Foreigners to Serve as Human Shields for His Palace"; the subhead claimed: "In US, Anti-War Protests; in Israel, Joint Missile-Defense Exercise with US Starts Today." The associated photo showed Iraqi citizens demonstrating their support for Saddam, burning the Israeli flag, and impaling an effigy of Bush.

The Third Period: The Build-up toward War

The reporting of the crisis in Israel's two leading newspapers reached its climax after February 2003, as there was a dramatic rise in the quantity of coverage. Although Israeli involvement in the war against Iraq seemed more remote than ever, the prominence of the war frame followed the developments of the crisis. Graph 11.1 shows a gradual escalation in the crisis, as well as a delineation of the salient gap between the phases. The headlines relate the national narrative like a dramatic storyboard building toward a gradual climax—initiation of the war on Iraq.

The turning point occurred at the beginning of the third phase, on January 28, 2003, the day President Bush announced that he was ready to attack Iraq even if the UN did not issue a mandate to do so. From this point on, there was a steady increase in the number of news reports about the impending war. Thus, according to *Yedioth Aharonot*, the "Road to War" was already paved. Daily reports began the day after Secretary's Powell report to the UN Security Council on February 6, 2003. As in a Hollywood movie, as the moment approached, daily headlines followed the storyboard until the climax on the day the war broke out (March 20, 2003), as seen in the many newspaper headlines. The headline "Horror Show"[17] reflected the psychological warfare being waged by Colin Powell. In his speech, he presented intelligence data confirming the existence of WMD in Iraq followed by an attempt to terrify Europeans who opposed the war. However, he was followed by the Chief of the UN Inspection Team and the UN secretary-general who argued in the Security Council that Powell had not presented new evidence nor had he provided adequate cause for launching a war. The confusing information by both sides caused a dilemma as revealed directly in the papers, as *Ha'aretz* reported: "At the UN: Agonizing Whom to Believe."[18]

Tension between France and the United States increased, and Israeli media reported in February: "Diplomatic Confrontation Descends into a Cultural War."[19] Once again, the eventuality of a missile attack on Israel was envisaged: "US: Saddam May Launch Missiles at Israel"[20] and the growing crisis between Europe and the United States was viewed as an "Opportunity To Push Europe out of Middle East."[21] At the same time, the United States' preparations for the coming attack on Iraq were described in *Yedioth Aharonot*: "Airtight Rooms Being Prepared in US"; "Saddam Moving Launchers into Mosques"; "When Will the Attack Take place?"; "US Will Attack Even Without Europe"; and "The War of Independence Begins."

In the course of the period from February 24 through mid-March, the United States and Britain conducted a lobbying campaign among the members of the UN Security Council in order to secure support for the bombing of Iraq. These efforts only produced two more supporters—Spain and Bulgaria.

At the same time, Israel's school system was already gearing up for war. From the last week of February 2003 and on, the media prepared schoolchildren for defense. One headline in *Yedioth Aharonot* declared[22] "Schoolchildren Facing War: a Defense Lesson," while another described the Ministry of Education's preparations for the missile attack on Israel: "Today We'll Learn How To Put on Masks."[23] "Emergency Guide for Parents and Children" and "Children in Wartime"[24] referred to the Ministry's brochure offering advice to families during the emergency. *Ha'aretz* reported that drills were conducted in schools in preparation for an actual attack: "Schools Prepare for War," read one headline.[25] The newspaper went on to deal mainly with the political and military aspects of the Iraq crisis, which by this time also included a worsening crisis between the United States and Turkey over deployment of forces on military bases on the Turkish soil.

By mid-March the United States presented Iraq with an ultimatum, set out in a headline "Powell: Final Deadline for Iraq Arrives—Disarmament or War."[26] *Ha'aretz* continued reporting threats of impending war: "Toward an Offensive: US Intensifies Bombings"[27] and "War Becomes Inevitable."[28] Following Powell's report to the UN Security Council, the United States continued attempts to secure a UN majority, while in Israel, the Israel Defense Forces (IDF) adopted the chief-of-staff's assessment that there was a low probability of a war involving Israel. In this state of affairs, *Yediot Aharonot* reported a threat made by the Israeli prime minister—"Sharon: If Attacked, We Will Not Relinquish Right of Self-Defense"[29]; a declaration that the Jewish people was entitled to defend itself if attacked.

On March 20, 2003, the war against Iraq began and U.S. forces entered Iraq, with their primary objective to apprehend Saddam Hussein and other leaders. The front-page headline of *Ha'aretz* portrayed the main protagonists in the unfolding drama: "Ultimatum Expires, US Forces Move toward Southern Iraq." The report described the start of the offensive in Iraq. This was followed by "Iraq," another headline that conjectured about Saddam's strategy and listed the possible number of fatalities and civilian casualties. "US," depicted the might and technological advantages of the U.S. army. Another news report in *Ha'aretz* dealt with Israeli public relations efforts, while "Education Ministry: Classes as Usual. Parents Prefer to Keep Kids Home" reported the presence of confusion in the Israeli educational system.

Yedioth Aharonot, in a dramatic headline, proclaimed "Out to Get Him." The report dealt with the start of the war, the declaration of placement of the defense forces on maximum alert, activation of a "silent channel" on Israeli radio for transmission of emergency announcements, and the order that civilians should carry gas masks when in public. Other stories reported that the U.S. army was "On the Road to Baghdad" and in the article entitled "Restraint, Please," the decision by President Bush and Prime Minister Tony Blair to go to war was discussed along with their instructions given to Israel not to interfere in the war on Iraq. Domestically, a newspaper report described great frustrations in the school system—"Classes One Big Mess" due to the lack of clear guidelines from the Ministry of Education about holding classes. Another item reported the recommendations issued by the Parents Committee not to send children to school. "In Emergency, Kids to Be Sent Home. Someone out There Has Gone Totally Crazy. A Lesson on How to Mess Up" the headline continues.

It is worth mentioning that three significant patterns of coverage can be distinguished in both newspapers. First, in terms of *frequency*, there were daily news reports on the crisis. Second, the *extent* of media treatment of the crisis steadily rose on a daily basis over the two month examined. The reporters exhibited their professional capabilities by keeping up with the unfolding international events, while their writing and editing maintained the suspense necessary for steady and dramatic escalation of the story line.[30] Unsurprisingly, the third pattern received the higher *prominence* of war discourse in *Yedioth Aharonot* than in *Ha'aretz*, even though the reports appeared on the same days in both newspapers.

Newspaper Headlines

Quantitative and qualitative measures were applied in this study to analyze the degree of prominence of newspaper headlines in the six months that preceded the war in Iraq. Two measures were applied: *prominence*, that is whether it was a main or a secondary headline as an indicator of the item's importance in the media agenda; and, *location* of the headline, in the upper or lower part of the page, if it was not the main headline.

The analysis of headlines reveals almost complete correspondence between the "proportions of front page coverage" throughout the crisis (Graph 11.1) and the "score" for headlines during the same period. The analysis shows that during Escalation the headlines with the highest prominence appeared in *Ha'aretz*, featuring a combination of main and secondary headlines. The use of main headlines (only) continued alternately during the crisis period but it was more comprehensive in *Yedioth Aharonot* (among other reasons because *Ha'aretz* included secondary headlines in the third phase). The most prominent pattern of the media agenda in respect to headlines was the use of secondary headlines by both newspapers at a high frequency for almost the entire period. In conclusion, while the crisis was covered in the first two phases it was reported, as a rule, in secondary headlines. Only at the time of the third phase the headlines were upgraded to become main and most important ones.

Countries Involved in the Crisis

One of the interesting aspects examined in the Israeli newspapers was the focus solely on two countries presumed to be relevant to the crisis—the United States and Israel. While the media reported on a possible involvement in the war of other countries as well as on the European attitude toward the crisis, we found that there was no deep and detailed discussion of the European perspective. The prominent protest demonstrations in Europe against the war on January 18, 2003 were treated as an isolated event and there was no follow up. Indeed, the study found that even in this case, neither paper represented directly the European perspective. *Ha'aretz* presented an integrated Israeli–U.S. perspective, while *Yedioth Aharonot* presented mainly the U.S. point of view.

In addition, the study examined three possible forms of involvement in the crisis that were represented in the news: Israeli involvement only, U.S. involvement only, or integrated Israeli–U.S. involvement. Graph 11.2 presents findings of the extent of reports in the news.

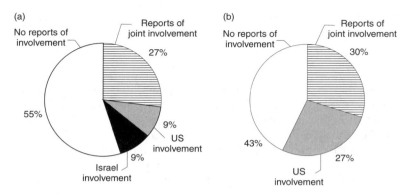

Graph 11.2 (a) *Yedioth Aharonot*: Involvement patterns as part of all issues; (b) *Ha'aretz*: Involvement patterns as part of all issues.

As it is seen on Graph 11.2, 45 percent of *Yedioth Aharonot* news reports primarily were concerned with some kind of involvement of Israel and/or the United States in the conflict, whereas in *Ha'aretz* the same kind of rate was higher, reaching 57 percent.

Analysis of the extent of different types of involvement as reported in both newspapers, too, was conducted. The most important finding in this regard was that references to the joint Israeli–U.S. involvement in the crisis was the highest in both newspapers, but it too was not particularly high per se (less than one-third in both newspapers). However, it was surprising to find single-country involvement patterns. *Ha'aretz* did not present any coverage of sole Israeli involvement and its view of the U.S. perspective was similar to its view on the joint involvement idea. In contrast, there is a coverage of each of the countries in *Yedioth Aharonot*; that is, separately, about the United States and Israel, but this appears to hold at an identically low level—only 10 percent of the sample.

In general, certain patterns were found for the appearances of the involvement issue during the first two phases of the crisis. In the first phase, the perspective that appeared in front-page news was that the entire crisis was the U.S. problem only and at a much lower rate a view of a joint U.S.–Israeli involvement was entertained. In the second phase, references to the crisis as a purely American problem developed further (especially in *Ha'aretz*). There were very few reports about the crisis as a joint venture, and none at all about the crisis as a purely Israeli affair. In the third phase, the frequency of references to the crisis was high, as both newspapers viewed the crisis mainly as the joint U.S.–Israeli problem. As already mentioned, there was no reporting of European perspectives on the newspapers' front pages.

Conclusions

The front pages of the newspapers faithfully represented the events of the Iraq crisis as they developed internationally and in close correspondence with local interests. The "news value" expressed in the main headlines was discernible throughout the period studied; that is it followed the development of the international crisis itself in the run up to the war on Iraq.

The main issue, for the purposes of this study, was the attitude and meaning of the Israeli news media during preparations for the U.S. war on Iraq. The findings of the study revealed, as expected, the presentation of any involvement in the crisis from a purely local Israeli viewpoint that represented both sides of a coin—one Israeli, the other American—both of which applied the same forms of expression and addressed similar needs. It is hardly surprising that both of the newspapers presented similar positions and identical references. It merits mention that the European perspective was entirely absent—even in the case of Britain, an active member of the U.S.-led coalition whose aims served Israel's interests.

The findings suggest that Israeli newspapers were recruited, or joined on their free will, in support of their government's policies, along with the support for the U.S. administration's positions. This enlistment intensified during the Escalation period and reached its climax with the outbreak of the war against Iraq.

Notes

1. A. Harel and A. Isacharoff, *The Seventh War* (Tel Aviv: Miskal/Yedioth Ahronoth Books and Hemed Books. 2004) (Hebrew).
2. A. Kurz and T. Maltz, "Stressed Routine—The Israeli Public at the Eve of War," in *In the Wake of the War in Iraq*, ed. S. Feldman and M. Grundman (Tel Aviv: The Ministry of Defense Publishing House, 2004) (Hebrew).
3. D. Dor, *Newspapers Under the Influence* (Tel Aviv: Babel, 2001). (Hebrew).
4. D. Johnson, "Senior Officials Tells Lawmakers of Iraq and Al-Qaeda Ties," *New York Time on the Web*. February 11, 2003 <http://www.nytimes.com> (accessed August 15, 2004).
5. A. Kurz and T. Maltz, "Stressed Routine."
6. A. Arian, "Israeli Public Opinion on National Security," *Memorandum No. 61* (Tel Aviv: The Jaffe Center for Strategic Studies: Tel Aviv University, July 2002). <http://www.tau.ac.il/jcss/memoranda/memo61.pdf> (accessed January 25, 2005). See also E. Yaar and T. Hermann, *The Peace Index: February 2003* (Tel Aviv: The Tammy Steinmatz Center for Peace Research, Tel Aviv University, 2003) <http://spirit.tau.ac.il/socant/peace/peaceindex/2003/files/feb2003e.doc.> (accessed January 25, 2005).

7. S. Lehman-Wilzig and A. Schejter "Israel," in *Mass Media in the Middle East: A Comprehensive Handbook*, ed. Y.R Kamalipour and H. Mowlana (Westport: Greenwood Press, 1994), 109–125.
8. T. O'Sullivan, J. Hartley, D. Saunders, M. Montgomery, and J.T. Fiske, *Key Concepts in Communication and Cultural Studies* (London: Routledge, 1994).
9. T.A. Van Dijk, *News as Discourse* (London: Lawrence Erlbaum, 1988).
10. S. Hall, "The Question of Cultural Identity," in *Modernity and Its Futures*, ed. S. Hall, D. Held, and T. McGrew (Cambridge: Polity Press in association with the Open University, 1996), 293.
11. M. McCombs and D. Shaw, "The Agenda Setting Function of the Media" *Public Opinion Quarterly*, 36 (1972), 176–187.
12. B. Cohen, *The Press and Foreign Policy* (Princeton: Princeton University Press, 1963), 12–13.
13. N. Fairclough, *Language and Power* (London: Longman, 1989).
14. Iraq War Timeline. *Infoplease Website* <http://www.infoplease.com/ipa/A0909792.html> (accessed July 25, 2005).
15. "Preparations?" *Ynet website* <http://www.ynet.co.il.> (accessed November 5, 2002).
16. Y. Evron, "Strategic Theories and its Implementation: The War on Iraq as A Case Study," in *In the Wake of the War in Iraq*, ed. S. Feldman and M. Grundman (Tel Aviv: The Ministry of Defense Publishing House, 2004) (Hebrew).
17. *Yedioth Aharonot*, (Daily Newspaper [Hebrew]), February 2, 2003.
18. *Ha'aretz* (Daily Newspaper [Hebrew]) February 6, 2003.
19. *Ha'aretz*, February 12, 2003.
20. *Ha'aretz*, February 12, 2003.
21. *Ha'aretz*, February 12, 2003.
22. *Yedioth Aharonot*, February 20, 2003.
23. *Yedioth Aharonot*, February 20, 2003.
24. *Yedioth Aharonot*, February 20, 2003.
25. *Ha'aretz*, February 20, 2003.
26. *Ha'aretz*, February 22, 2003.
27. *Ha'aretz*, March 3, 2003.
28. *Ha'aretz*, March 6, 2003.
29. *Yedioth Aharonot*, March 12, 2003.
30. Iraq War Timeline, *Fact Index website* <http://www.fact-index.com/ir/iraq_disarnament_2001_2003.html> (accessed July 25, 2005).

EURASIA

Chapter Twelve

Why The Russians Did Not Support the 2003 Iraq War: A Frame Analysis of the Russian Television Coverage of the Coming of the War in Iraq

Alexander G. Nikolaev

This chapter examines how Russian mass media covered the coming of the 2003 Iraq war. The main focus of this work is what type of frames dominated the Russian television coverage of the coming of the war. This should shed some light on the pattern of political thinking and on the criteria used by the Russians when they decided to oppose the 2003 war in Iraq.

Russian print media can be excluded as a valid source of material for analysis. Since 1991, newspaper readership in Russia has dropped dramatically. The percentage of the Russian population who regularly read newspapers is miniscule. Papers belong either to certain political parties or they promote interests of separate wealthy individuals (so-called oligarchs). In either case, Russian people are not interested in propaganda or cheap publicity. Besides that, since the collapse of the Soviet Union the newspapers have been considered by general population as agents of foreign influence and tools of the social destruction. All this led to a deep distrust between Russian print media and the Russian general public.[1] Therefore, first of all, any kind of print material would reflect only the position of a tiny part of the Russian society. Second, the effect of such publications is really negligible.

But television in Russia has a really great potential to provide interesting material for analysis. It is important to note that there is still some mistrust and skepticism on the part of the Russian public toward TV programs. But there are several factors that, to some extent, neutralize or at least mitigate this skepticism. First, the two main Russian TV channels are not owned or operated by any party or any private company. Second, they are financed either from the state budget or from a public stock offerings that, at least theoretically, are accessible to everyone. Third, Russian TV gatekeepers go to a lot of trouble to demonstrate their patriotism and, at the same time, show their impartiality in political matters to the Russian citizens. Finally, television in Russia is really a ubiquitous medium—there are few families in the country that do not have one or two TV sets in the household. Overall, in the absence of other easily accessible, reliable, and relatively credible sources of information, television becomes the main source of information for the general Russian public.

Let me briefly describe the structure and ownership of the two Russian main TV channels—TV1 (Public Russian Television) and RTR (Russian TeleRadio Company). They are available in the entire territory of the Russian Federation and can be picked up with a regular home broadcast antenna. The programs are broadcast free of charge through a series of powerful retranslators throughout 11 time zones. (The cable TV industry is not developed in Russia because of the price of the technology and services, lack of programming, and weak Russian communication infrastructure.)

The Public Russian Television (TV1) Company is a nongovernmental commercial enterprise that is funded through advertising revenue and sponsorship. Its shares are publicly traded on the Russian stock market.

The Russian TeleRadio Company (RTR) Company is officially associated with the Russian government. Although it is also mostly financed through advertising revenue, the Russian government has a considerable interest in this enterprise and provides a substantial financial support for all its operations. Although the government made an official pledge not to interfere with the editorial policy of the both channels, the 2003 parliamentary elections clearly showed that Kremlin still has a significant influence on what and how different issues are covered by TV1 and RTR journalists. But this influence is very well camouflaged by the outward appearance of objectivity that actually makes the channels quite credible for many Russians.

It seems that television would provide the ideal source of information for a serious political news analysis in Russia, since these channels arguably are the most credible sources of political information the Russians have (except, probably, for the Internet, which is still in its infancy in Russia). This credibility mostly comes from the fact that these companies are not private enterprises. This is where cultural factors highlighted by de Smaele come into play.[2] The Russian mentality sees mostly low credibility in anything private— including mass media. The outward appearance of objectivity and impartiality evidently has at least some effect on the channels' audience. Then, they are free of charge (which is important for poor Russian people) and really pervasive (almost 100 percent of the Russian population can watch them). And even the fact that they reflect the position of the Russian government is a plus for the purpose of this study. To some extent we can see the general position of the current Kremlin administration on certain political issues as it was reflected in TV1 and RTR programs. And if we take into account that during the 2004 presidential elections 70 percent of the Russians supported President Putin mostly because of his stance on international and military issues, we can say that by analyzing the TV coverage of the coming of the 2003 Iraq war we can indirectly see the reflection of the opinion on this war of the majority of the Russian population.

Because of the demise of the print media and the importance of television, most good and famous Russian journalists moved to work on TV (even if just part-time). They brought with them many journalistic genres that they favored when they had been working in other types of media. This is how, for example, the newspaper editorial became a part of the television repertoire. And the best example of such a novelty became an analytical prime-time program called "Odnako" ("However"). It was created, and until recently was anchored, by a group of prominent Russian syndicated columnists—Leontyev, Sokolov, and Privalov. Before creating this program, all of them became famous for their political editorials and columns in different Russian major newspapers, magazines, and on the Internet.

Until recently, the program was aired four times a week (Monday, Tuesday, Wednesday, and Thursday) in prime time—right after the main evening newscast on the TV1 channel. The program is not exclusively about international issues. But up to 50 percent of these programs, in one way or another, touch upon political issues of international importance.

As a genre, the program represents a political column creatively moved on to the television soil, so to speak. Each of the hosts (or commentators) mentioned above prepares his own program on a topic of his choosing. (It is important to note here that they work absolutely independently from one another.) Then, each of them simply sits in from of the camera and reads his text from a teleprompter. In order to avoid boredom or to illustrate some points more vividly clips from classic Russian movies and short information pieces are inserted in the text of the programs. But the text itself represents a regular editorial or political column piece.

In general, "Odnako" was created and kept on TV1 for years because it was well in line with the political ideology of this channel that, as I already mentioned above, coincided with the Putin government political positions, which in turn, were basically approved by 70 percent of the Russian population during the 2004 Russian presidential elections. Therefore, by analyzing this program we can uncover the political position of the main Russian mass medium (television), we will see the reflection of the official Russian government's position on the issue, and gain some impression as to how the general Russian public saw (and, partly, was told to see) the upcoming 2003 Iraq war.

Frame Analysis as Method

Scheufele believes that in relation to political communication framing has to be defined and operationalized on the basis of social constructivism. The mass media are active in setting the frames of reference that public uses to interpret and discuss different events.[3] The media construct social reality "by framing images of reality . . . in a predictable and patterned way."[4] Some researchers define framing as a "spin" given to a certain story.[5]

There are many working definitions of media frames. For example, Kinder and Sanders believe that frames are "devices embedded in political discourse."[6] Entman defines framing simply as "a scattered conceptualization."[7] Gitlin defines frames as "principles of selection, emphasis and representation composed of little tacit theories about what exists, what happens and what matters."[8] He also writes that frames "largely unspoken and unacknowledged, organize the world both for journalists who report it and, in some important degree, for us who rely on their reports."[9] Friedland and Zhong say that frames are "bridges between larger social and cultural realms and everyday understanding of social interaction."[10] Gamson and Modigliani state that a media frame is "a central organizing idea or story line that provides meaning to an unfolding event . . . The frame suggests what the controversy is about, the essence of the issue."[11] Tuchman simply says "The news frame organizes everyday reality. . . ."[12] Entman gives a deeper consideration to the process of framing: "To frame is to select some aspects of a perceived reality and make them more salient in a communicating text, in such a way as to promote a particular problem definition, causal interpretation, moral evaluation, and/or treatment recommendation."[13]

Shoemaker and Reese identified five factors that may influence how journalists frame a certain issue: social norms and values, organizational constraints, pressure of interest groups, journalistic routine, and ideological and political orientation of journalists.[14]

Scholars have also devoted their attention to how frames work. Pan and Kosicki identified four types of structural dimensions that influence the formation of frames: syntactic structures (words and phrases), scripts structures (the general newsworthiness and the communicative intent), thematic structures (the cause-and-effect logic imposition), and rhetorical structures (the stylistic choices).[15] Entman identified five features of media texts that set a certain frame of reference: importance judgments; agency (who did it); potential victim identification, categorization (labels), and generalization (context).[16]

The issue of the frame effects has also been addressed by the communication scholars. Tankard suggests that "power of framing comes from its ability to define the terms of a debate without the audience realizing it is taking place."[17] Price, Tewksbury, and Powers found a very interesting effect that they called "a kind of 'hydraulic' pattern, with thoughts of one kind, simulated by the frame, driving out other possible responses."[18] Nelson, Clawson, and Oxley also found that "frames influence opinions by stressing specific values, facts, and other considerations, endowing them with greater apparent relevance to the issue than they might appear to have under an alternative frame."[19]

Another aspect of the effectiveness of frames is their accessibility. Accessibility refers to the "ease in which instances or associations could be brought to mind."[20] That is, the most accessible frames are those that are most easily available from memory.[21] Therefore, journalists often use stereotypical, simplistic, and/or value-based ideological terms familiar to all the people brought up in that particular society.

Scheufele believes that frames are built in three stages or the process of frame building has three sources. The first source is the individual frames of the journalists. The second source is organizational in its nature. Organizational standard procedures as well as political orientation of the medium may play a role here. Finally, the third source of influence on the frame building process is the external pressures and constraints that may originate with political actors or authorities, interest groups, and country's elites.[22]

In reality, the process of frame formation and development is quite complex; it is actually "the interplay between two levels—between individuals who operate actively in the construction of meaning and socio-cultural processes that offer meanings that are frequently contested"[23] through the national media system.

At the individual level, personal frames are not exclusively the result of the human–media interaction. Individual frames are also products of such factors like the emotional makeup of each individual, cultural environment, educational background, familial circumstances, religious affiliation, social class association, as well as racial and ethnic origin of the person. All these elements work together in a very complex manner to form what can be called the individual frame of reference. Then, journalists who possess certain types of frames actively choose or are chosen to work for certain media outlets where they are further trained and indoctrinated. But this is not where the process of frame formation ends. Journalists themselves are members of the audience. They themselves are susceptible to the effect of their own media outlets as well as other media outlets they use as sources of information for personal use (the factor of selective exposure is important here). These media frames reinforce their personal frames that the journalists continue to use in their next reports and materials. Therefore, the process of frame formation is not a hierarchical drop-down top-to-bottom process but rather a circular or spiral self-reinforcing cyclical process where individual frames of the journalists help to create media frames that in turn help to reinforce and reproduce the existing personal frames of the journalists. This phenomenon was labeled the "news wave" by Fishman.[24]

Therefore, any frame analysis may be complete only if we take into account all the factors and elements in this process—individual frames, organizational factors, and social or national influences. This is exactly what this article attempts to do.

Time Frame

The material for this study was collected from the Internet. As it was mentioned earlier, all the transcripts of all the "Odnako" programs are available online on the official web site of the TV1 channel at <http://www.1tv.ru> All the programs between January 29, 2002 and March 19, 2003 were examined. Only those that had anything to do with the Iraq issue were analyzed. January 29 and March 19 were chosen because of their significance to impending war. On January 29, 2002 Bush delivered what became known as the "Axis of Evil Speech." In this speech President Bush revealed a new doctrine of preemptive action against America's enemies and he named the members of the so-called axis of evil—Iran, Iraq, and North Korea. It was the first time when he publicly (even though indirectly) threatened Iraq. It is also when the weapons of mass destruction theme was used for the first time as the justification for future wars. September 12, 2002 is the date when President Bush delivered his speech to the UN General Assembly. In this speech he used the full set of arguments in support of the war. It is also the day when he clearly and directly announced to the Iraqi government and the entire world his firm intention to go to war.

Overall, 27 program transcripts were analyzed. The main issue-specific frames were identified from the texts using "keywords, stock phrases, stereotyped images, sources of information, and sentences that provide reinforcing clusters of facts and judgments."[25] Then, each frame was analyzed longitudinally (when it appeared, how it developed over time), from the strength point of view, frequency, as well as how each transcript frame is related to the known individual frame of reference of each of the three commentators.

Analysis

Each segment of analysis is preceded by some information on the individual frame of reference for each Odnako analyst. This information will help the reader to understand their personal political positions and, later, to separate personal frame elements from commonly repeated frame elements across all three commentators.

Leontiev

Before becoming a journalist, Mikhail Leontiev[26] was a professional economist. He holds an advanced degree in economics. This economics background will be evident in his commentaries. In addition, he is the one among the three analysts who demonstrates the biggest interest toward international affairs. That is why he actually authored 16 out of 27 pieces. Leontiev is known for his anti-American political stance. He can be classified as "gosudarstvennik," which means "statesman" in Russian. He believes in the idea that Russia must develop eventually again into a strong superpower—militarily and economically.

Leontiev systematically reproduced five main frames in his TV editorials.

The American internal economic crisis and
economic interests frame
Leontiev's arguments suggest that the entire war was nothing more than a giant ploy to overcome the internal economic crisis in the United States.

In the program aired on September 11, 2002—the first anniversary of the 9/11 attacks—he proclaims that "American systemic economic crisis had started one and a half years before [the 9/11 events]. Its coming and the general inability to stop it were very well realized by the American elite" (September 11, 2002). Then he shows how official American economics statistics had been revised downward by the American officials themselves and that the new statistics show strong negative trends in American GNP and GDP, capital investments, trade balance, and so on. Then, he gives the following vision of the real roots of the Iraq problem:

> 9/11 gave America a break. It provided an opportunity to postpone, to distract, to "cast a spell" on the crisis. But the crisis itself did not go away. However, the anesthesia is wearing off. They need new means, even stronger ones. The United States is addicted to the drug of the struggle with satanic threats. This is where Iraq came from. This is where we can find the roots of a stupendous readiness of America to sanction any violent requests of the administration. . . . The "strongmen"—the Cheney–Rumsfeld group—believe that the best medicine [against the crisis] is total and direct dictatorship of the United States over the entire world. But by now the United States has only one advantage—total military might. And exactly this might they are going to use to suppress the crisis by simply transferring it from economic to the military dimension. . . . Maybe indeed Cheney and Rumsfeld more adequately see the real situation in the American economy. Here you see . . . such adequate maniacs. (September 11, 2002)

This frame of the internal economic crisis goes through the entire set of his Iraq commentaries. In early October 2002 he writes, "Donald L. Evans, the U.S. Secretary of Commerce, admitted in Houston in the couloirs of the World Energy Forum that the war against Iraq would be conducive to the rise of the American economy. . . . Otherwise, if the Americans will not succeed in realizing their plans, it means that the crisis will become a collapse" (October 3, 2002).

There are three sub-elements in this frame. The first two are oil prices and the pumping of devalued money into the American economy and, especially, into the military–industrial complex. The third sub-element is the idea that this war provides a perfect pretext for the Bush administration to put direct pressure on every country in the world not only in the military but also in economic sphere.

For example, on September 17, 2002 Leontiev writes that for the United States "10 dollars per barrel is the only chance to come out of the crisis" (September 17, 2002). As to the monetary issue, Leontiev quotes Alan Greenspan's speech in November 2002 where he, according to Leontiev, suggested defaulting on the current American credit obligations, to dump on the financial market more state bonds, and to simply print more money. And all this, Leontiev says, should lead to "wild inflation and devaluation of the dollar" (November 28, 2002). But all this should "give a boost to the American economy and, at the same time, will pay huge expenses for the war in Iraq" (November 28, 2002).

Finally, in two of his commentaries Leontiev shows direct American attempts to use threats of economic sanctions to demand cooperation from other countries. But he emphasizes the threats made against Russia. For example, he quotes a Russian newspaper, which in turn quotes "a high-level American diplomatic official," that if Russia will not support the United States on the Iraq issue "it will have to pay for it" (March 6, 2003). And on March 18 he analyzes what he calls "the Vershbow ultimatum" where he examines some potential consequences of some possible American sanctions on the Russian economy.

This idea of the American internal economic crisis as the main driving force behind the war is main Leontiev's idea. And on the first day of war he summarizes his entire argument:

America—now very few people would dare argue with this—is in deep economic crisis. . . . The 9/11 events gave an opportunity for the U.S. administration to throw out liberal monetarism and start a budgetary pumping of the economy . . . And the war on terror, on Saddam, on whatever was just a pretext for a colossal money pump to start working and, by the way, for testing different instruments of the international economic pressure. . . . Analysts agree that the war will revitalize the American economy for a while. . . . The dying American economy is capable of perpetrating many things. Even a war. For now—just with Iraq. But all this presents an obvious threat not only to security but also even to mental health. Just recall Powell shaking that test-tube in the U.N. Security Council. (March 20, 2003)

The effect on the Russian national interests frame

As a *gosudarstvennik* ("statesman"), Leontiev pays a lot of attention to the effect of the upcoming war on the Russian national interests. He strongly believes that this war will negatively affect the Russian economy and that the Russians have nothing to gain from participating in America's Iraq adventure. He also believes that the increased American aggressiveness, and especially the preventive strike doctrine, will have a very dangerous effect on Russian national security. He also thinks that the American foreign policy is deliberately and very aggressively anti-Russian. He, for example, feels that the United States "throw out Russia from some regions of the world that are vitally important for Russia. The next logical step is the appearance of the American special forces in Kazan' or Izhevsk [two Russian ethnic provincial towns]" (March 12, 2002).

According to Leontiev, the choice for the Russians—whether or not to support the war—seems difficult, but, in reality, is very easy: "There is no bonus waiting for Russia under any circumstances from American actions against Iraq. Even if we would run ahead of the American rangers on Baghdad. Our choice is the lesser evil. And the lesser evil is not to let drag us into this American adventure. . . . In this case we will keep at least some political capital" (October 3, 2002).

He also mentions Russian economic interests in Iraq—especially, interests of the Russian oil companies—and how they will inevitably suffer from the war. But because of his deep mistrust of the United States he strongly believes that even if the Russians supported the war—it would not change anything: "[A]ny kind of preservation of the Russian companies' serious economic positions in Iraq in case of a violent change of regime by the Americans is impossible in principle, even if we support 10 resolutions" (October 9, 2002).

Leontiev does not see any reason at all for any partnership with the United States because, in his opinion, it is not worth being loyal to the United States. He thinks that "[I]n this Cheney–Rumsfeld logic, there is no place for Russia anywhere, even as a junior partner. Therefore, any efforts to preserve any special or intimate relations with the United States of America from our side lose any meaning" (September 17, 2002). "Relations with the USA and their reciprocal actions are not determined by any means by your loyalty toward America, but only by the degree of degradation of those objects that are of some interest to them [the Americans]. That is, our fate is determined exclusively by the degree of our own degradation but not by the degree of the partnership with the United States" (March 6, 2003). That is, the main idea is that it does not matter whether Russia supports or opposes the war. Future relations between Russia and the United States are determined exclusively by the economic and military strength of the Russian state and by nothing else.

Finally, he talks a lot about how so-called war on terror and the Bush strategic doctrine (that directly justifies aggression) untied the hands for the American hawks to practically start a large-scale anti-Russian aggression in the former Soviet republics. He cites many examples where American military and intelligence services directly incite anti-Russian military and political actions. Leontiev sees direct anti-Russian interference by the Americans in several former Soviet republics: Georgia, Azerbaijan, Lithuania, Latvia, Tajikistan, Uzbekistan, and the Ukraine. And this is already a serious business. In his opinion, it is a direct incitement of the Russian neighbors toward aggression against Russia. In addition, it is a direct accumulation and strengthening of belligerent military forces (including NATO) right on the Russian borders. And of course, Leontiev believes that the Russians must be crazy to support American aggressiveness at the time when this aggressiveness threatens most of all the Russians themselves. On the contrary, Russia must resist and contain this American aggression everywhere—including Iraq.

The geopolitical and global security frame
Leontiev saw the upcoming war as a turning point of the contemporary political history—the complete collapse of the modern cooperative world security system. Already in the spring of 2002, when the Cheney–Rumsfeld doctrine of preemptive wars was intensively discussed all over the world, Leontiev proclaimed: "Permanent anti-terrorist operation provides [facilitates] the United States with unlimited and unceremonious penetration into all the points of the world geopolitical space, all the points they choose themselves. . . . Throughout the six months that have passed since 9/11 the United States succeeded only in one respect: they proved to all that there is no right but might" (March 12, 2002).

This, in his opinion, is the main goal of all the American actions—to destroy the contemporary cooperative world security system that limits the U.S. actions and to establish a new world order—the complete United States dictatorship all over the word. The basis of this new world security system will be the brute U.S. force—as the only instrument of international politics. Consequently, he believes that the largest danger the world faces right now is the United States. Leontiev writes that

> [A]ll their problems—that multiply constantly—the United States created
> themselves. . . . The United States crazily have grown a huge force and lost all
> the technologies of international politics, technologies of world politics.
> They were replaced by unlimited projection of force. . . . The Americans,
> who over many years forced upon the world the ideology of the armed-
> upto-teeth political correctness—including such Clinton legacy as so called
> humanitarian interventions—now decided to throw away any ideology at all.
> Now, it is just global isolationism—"those who are not with us are against
> us." This idea is very ambitious but it may have some unforeseen conse-
> quences. Because, automatically, it turns out that those who are not with
> them are against them. (April 17, 2002)

He believes that American belligerence is spinning out of control and
borders on insanity: "That is, we do not assert that the United States went
completely mad. But an obvious tendency toward this is clearly seen"
(December 16, 2002).

Leontiev saw the Bush ultimatum to Saddam Hussein as directed "not
even to Saddam Hussein . . . but the ultimatum to the entire world community, to the United Nations, and, specifically, to those countries that did
not support the war. That is to us [the Russians] as well" (March 18, 2003).
He believes that the United States violated all the norms of the international
law and destroyed all the main elements of the stable and secure world system. To support the United States means to help them in this process and
become similar to them. To oppose the United States too actively does not
make any sense either because America does not pay attention to anybody
anyway. Therefore, the only choice is to strengthen one's own economy and
military force and to conduct one's own independent international policy—
no matter what America thinks about it.

The Americanization of the Arab world and the
Middle Eastern beachhead frame

This frame is slightly related to the previous one because it has a geopolitical
subtext to it. But still it is a separate and very salient frame. According to
Leontiev, a very special goal of the 2003 Iraq war was Americanization of
the Arab world and, in particular, of Iraq. But this is not the ultimate goal.
The ultimate regional goal of the war is, through this Americanization
process, to establish a strong beachhead in the region for future aggressions
against other countries that don't want to serve the Americans.

Very early in the debate Leontiev had already proclaimed: "They [the
Americans] entirely focused on Iraq. They need Iraq in relation to their

far-stretching plans of Americanization of the entire Arab world" (April 1, 2002). And this will be achieved through creating an American beachhead in the region: "The puppet regime in Iraq is needed as the key to open 'mop-up' operations against the rest of the Arab world" (September 12, 2002).

On the first day of the war, Leontiev said in his summary commentary: "Saddam Hussein traditionally has been the most effective instrument of the American foreign policy in the Gulf region. . . . The United States have to thank him specifically for the fact of their massive military presence in the region, which they—without any basis for that—consider their most strategic part of the world. And today Saddam Hussein has to render his last services to America" (March 20, 2003). That is, as he sees it, the entire "war on Saddam" is just a pretext to increase the American military presence in the region and to move American military forces closer to the next objects of aggression—Iran and Syria.

The bloody farce and hypocrisy frame
This frame[27] appears quite early in the prewar debate process. Already in March 2002, Leontiev noticed a strange tendency in the American war on terror. Americans were threatening to attack Iraq and North Korea but cooperated with and actually helped the countries from whose territories terrorism actually originated—Saudi Arabia, Pakistan, and Georgia (March 12, 2002). It was already the beginning of the policy of hypocrisy frame. Later, he called the American policy on the Middle East "a comedy, which is even senseless to comment on. . . . such a bloody comedy" (April 1, 2002).

Leontiev strongly believes that the real roots of the upcoming war in Iraq lie in other dimensions, the ones described above—economic, strategic, and geopolitical. Consequently, from the very beginning he perceives other justifications for the war as just a smoke screen set up to cover real goals of the war. "The UN sanctions, the Security Council, the access for the inspectors—all this is just tactics. Strategically, the United States' decision about Iraq has already been made. Indeed, they don't even care if actually Iraq does have weapons of mass destruction or any connections to Al Qaeda. The United States themselves certainly have more connections with Al Qaeda than Iraq" (September 17, 2002). Thus, he sees the entire American propaganda campaign as a huge farce. He says that the "entire situation around Iraq . . . is becoming more and more indecent" (December 12, 2002).

But nowhere is this feeling of a huge farce more evident than in the commentary devoted to the presentation delivered by the U.S. Secretary of State Colin Powell in the United Nations. He saw that presentation as a climax of this farce and called it "pathetic babble" and "rubbish" (February 6, 2003).

Here are just some excerpts from that commentary:

> I can only feel sorry for a very authoritative general. I believe that if anybody delivered this kind of report at his staff meeting, he would simply throw that person down the stairs. . . . Then, Powell, shaking a test tube with some white substance inside, delivered a lecture about the harm of Saddam Hussein for all the humanity and about the connections, that were allegedly found by the American special services, between the Iraqi special services and Al Qaeda. This test tube with a white substance inside—it is just a piece of stand-up comedy. It is very difficult even to imagine the circumstances that would force leaders of the world's most powerful country to play the role of a cheap provincial magician. (February 6, 2003)

In general, it is clear that Leontiev's individual frame affects the way he framed the Iraq war debate events. His educational background as an economist and his anti-Americanism are clearly seen in his commentaries. At the same time, they just must reflect at least some attitudes and ideas that would shed some light on why and how the Russians decided to oppose the 2003 Iraq war. The question is: What frames can be attributed to his personal frame of reference and what frames can be considered relatively universal for this country. The only logical way to find out is to compare his frames with frames of other journalists who have different backgrounds and political views to see if there are any common elements in their commentaries that are relatively universal for this country.[28] Therefore, in the next two sections, Leontiev's frames will be compared with those of his colleagues.

Sokolov

Maxim Sokolov is a centrist—he neither hates nor loves America. He also can be classified as "gosudarstvennik" (statesman). He believes that the wisest policies are those that safeguard vital Russian interests; therefore, alliances and particular political actions should be chosen on the case-by-case basis. This type of realist political philosophy should be seen in almost all of his commentaries.

These are the frames that were consistently identified in his commentaries.

The geopolitical and global security frame

This frame appeared in Sokolov's commentaries early in the debate. He believes that the growing aggressiveness of the current American administration leads to a sharp increase in the aggressiveness of all its puppet states, which threatens stability and peace all over the world. Already in September of 2002 he places a special emphasis on the words of the

German Chancellor Gerhard Shreodor that the war in Iraq "will have unpredictable consequences" and that it "for sure, will weaken and destroy the anti-terrorist coalition" (September 10, 2002). And the collapse of the coalition, according to Sokolov, will have a devastating effect on the world cooperative security system. The Americans are destroying this system.

He also believes that the American state is on the path toward destruction of the entire contemporary international law system: "Russia against [the Iraq war] because, if everything continues going like this in the future, the entire system of international law as well as the very idea of state sovereignty will simply disappear. At the same time, the universalists[29] [obschecheloveki—in Russian] absolutely don't give a damn about the law or sovereignty—remember how they respected all these things four years ago when they bombed Yugoslavia" (March 4, 2003).

And according to Sokolov, the only way to resist the American threat to world peace and international security (and to save one's sovereignty) is to resist the United States in each of its aggressive intention: "The Iraq crisis reached such a point that the entire problem is already not in Saddam Hussein, but in the question whether France, China, or Russia will keep their status of sovereign states or not" (March 11, 2003).

The negative effect on the Russian national security interests frame
Sokolov pointed out how the increased aggressiveness of the U.S. government led to a growth in the level of aggressiveness of many of the puppet regimes installed by the Americans. He refers to such countries as Georgia, Azerbaijan, Latvia, and Lithuania where nationalist leaders not only violate human rights and conduct genocidal policies against ethnic minorities but also create direct provocations on the Russian borders. Sokolov is afraid that feeling unconditional support of the Big Brother they may do something foolish which would leave Russia with no option but to respond to their aggressive actions adequately. This entire situation may entail a war. And, according to Sokolov, the United States does everything to make this entire situation even worse (February 12, 2002 and February 4, 2003).

The low value of partnership with America frame
Just like Leontiev, Sokolov does not see any value for the Russians to become an American partner in the Iraq adventure. His main reason is that America is so arrogant that it does not value loyalty anyway: "Uncle Sam has no right to speak to Germany like that because Germany is not a South American banana republic—but what do you know—he did! . . . Now Richard Perle has started to decide who should be the Chancellor and who should not" (October 2, 2002). That is, Sokolov believes that it is good to be an American partner as long as one blindly follows the orders from

Washington, but if one dares disagree with Uncle Sam even once—the benefits of partnership immediately disappear. Therefore, it does not make any political sense to be loyal to the United States: "You see, according to the example of Germany, it is really good to be a close American ally. But don't move too abruptly, because, all of a sudden, it becomes not that good" (October 2, 2002).

The hypocrisy and double-standards frame
This is one of the prevalent Sokolov's frames. He several times addresses the issue of double standards in America's support for political regimes that harbor terrorists and conduct genocidal politics regardless of Washington's official rhetoric of human rights and of the war on terror (February 12, 2002 and February 4, 2003).

One of his favorite topics is the American hypocritical concern over the freedom of speech in other countries. Here he uses his favorite rhetorical tool—the irony:

> The New York Times published information that the Department of Defense of the USA is currently creating a "division of strategic influence" with a "multimillion" budget, which will be conducting propaganda in friendly as well as unfriendly countries. This division is given a wide authority to provide foreign mass media with disinformation and conduct other covert operations. . . . When the administration and Congress of the USA are deeply concerned with the problem of the freedom of speech in Russia, as equally in some other countries—it is certainly explained by their unselfish love for freedom. Wow—can there be a more beautiful and pure motive?! . . . In response to an [American] ardent demarche in defense of the freedom of speech, an interlocutor now can ask—"You mean that you have problems planting disinformation in our press?" (February 19, 2002)

In discussing the Iraq problem, Sokolov simply believes that "Bush went mad" and that he "is possessed by the idée fixe to bomb Iraq" (September 10, 2002). He also believes that "the upcoming war with Iraq has a goal of distracting the Americans from their domestic problems" (October 2, 2002). Finally, he thinks that geopolitically the United States just tries to remove from power all the dissident political leaders in the world—whoever they are: "It turns out that for the triumph of peace Saddam Hussein is not the only person who has to go away" (October 2, 2002). (He means here Richard Perle's attacks on the German Chancellor Gerhard Shreodor.) Consequently, all the other justifications for war—such as violation of human rights in Iraq, weapons of mass destruction, and the terrorist connections—according to Sokolov, represent just a political theater meant to cover the real causes and goals of the war.

It is interesting that a moderate Sokolov highlighted many of the same frames previously highlighted by more anti-American Leontiev. In particular, they are the geopolitical and global security frame, the negative effect on Russian national security frame, the low value of partnership with America frame, and the hypocrisy and double-standards frame. It seems like these two commentators consistently point out the same issues regardless of their personal background and political convictions.

Privalov

Alexander Privalov is slightly more pro-American and pro-Israeli than the other two columnists. He prefers to deal in his commentaries with small domestic issues. He does not often address international issues. Consequently, it was not expected that he would offer many commentaries on the issue. Nevertheless, it was quite surprising to find that over the 15-month period he made just three programs even remotely related to the problem at hand. With this amount of material it was difficult to find any clear and stable frames. But it is very instructive to see some elements of his commentaries on the subject.

He mentioned the name of Saddam Hussein for the first time in 2002, just on April 8. In that program, he clearly connected the entire Saddam Hussein affair with the issue of the oil prices, but did not develop this theme any further.

In the same month, he made another program that was entirely devoted to the oil problem and the visit of a Saudi prince Abdullah to America. Privalov once more highlighted that the main concern of the United Sates in the region is oil. And although he blamed the Clinton administration for the "current nightmare in the Middle East" (April 26, 2002), he emphasized that Russia should support Israel in its fight against Islamic terrorism.

Then, he skipped almost an entire year—11 months—without writing anything about Iraq. It is unclear why. Probably, he did not want to jump on the bandwagon of the Iraq war debate or he did not like too much what the Americans were doing and preferred not to talk about it.

But he just had to break his silence in the first days of the war. On March 26, 2003, he issued a big program devoted to the war in Iraq. His program had three main motives.

First, he did not say that America deceived the world; rather, he said that all the American problems in Iraq were the products of American *self*-deceit. Poor planning and intelligence as well as many unjustified illusions led Americans into this mess—these were the actual roots of all the American initial military woes.

But even he mentioned American hypocrisy when he talked about the preposterous American allegations that Russia supplied Iraq with some modern military weapons: "Well, it's time to find a scapegoat. Of course, it cannot be the [American] generals who promised that the Iraqis would quickly defeat themselves. And they have found the scapegoats—it's us" (March 26, 2003).

But what is interesting is the end of that program. Although Privalov believes that Russia has to support the American war on terror, he also believes that the war in Iraq and the American military misfortunes in that country will have a very clear negative effect on Russian national security. He believes that American failures in Iraq will give confidence to the terrorists. "And the problem is that, excited by the weakness of their victims, terrorist forces will have to be convinced over a long period of time that they have nothing to be excited about. And this convincing will have to be done rather by us [the Russians] then by the Americans: we are located right here," he says (March 26, 2003).

It is quite remarkable that even Privalov in just three programs manages to stumble on the two of the four common topics highlighted above—the hypocrisy issue and the problem of the negative effect of the war in Iraq on the Russian national security interests. It says at least something about how important these two matters are for the Russian national political thinking.

Conclusion

There are four dominant frames in the works of the three prominent Russian TV commentators, regardless of their personal background or their attitude toward the United States: hypocrisy; low value of any partnership with the United States; geopolitical and global security frame; and Russian national security interests. The last frame emphasizes the aggressively anti-Russian American policy right on the Russian borders—in the former Soviet Union region.

The best way to see how well Russian television reflected main Russian political concerns and considerations is to use what Lasorsa calls the "external criteria" that "deal with comparison of news reports to independent standards, such as experts and official statistics."[30]

The real-world events of the last several years in the former Soviet Union region are well documented in the media reports all over the world and speak for themselves. Here are just some examples that may explain where the highlighted frames come from. For most Westerners all that follows will be a revelation because Western media mostly ignore these facts.

The United States of America gave a political asylum to Ilyas Akhmadov, an internationally wanted terrorist who was directly involved in terrorist acts and horrendous crimes against civilians on the territory of Chechnya. The Americans installed and currently support the regime of Mikhail Saakashvili, a Georgian nationalist whose forces are poised to renew the campaign of genocide against the population of Southern Osetiya (an ethnic region in the republic of Georgia). The United States is directly financing and training the military forces of this dictator. Actually, the United States spent 64 million dollars to equip and train the Saakashvili forces.[31] Some time earlier Russian forces stopped genocide in that region and signed a special agreement with the previous leader of Georgia—Shevardnadze.[32] And now the only force that stands between the Saakashvili army—trained, equipped, and led by American instructors—and the population of Southern Osetiya is a small (about 500 soldiers) contingent of the Russian peacekeepers (stationed there according to that previous agreement).[33] American administration many times expressed an explicit and official support for Saakashvili's actions. Feeling this support, he started threatening to sink Russian tourist ships in the Black Sea. Still, America supports his policies and actions.

In the former Soviet Baltic republics (Latvia, Estonia, and Lithuania) ethnic Russians are deprived of their citizenship and of the right to vote. They are thrown out from their apartments only because they are Russians. Their housing is taken away. Their schools and mass media outlets are closed. Some members of the ruling regimes in these countries call ethnic minorities "civilian occupiers" and call for their expulsion from their countries by force. Those regimes erected right in the middle of their cities monuments to the nazi SS divisions famous for their horrendous atrocities.[34] These are the only countries in Europe that refuse to celebrate the 9th of May—the day of victory over fascism in Europe—because they consider this date a sad day in their history. They call *Salaspils* (one of the most brutal nazi concentration camps) simply "a corrective camp."[35] The school textbook in which this particular statement was made "was published with support from the chancellery of Latvian President and the U.S. Embassy."[36] And the governments that commit these terrible violations of human rights and idolize fascism are again officially, explicitly, and strongly supported by the United States of America.

The United States keeps moving its European military bases closer and closer to the Russian border. New bases are now being opened in Lithuania, Poland, and Bulgaria. The question of "Why?" has never been clearly answered by the United States.

The list of policies and events like these can go on forever including Tajikistan Uzbekistan, Azerbaijan, Moldavia, Ukraine, Belarus, Kyrgyzstan, and so on. They are not known in the United States but they are well known to every Russian. They directly threaten Russian national security and the security of every Russian citizen. If a war starts it will affect each of them at a very personal level.

One of the recent major examples of a hypocritical and utterly anti-Russian and threatening American foreign policy right on the Russian border is the Ukrainian 2004 presidential election.[37] And the word "hypocrisy" came not from a Russian source but directly from the depths of the United States Congress. Delivering his speech before the House of Representatives International Relations Committee, Representative from Texas Ron Paul said:

> Unfortunately, it seems that several US government agencies . . . sent US taxpayer dollars into Ukraine in an attempt to influence the outcome. . . . We do know that much of that money was targeted to assist one particular candidate, and that through a series of cut-out non-governmental organizations (NGOs)—both American and Ukrainian—millions of dollars ended up in support of the presidential candidate, Viktor Yushchenko. . . . Simply, it is none of our business who the Ukrainian people select to be their president. . . . This [Chinese] foreign funding of American elections is rightly illegal. Yet, it appears that that is exactly what we are doing abroad. What we do not know, however, is just how much US government money was spent to influence the outcome of the Ukrainian election. . . . Nor do we know how many other efforts, overt or covert, have been made to support one candidate over the other in Ukraine. . . . President Bush is absolutely correct: elections in Ukraine should be free of foreign influence. It is our job here and now to discover just how far we have violated this very important principle, and to cease any funding of political candidates or campaigns henceforth.[38]

Other sources give some estimates as to how much of the American taxpayers' money went to finance anti-Russian and anti-government forces in the Ukraine. The Russian TV 1 Channel reported that over the last two years the United States spent on this program over 65 million dollars.[39] But recently—specifically for the 2004 presidential elections—"Official Washington and George Soros . . . provided 13 and 8 million dollars respectively."[40] The British *Guardian* believes that "In Ukraine, the figure is said to be around $ 14 million."[41]

What was going on in the Ukraine was called not by Russian but by British newspapers "the CIA-sponsored coup d'etat" and "American mischieff."[42] The British newspaper actually believed that "Ukraine has been turned into a geostrategic matter not by Moscow but by the US, which refuses to abandon its cold war policy of encircling Russia and seeking to pull every former Soviet republic to its side."[43]

What is striking is that what was going in the Ukraine had all the elements of all the previous CIA-sponsored coup d'etats in Eastern Europe and even in Latin America. The British *Guardian* wrote about it:

> Funded and organised by the US government, deploying US consultancies, pollsters, diplomats, the two big American parties and US non-government organisations, the campaign was first used in Europe in Belgrade in 2000 to beat Slobodan Milosevic at the ballot box. Richard Miles, the US ambassador in Belgrade, played a key role. And by last year, as US ambassador in Tbilisi, he repeated the trick in Georgia, coaching Mikhail Saakashvili in how to bring down Eduard Shevardnadze. Ten months after the success in Belgrade, the US ambassador in Minsk, Michael Kozak, a veteran of similar operations in central [*sic*] America, notably in Nicaragua, organised a near identical campaign to try to defeat the Belarus hardman, Alexander Lukashenko. . . . But experience gained in Serbia, Georgia and Belarus has been invaluable in plotting to beat the regime of Leonid Kuchma in Kiev.[44]

It did not quite work out to install a Somoza-like regime in Belarus but it did finally work in the Ukraine. And it was done with the traditional CIA disregard for decency and ethics. In the Ukraine, American agents trained under-aged youth—as young as 14 years old—as to how to create riots on the streets and disobey police orders in case a pro-Russian candidate won elections. They organized those kids in a clandestine small-cell terrorist organization called "Pora."[45] The police found explosives in the possession of at least one such cell. This organization was the main force of the antigovernment campaign in the Ukraine.

Each participant of the antigovernment rallies in Kiev in 2004 received a daily payment of 50 Ukrainian grivnas (which is equal to 300 Russian rubles or about 11 American dollars). In addition to that, each participant (dozens of thousands of them) received a one-time gift of an expensive item of clothing—jackets, fur coats, winter boots, and so on.[46] It is clear that all this required an enormous amount of money that simply could not come from within the Ukraine.

And the question is: Why to go into all this trouble and expense? The answer may lie in the fact that "Yet in May, during hearings in the United States Congress the representatives of the State Department, Council on Foreign Relations, and the Carnegie Foundation openly declared that a [electoral] victory in the Ukraine of any kind of political force that would be oriented on good neighborly relations with Russia is not in the interests of the United States."[47] For the Russians it is very difficult to understand why the United States continues its cold war policy against them.

This situation clearly demonstrates from where media frames of hypocrisy, geopolitical and global security menace, and threat against Russian national security interests come from. Russians have a right to perceive American foreign policy in general as belligerent and anti-Russian.

All these real-life facts (even more can be found in the end-notes section of this chapter), serving as "external criteria," as Lasorsa would argue,[48] clearly support the veracity of the frames used by the commentators. This is where the frames of double standards and hypocrisy, of the global geopolitical threat, and of the threat to Russian national security came from. These frames and attitudes are actually rooted in American policies. America was once loved and admired in Russia but normal instincts of self-preservation and self-protection changed all that.

This sheds a clear light on the pattern of political thinking and on the criteria used by the Russians when they decided to oppose the 2003 war in Iraq. The Russians did not support this war because it was not in their national interests to support it. And these are the elements—frame by frame—that helped them make this decision.

Geopolitically, the Russians see the United States crushing the cooperative international security system, which has been working since the end of World War II. And the Russians believe that it is in their national interests to protect and maintain this system.

Second, the Russians feel real threats from some of their belligerent neighbors. And they strongly believe that those threats would not simply exist without a direct American financial, military, and political support and intervention. Therefore, they perceive America as a major anti-Russian force that directly threatens Russian national interests and Russian national security.

Further, the Russian don't see any benefits from any cooperation with the United States. The examples of France and Germany once more showed to all the Russians that even a long-time faithful service does not guarantee you American favor if you dare disagree with the United States even once. These events just supported the conclusions made by the Russians after the years of the Yeltsin regime. That is, for every Russian, the perceived value of any partnership with the United States—political, economic, or military—is really very low.[49]

Finally, the Russians feel an outrage against American hypocrisy. The United States proclaimed war on terror but, at the same time, they continue harboring and supporting terrorists (Ilyas Akhmadov and the Ukrainian *Pora* organization). They proclaim their concern for human rights but they support regimes that violate them and admire fascism. Consequently, the Russians perceive the American war on terror as a "bloody farce" and do not associate it in any way with the war on terror conducted by the Russian state.

Russian TV journalists showed the general mood of the Russian public as well as at least some of the main motives behind the Russian government's decision not to support the 2003 Iraq war. And it seems that the reason for these attitudes and decisions was not simply a legacy of the cold war or some kind of Russian irrational anti-Americanism. The real reason was the set of international policies in the world in general and in relation to Russia in particular that the Clinton and Bush administrations were conducting.

On the first anniversary of the 9/11 events, Leontiev wrote in one of his *Odnako* commentary: "If exactly one year ago there were some illusions that shaken America would somehow change and would make some conclusions, including those that somehow concerned our [Russian] problems, today, on the contrary, there is a general feeling that America made no conclusions and learned nothing" (September 11, 2002). He accurately summarizes the general feeling of the Russian population as well as people in many other countries. In September 2001, people all over the world hoped that America would finally understand the fight against terrorism conducted by other countries, would understand the real meaning of human rights, and would start helping others to fight for what is right. But it seems that what has mainly changed is rhetoric but the policies in relation to other countries either stayed the same or became even more aggressive. Under these circumstances any support for any American war actions was absolutely impossible on the part of the countries that felt discriminated against.

It is important to make one last observation. The American media talked a lot about Russian economic interests in Iraq and Russian political ties with the Hussein regime as the reasons why Russia (and some other countries— such as France) opposed the war. But this research seems to indicate that an absolutely different set of considerations took the front stage when the Russians were forming their opinion on the issue. And some of them—such as, for example, the American-sponsored threats to Russian national security— are absolutely unknown to the American public and have never been mentioned by the American media or politicians.

This seems to be the problem. Members of the news media as well as politicians all over the world often have very distorted, unwarranted, stereotypical, and prejudiced ideas about the motives and reasons that underlie other countries' foreign policy decisions. (This is exactly what is called by Jonsson "the fundamental error of attribution."[50]) And studies like this one should help everybody realize that it is necessary to explore other countries' positions deeper and to negotiate with them better in order to *really* understand how and why certain international political decisions are made.

Notes

1. O. Manaev, "The Disagreeing Audience: Change in Criteria for Evaluating Mass Media Effectiveness with the Democratization of Soviet Society," *Communication Research* 18:1 (1991): 25–52.

2. H. de Smaele, "The Applicability of Western Media Models on the Russian Media System," *European Journal of Communication* 14:2 (1999).
3. D.A. Scheufele, "Framing As a Theory of Media Effects," *Journal of Communication* 49:1 (1999). See also G. Tuchman, *Making News: A Study in the Construction of Reality* (New York: Free Press, 1978).
4. D. McQuail, *Mass Communication Theory: An Introduction*, 3d ed. (Thousand Oaks: Sage, 1994), 331.
5. R.W. Neuman, M.R. Just, and A.N. Crigler, *Common Knowledge: News and the Construction of the Political Meaning* (Chicago: The University of Chicago Press, 1992), 120.
6. D.R. Kinder and L.M. Sanders, "Mimicking Political Debate with Survey Questions: The Case of White Opinion on Affirmative Action for Blacks," *Social Cognition* 8 (1990): 74.
7. R.M. Entman, "Framing: Towards Clarification of a Fractured Paradigm," *Journal of Communication* 43:4 (1993): 51.
8. T. Gitlin, *The Whole World Is Watching: Mass Media in the Making and Unmaking of the New Left* (Berkeley: University of California Press, 1980), 6.
9. Ibid., 7.
10. L.A. Friedland and M. Zhong, "International Television Coverage of Beijing Spring 1989: A Comparative Approach," *Journalism and Mass Communication Monographs* 156 (April 1996): 13.
11. W.A. Gamson and A. Modigliani, "The Changing Culture of Affirmative Action," in *Research in Political Sociology*, ed. R.G. Braungart and M.M. Braungart, vol. 3 (Greenwich: JAI Press, 1987), 143.
12. G. Tuchman, *Making News*, 193.
13. Entman, "Framing: Towards Clarification of a Fractured Paradigm," 52.
14. P.J. Shoemaker and S.D. Reese, *Mediating the Message: Theories of Influence on Mass Media Content*, 2d ed. (White Plains: Longman, 1996). See also Tuchman, *Making News*. See also Scheufele, "Framing As a Theory."
15. Z. Pan and G.M. Kosicki, "Framing Analysis: An Approach to News Discourse," *Political Communication* 10 (1993).
16. Entman, "Framing: Towards Clarification of a Fractured Paradigm."
17. J.W. Tankard, "The Empirical Approach to the Study of Media Framing," in *Framing Public Life: Perspectives on Media and Understanding of the Social World*, ed. S. Reese, O. Gandy, and A. Grant (Mahwah: Lawrence Erlbaum, 2001), 97.
18. V. Price, D. Tewksbury, and E. Powers, "Switching Trains of Thought: The Impact of News Frames on Readers Cognitive Responses" (Paper presented at the Annual Conference of the Midwest Association for Public Opinion Research, Chicago, November 1995), 23.
19. T.E. Nelson, R.A. Clawson, and Z.M. Oxley, "Media Framing of a Civil Liberties Conflict and its Effect on Tolerance," *American Political Science Review* 91 (1997): 569.
20. A. Tversky and D. Kahneman, "Availability: A Heuristic for Judging Frequency and Probability," *Cognitive Psychology* 5 (1973): 208. See also S.D. Hodges and T.D. Wilson, "Effects of Analyzing Reasons on Attitude Change: The Moderating Role of Attitude Accessibility," *Social Cognition* 11 (1993). See also D.A. Houston and R.H. Fazio, "Biased Processing As a Function of Attitude Accessibility: Making Objective Judgments Subjectively," *Social Cognition* 7 (1989).

21. R. Hastie and B. Park, "The Relationship Between Memory and Judgment Depends on Whether the Task Is Memory-Based Or On-Line," *Psychological Review* 93 (1986). See also S. Iyengar, "The Accessibility Bias in Politics: Television News and Public Opinion," *International Journal of Public Opinion Research* 2 (1990).

22. Scheufele, "Framing As a Theory." See also H. Gans, *Deciding What's News* (New York: Patheon, 1979). See also Shoemaker and Reese, *Mediating the Message.*

23. W.A. Gamson, "The Social Psychology of Collective Action," in *Frontiers in Social Movement Theory*, ed. A.D. Morris and C. McClurg Mueller (New Haven: Yale University Press, 1992), 67.

24. M. Fishman, *Manufacturing the News* (Austin: University of Texas Press, 1980). See also L. A. Rhodebeck, "Framing Policy Debates on Old Age" (Paper presented at the Annual Conference of the Midwest Political Science Association, Chicago, April 1998). See also Scheufele, "Framing As a Theory."

25. Entman, "Framing: Towards Clarification of a Fractured Paradigm," 52.

26. All the quotes in the Analysis section are taken exclusively from the Odnako programs. Full transcripts of all these programs (in Russian) are readily available on the official web site of the Channel One TV Company at <http://www.1tv.ru> And the analysis goes author-by-author. Consequently, the name of the author of each quote is indicated in the heading of each particular subsection.

27. The word "bloody" is used here not in its British sense, which can be translated into American English as "damn" or "god-damn." It is used here in its literal meaning—"with blood all over" something.

28. Certainly, the term "universal" is used here in its most relative sense since we do not have a chance to study all the journalists from all the media outlets in this country.

29. Universalists—people who believe that their personal ethical and political views must be universal and try to impose their views on the rest of the world (often by force).

30. D.L. Lasorsa, review of *Measuring Bias on Television*, by Barrie Gunter, *Journal of Communication* 48:3 (1998): 162, 163.

31. ITAR-TASS, "USA Trained for Georgia over 2 Thousand Troops," *ITAR-TASS News Agency on the Web*, Monday, December 13, 2004 <http://www.itar-tass.com> (accessed December 13, 2004).

32. Before Saakashvili, America installed, supported, and protected in Georgia the Shevardnadze regime that harbored international terrorist camps on its territory—in the Pankissi Gorge. It is ironic that many of the terrorists trained in those camps are now fighting in Iraq against American forces. Shevardnadze also conducted ethnic cleansing campaigns in three ethnic minority provinces of Georgia—Southern Osetiya, Adzharia, and Abkhazia. His forces also were financed, equipped, and trained by the Americans.

33. It is also important to note that the absolute majority of the people of Southern Osetiya are Russian citizens.

34. In Latvia, during the SS celebration days, SS veteran marches were protected by Latvian police from anti-fascist protestors.

35. ITAR-TASS, "Latvians to Amend Libelous Book on Country's History," *ITAR-TASS News Agency on the Web*, Monday, March 4, 2005 <http://www.tass.ru> (accessed March 4, 2005).

36. Ibid.

37. It is important to note that the Ukrainian presidential elections were certified as valid by observers from all over the world except for the European Union and American observers. But the main fact is that the representatives of Viktor Yushchenko—the opposition's candidate—had signed and certified as true and valid all the final tally documents at all the polling stations in the country before they started alleging certain violations. Besides that, even if we assume that certain violation did take place they were definitely committed by both sides equally.

38. R. Paul, "U.S. Hypocrisy in Ukraine," Speech delivered before the U.S. House of Representatives International Relations Committee, December 7, 2004, *United States House of Representatives on the Web*, <http://www.house.gov/paul/congrec/congrec2004/cr120704.htm> (accessed December 10, 2004).

39. "USA: 'Ukrainegate' Will Not Happen. Editorial Comment," *Channel One (Public Russian Television) on the Web*, Saturday, December 11, 2004 <http://www.1tv.ru/> (accessed December 11, 2004).

40. "The Cost of the Confrontation Still Dragging on in the Ukraine Is High for the Society. Editorial Comment," *Channel One (Public Russian Television) on the Web*, Thursday, November 25, 2004 <http://www.1tv.ru/> (accessed November 25, 2004).

41. I. Traynor, "US Campaign behind the Turmoil in Kiev," *Guardian Unlimited*, Friday, November 26, 2004 <http://www.guardian.co.uk/ukraine/story/0,15569,1360236,00.html> (accessed November 26, 2004).

42. J. Steele, "Ukraine's Postmodern Coup D'etat,"*Guardian Unlimited*, Friday, November 26, 2004 <http://www.guardian.co.uk/Columnists/Column/0,5673,1360296,00.html> (accessed November 26, 2004).

43. Ibid.

44. I. Traynor, "US Campaign behind the Turmoil in Kiev."

45. I. Zeinalova, "The Central Election Committee of the Ukraine De Facto Certified Viktor Yushchenko as the Winner of the Presidential Elections," *Channel One (Public Russian Television) on the Web*, Monday, November 22, 2004 <http://www.1tv.ru/> (accessed November 22, 2004).

46. V. Golubev, "The Cost of the Confrontation Still Dragging on in the Ukraine Is High for the Society. Live Report from the Opposition's Headquarters," · *Channel One (Public Russian Television) on the Web*, Thursday, November 25, 2004 <http://www.1tv.ru/> (accessed November 25, 2004).

47. A. Panov, "USA: 'Ukrainegate' Will Not Happen. Live Report from Washington, DC," *Channel One (Public Russian Television) on the Web*, Saturday, December 11, 2004 <http://www.1tv.ru/> (accessed December 11, 2004).

48. Lasorsa, *Measuring Bias on Television*.

49. Another example here is the fate of Ahmed Chalabi—a long-time faithful American servant who was blamed for all the American problems in Iraq. His loyalty was not appreciated either.

50. C. Jonsson, "International Negotiations and Cognitive Theory: A Research Project," in *Process of International Negotiations*, ed. F. Mautner-Markhof (Boulder: Westview Press, 1989), 263.

CHAPTER THIRTEEN

CLASHING WORLD VIEWS: COVERAGE OF THE PREWAR IRAQI CRISIS IN THE CHINESE PRESS

Louis Mangione

This chapter examines how the Chinese press treated the build up to and commencement of the war in Iraq.[1] It studies the prewar coverage of five Chinese newspapers over a period of almost three months in 2003, beginning in early January and ending with their March 21 editions. Two of the newspapers used are published directly by the Communist party. One of them, the *People's Daily*,[2] is a national newspaper. The other, the *Zhejiang Daily*, is published in Zhejiang by the provincial party branch and has a circulation that is, for the most part, limited to the province. A third paper consulted is the *Jinhua Evening News*, which is published under the auspices of the *Jinhua Daily*, a newspaper published by the local branch of the Communist party. Its circulation does not extend much beyond Jinhua, a medium-sized city in central Zhejiang. A fourth paper, the *New People's Evening News* is published in Shanghai and has a readership that is well beyond that city. The final paper consulted is a weekly, *Southern Weekend*. It is published in Guangzhou and read throughout the country. Because of the extensiveness and depth of the prewar coverage, it has been necessary to be selective in deciding what to focus on. The items chosen for discussion are either typical of articles concerned with a particular story or direction of analysis or provide an overview of the most important content of a wide range of published material.

The newspapers consulted share an overall approach to the Iraqi crisis, which can be understood in terms of two interrelated narratives. One of the narratives concerns the efforts of most of the international community to resolve the Iraqi crisis by working through the United Nations. Central to this narrative are the Security Council's mandated inspections to determine if Iraq was in compliance with resolutions like 1441 that prohibited it from possessing weapons of mass destruction (WMD) and Iraq's response to these resolutions and inspections. The other narrative describes a relentless move toward war by the implacable United States and its allies. In this narrative, the United States and Great Britain are seen as trying to manipulate and finally pressure the Security Council into authorizing their inalterable decision to use force against Iraq. Some of the analysis and commentary embedded in this account held that America's conduct with respect to Iraq arose from its ongoing pursuit of the long-term goal of imposing and maintaining a world order that serves its own narrow interests. Frequently, the United States' actions were characterized as unilateralist and hegemonic in orientation. Within this context, much attention was paid to explaining the reasons for the divisions within the Western alliance over the United States' insistence on the use of force in Iraq.

In the following pages we discuss the prewar coverage in terms of the two narratives, (1) the efforts to achieve a political solution and (2) the build up to war. In discussing the latter narrative, we pay particular attention to the accounts given about what underlay the United States' insistence on the use of force and the opposition that such position provoked from some of its major allies.

Efforts to Achieve a Political Solution

Central to this narrative are the Security Council's actions and debates and the work of the two inspection teams sent by the United Nations to determine if Iraq was in compliance with the Security Council resolutions passed after Iraq's invasion of Kuwait in 1990. Also important to this narrative is the gradual change in Iraq's approach to the inspections from passive, insincere cooperation to a willingness to actively and on their own initiative cooperate with the inspectors.

Articles about the inspections often reported on the discoveries of weapons or other materials that violated Security Council resolutions. A typical article of this kind is "Inspections, Once Again [They] Discover Four Empty Shells" from the *Jinhua Evening News*.[3] The article begins with the simple reporting of a fact, that the relevant UN inspection team announced the discovery of four more "empty shells that could be used to carry chemical weapons."[4] This then is put into the context of earlier discoveries, subsequent discussions between a UN inspection group and Iraqi authorities, and the Iraqi explanations. Director General Mohamed ElBaradei of the International Atomic Energy Commission is then reported to have said that the talks were making "some progress," but this was qualified by also reporting that ElBaradei and Dr. Hans Blix, the Executive Chairman of the UN

Monitoring, Verification and Inspection Commission (UNMOVIC), "strived hard in the talks to let the Iraqi authorities clearly realize that there was already not much time remaining and that Iraq should take a 'pragmatic, positive' attitude."[5] Further qualification was then provided by citing Blix's view that what had been found so far was not " 'substantive proof' of Iraqi violations of Security Council resolutions that could lead to a war."[6]

There were also a number of articles that dealt with the lack of Iraqi cooperation and its possible consequences. One such article published in the *Zhejiang Daily* reported that ElBaradei expressed the "hope that Iraq would offer greater active and sincere cooperation to prove that it did not have weapons of mass destruction."[7] Blix was also reported as having indicated a number of times that Iraq "actually hasn't offered enough cooperation, especially substantively sincere cooperation."[8] The article then went on to report on public opinion, which held that "it was very possible that the US would use Iraq's not having fully cooperated with the inspectors as a reason to use force against Iraq."[9]

Many articles like the two described above reported that the inspections were being conducted in a thorough manner, that no significant violations that could lead to war had been found, that the inspectors were requiring strict and verifiable compliance and improved cooperation from Iraq, and also that Iraq had explanations for some discoveries of noncompliance. In spite of the difficult situation, these articles created the impression that there were grounds for optimism about resolving the crisis through inspections. At the same time, these articles recognized that war was still possible as shown by the report about the concern that a lack of Iraqi cooperation could provide the United States with a justification for war.[10] By singling out the United States here, rather than seeing responses to Iraq's lack of cooperation as involving the Security Council as a whole, this last observation was especially significant because it implied that unlike other countries the United States was looking for reasons to go to war.

During the period under consideration, the first major event in the narrative about the inspections was the inspectors' preliminary report to the Security Council on January 27, 2003. Articles on this report followed what had already become the familiar pattern of presenting the inspections in a positive light, leaving no doubt that most of the international community insisted on full active compliance by Iraq, and portraying the United States and Britain as committed to waging war. An article that appeared in the *New People's Evening News* offered the observation that "as for the content of the inspectors' report, the news media had already previously reported it."[11] According to this article, the new story was that both sides of the debate over whether to use force could find in the report support for their positions.[12] The *People's Daily* published an article, "A Gray Report," which took its title from an article that appeared in the *Washington Post.*[13] Ding Gang observed in this article that "Blix's report actually gave the US and Britain evidence to use to win over the support of public opinion."[14] He also observed that most, regardless of their position on the inspections, did not expect a definitive conclusion after only 60 days of inspections.[15] He further reported that most countries on the Security Council believed "that now is still not the time to determine whether Iraq has committed substantive violations."[16] Three short articles published together under a single title in the *Zhejiang Daily* captured much of the tone of the coverage on the inspectors' preliminary report. In the first article, Secretary-General Kofi Annan was reported as asserting that "he expects the Security Council to give the inspectors more time to complete their work of inspection in Iraq."[17] In the second report, the Iraqi foreign minister was paraphrased as saying that the report "proves that the American and British accusations that Iraq possesses prohibited weapons are unadulterated lies."[18] The third report focused on Great Britain and the United States. It first reported that Britain would request an ultimatum from the Security Council, suggesting that "the purpose for bringing forth this proposal was to secure more time for the US and Britain to finish all their prewar preparations."[19] In this article's final paragraph there was a shift to the United States, which was reported as "not [having] rule[d] out the possibility of using nuclear weapons against Iraq if Iraq deploys weapons of mass destruction against the US and its allies."[20]

These and other articles about the inspectors' preliminary report consistently emphasized uncertainty over whether Iraq was in substantive violation of Security Council resolutions and also emphasized the charge that Iraq was not sincerely cooperating with the inspections. Many articles also focused on the desire of the majority of Security Council members to have the inspections continue and lead to a political resolution of the crisis. Throughout, Iraq was consistently treated as having a perspective on the developments worthy of consideration. In notable contrast, the United States and Britain were usually seen as committed to the use of force and uninterested in finding out if inspections could be used to resolve the crisis.

The next major development in this narrative was the presentation to the Security Council by the American Secretary of State Colin Powell. There were articles that gave straightforward accounts of Powell's presentation and responses to it from other Security Council members. However, two articles that appeared in the *Zhejiang Daily* on the same page shortly after his presentation captured the orientation of much of the reporting on his presentation. In an article designated as "news analysis," the authors identified what they believed the Bush administration hoped to achieve through Powell's speech.[21] The goal was "not only to win over the wide spread support of world opinion in order to win a high starting point in the diplomatic struggle centered on securing authorization to use force, but even more so to calm domestic antiwar public opinion and to construct an atmosphere for war in which the Iraqi threat to the American people is in front of their eyes."[22] This analysis concluded asserting that even "after [Powell's] proof of [Iraqi] guilt, the great majority of Security Council members did not positively respond but called for the UN to continue conducting weapons inspections for Iraq, in order to find a peaceful solution to the Iraqi problem."[23] In the other article Amer Al-Saadi, the presidential science advisor in Iraq, was paraphrased as asserting that Powell's presentation was done to "destroy the work of the UN weapons inspectors and to create public opinion favorable to an American initiation of war on Iraq."[24] Al-Saadi went on to cite a number of problems with the presentation including that "information contributed by Iraqi traitors is . . . not credible."[25] Attacks on Powell's presentation by two other Iraqi officials were also reported on, including the assertion that "there was no difference between Powell's speech . . . and reports on Iraq in American and Israeli media."[26]

From this point on, reporting and analysis became concerned with the open conflict between the vast majority of Security Council members, who favored continued and later strengthened inspections, and the United States, Britain, and their supporters, who worked to secure a new resolution authorizing force. A week after the Powell presentation, the Security Council received another report from the inspectors. Coverage of this report provided a new context for the press to use in exploring the conflict between the two factions on the Security Council.

In their second report the inspectors noted that there had been progress in the inspections but also that new problems had arisen like the discovery of Samoud-2 guided missiles with ranges in excess of what was permitted.[27] Ding Gang paraphrased Blix as asserting that "although he cannot confirm that these weapons [WMD] still exist, he cannot rule out this kind of a possibility."[28] Given the then current situation, ElBaradei called on Iraq to avoid war with the United States by fully cooperating with the inspectors.[29] In the same news item, Bush was reported as having challenged the UN to join him in opposing Saddam or face the possibility that it would "in the form of an incompetent, unimportant debating society gradually disappear from history."[30] An article from the *Jinhua Evening News* entitled "The Inspections' Voice Overwhelms the US and Britain" gave an overview of the situation after the second report from the inspectors, much of it explicitly from the Chinese point of view. China's foreign minister Tang Jiaxuan's reaction to the report and subsequent debate was paraphrased as "China agrees with the opinion of most members that the inspections have a use, that continued inspections should be supported, and that the inspectors should be given the time needed to carry out Resolution 1441."[31] The U.S. position was seen as "hardening" with Secretary Powell being reported as holding the view that "the Security Council cannot allow the inspections in Iraq to be extended 'endlessly.' "[32] It also reported in the section dealing with the U.S. position that "[a]t the same time as this, the US was intensifying its military activity in the Gulf region."[33] In contrast to the United States, Britain was seen as softening its position, having "agreed to give the UN inspectors more time to carry out their inspections in Iraq."[34] Also reported in the same article in a subsection captioned "Iraqi Cooperation" was the issuing of a presidential order by Saddam "prohibiting the manufacture and importation of nuclear weapons [and] biological and chemical weapons."[35]

After the second inspectors' report, the U.S. position was presented as hardening and more dismissive of the UN. Reacting to this development in a commentary entitled "The Security Council's Authority Should Not Be Damaged" Ding Gang wrote, "In the Bush administration's view, if the Security Council did not act according to the U.S. demands, it damaged the Security Council's [own] prestige."[36] Ding also characterized the U.S. adherence to international agreements and treaties as being highly selective and as respecting only those that were in its own interest.[37] Further, Ding contrasted the Bush administration's views with those of the vast majority of Americans, who, according to polls, supported inspections within a UN context.[38] He also stated that the Bush administration's views ran counter to the unprecedented need in the world to support the United Nations and the Security Council.[39]

In late February and early March much of the coverage focused on Iraq's increasing willingness to cooperate with the inspections. On March 1, 2003 the *People's Daily* reported that Iraq had agreed to destroy its missiles with ranges beyond those permitted by the Security Council.[40] There were also reports as in the *New People's Evening News* about Iraq's announcement that it would provide another report on its earlier destruction of WMD.[41] These and other Iraqi efforts led to an assessment by Blix that "since the end of January, there has been definite improvement with respect to the problem of Iraqi cooperation, on substantive questions they have offered cooperation on their own initiative and the inspection commission expresses welcome towards this."[42]

Commentaries like the one that appeared in the *People's Daily* on March 5, 2003, continued to emphasize the need for a peaceful resolution through strengthened inspections while arguing that the United States lacked justification to go to war.[43] In the same commentary, the Chinese commitment to international organizations and its efforts to promote peace were discussed and it was noted that "[a] peaceful resolution to the Iraq question not only would benefit world peace and development, but also was compatible with everyone's interests."[44]

Another commentary from the *People's Daily* that put the final prewar weeks of diplomatic effort in the Security Council into perspective looked specifically at international law. The overall thrust of the analysis was that the use of force by the United States and Britain against Iraq would be in violation of the UN charter and international law.[45]

Other than elaborations like the two discussed above, the treatment of the debates among members of the Security Council had a high level of predictability in the weeks just before the war. The narrative about the UN inspections ended with the beginning of the U.S. led attack on Iraq.

The Build Up to War

Throughout the period under consideration there were many articles reporting U.S. and British military deployments in the Gulf region, the call up of reserves, and increased military action against Iraq in preparation for an invasion. Besides reports on military activity, a number of articles reported on statements by Bush, other U.S. officials, and some British political leaders that left little doubt that they considered war inevitable. For example, an article on Bush's declaration that "the game was over" appeared in both the *People's Daily* and also in the *Zhejiang Daily*.[46] The American secretary of defense Donald Rumsfeld's statement that the international community had to prepare for war was also given prominent coverage in the *Zhejiang Daily*,[47] as was Bush's statement that "Iraq had lost its last opportunity."[48] These and other reports created the impression that war was imminent.

All of the newspapers consulted provided extensive coverage of antiwar activities throughout the world, with much of it emphasizing the link many antiwar demonstrators drew between the U.S. policy toward Iraq and its interest in Middle Eastern oil. Some articles carefully mixed highly emotional accounts of people's efforts to promote peace with more general descriptions about antiwar activities. An example of this kind of reporting occurred in an article that appeared in the *People's Daily* on January 10, 2003. This article reported on an antiwar visit to Iraq by Americans who had lost relatives in 9/11 to meet with Iraqis who had lost relatives to war.[49] The same article also reported, "People from many countries were using all kinds of forms to express their determination to oppose the fires of war again igniting in the Gulf region and [that they were] advocating the peaceful resolution of the Iraq problem within the framework of the UN."[50]

Not only was there detailed coverage of protests with numerous photographs in the newspapers consulted, but there were also reports about Iraq's response to them. This coverage of the Iraqi response included a report that "Saddam was elated [over the antiwar protests] and believed that the world-wide antiwar demonstrations showed international support for Iraq."[51]

An important aspect of the treatment of the build up to war was a focus on what it and war itself would mean to ordinary people. In an article in the *People's Daily* of March 6, 2003, Liu Aichang examined this question with respect to the United States.[52] Liu reported that the American build up "has created a tense atmosphere for many ordinary Americans, especially in terms of the spiritual and economic pressure on lower middle class people, which is becoming greater and greater."[53] Liu went on to point out that a disproportionately high percentage of American soldiers were either from poor white backgrounds or members of minorities.[54] The article presented this phenomenon as a long established fact about the American military, observing that as early as the American Civil War affluent people could buy their way out of the draft.[55] Liu then asserted that the reasons for the current make up of the all volunteer army mainly involved either attempts by immigrants to resolve problems with their status through military service, or the desire of some high school students to receive financial support for college after their discharge, or people using the military to escape economic hardships or unemployment.[56] According to the article, people of these backgrounds faced the risks of battle and endured its consequences in loss of life and other harms.[57]

The article continued, "Besides this, the economic pressure war brings makes it harder for more and more lower middle class Americans to endure."[58] After drawing a link between military expenditures and the American government's deficit, the article pointed out that these expenditures were occurring while funds for education were being cut amounting to an indirect "war tax" on poorer students.[59] Concern about the war also was seen as hurting the economy by depressing consumption.[60] Liu further suggested that increased oil prices brought on by the war also affected many before concluding the article by writing, "Although the war has yet to begin, many lower middle class Americans already have a worried look written all over their faces. This is also one of the reasons why so many from among them oppose this war."[61]

Accounts of what some Americans confronted because of the impending war paled when compared to reports about the suffering endured by the Iraqi people. One representative article about their plight appeared in the *People's Daily* on January 16, 2003. In this article, Wu Wenbin described how Iraq went from being "called by the United Nations 'the world's fastest developing country' " before the Iran–Iraq War to a nation enduring grueling economic deprivation and the loss of much life due to that war, the war in Kuwait, and the subsequent imposition of international sanctions.[62]

Iraqis were reported to be living with 60 percent unemployment and inadequate wages.[63] Citing information from the ministry of health, Wu reported that "Iraq has already had more than 1.7 million people die from hunger and basically treatable diseases, among whom nearly half were children, with children under five making up the highest proportion."[64] Wu continued by describing the meagerness of the rations Iraqis receive. In conclusion, the reporter wrote, "In spite of the Iraqi people already being exhausted in body and mind due to unending, totally inhumane economic sanctions, they have not given up to despair but still tenaciously resist in order to win an early lifting of the bans."[65]

Besides the articles that reported on the horrible suffering endured by ordinary Iraqis along with portrayals of them as having an indomitable spirit, there were articles that presented Saddam sympathetically. One such article of much greater length than many examined took up nearly an entire page of the *Zhejiang Daily* on February 8, 2003. Under the caption "A Strong Man Who Bears the Ideal of Rebirth," a subsection of the article gave a brief biographical sketch of Saddam.[66] According to this account, he was born after the death of his father and grew up under harsh, impoverished conditions.[67] Early in his life, he committed himself to the struggle for the rebirth of Iraq, and it was this commitment that led him to join the Baath party.[68] His rise to power was described in favorable terms and the benefits that Baathist rule brought to Iraq and its people during the 1970s were presented as major achievements.[69] His wars with Iran and Kuwait were put into a context that provided explanations for his decisions that could be seen as reasonable from an Iraqi perspective.[70] His failure to leave Kuwait when confronted with an ultimatum was characterized as an "error in judgment."[71] This and other articles created an image of Saddam as a strong leader, who was committed to the welfare of his people and the development of his country, and who enjoyed the support of his people.

Much of the coverage so far discussed can be summarized as showing the United States and its allies as determined to go to war in spite of the likelihood that the UN inspections could solve the Iraq problem. Their determination to use force also was made in the face of widespread diplomatic opposition and ran counter to public opinion throughout the world, including in the United States. In addition, the price to be paid by many Americans in life, physical harm, and economic hardship from a war would be great. Further, the humanitarian disaster then taking place in Iraq would become even more devastating if force were used against that country. Within this context, the coverage examined developed explanations for why the United States was inalterably committed to initiating a war and why some of its European allies strongly opposed this decision.

Much of the coverage on the motivation underlying the U.S. policy toward Iraq did not treat the expressed concern about WMD as a credible reason for why the United States was determined to go to war. For one thing, the U.S. objection to WMD could be seen as a recent development. Wen Xian in an article entitled "The US and Iraq also Used to Be Allies" wrote that during the Iran–Iraq War the Reagan and elder Bush administrations permitted the sale of materials that could be used in the manufacture of biological and chemical weapons.[72] Wen also reported that because the United States saw Iran as threatening Gulf area allies and oil supply lines "it provided intelligence to Iraq and sold it weapons."[73] Wen went on to assert that whatever its reasons may be, the United States "is only thinking about its own interests."[74]

Many articles asserted that considerations about oil underlay the U.S. decision to go to war. Some articles, while acknowledging the importance of oil to U.S. foreign policy in general and specifically to its policy toward Iraq, offered a more complex account of U.S. motivation. For example, in an interview with two academically based economists, Huang Zemin and Zhang Jikang, Liu Liang explored in detail some of the economic issues underlying the United States' desire to remove Saddam from power.[75] In this interview, Huang asserted that the size of Iraq's oil reserves was not the main reason for the United States' determination to go to war.[76] Both economists saw the U.S. moves in Iraq and concerns about oil as part of a larger overall strategy being implemented in the pursuit of American economic hegemony.[77] They recognized both the short-term costs and benefits of a war to the United States and long-term U.S. strategies to maintain economic and financial dominance.[78] They also identified many factors likely to make the U.S. pursuit of hegemony unsustainable over time, giving special importance to the historical trend toward multipolarization as ultimately undermining attempts to establish a lasting U.S. hegemony.[79]

Coverage about the reasons for the split over policies toward Iraq between the United States, and some of its traditional allies as well as with other countries was closely aligned to the accounts given for why the United States was determined to use force. Some of this coverage also explored the split by looking at many other factors like the lack of U.S. evidence that Iraq was in violation of Security Council resolutions, differences in the historical experiences of war among various countries, and differences in culture. In many articles, the split over Iraq was portrayed as one aspect of much larger political trends and conflicts of worldwide scope in which U.S. unilateralism was seen as inherently incompatible with the commitment made by most countries to international law and multilateral organizations. In almost all of the accounts, great attention was given to what was characterized as conflicts arising from America's attempt to impose an order of its own making on the rest of the world.

In an article that appeared in the *Jinhua Evening News* on January 25, 2003, the split between the United States and several of its major European allies was accounted for in terms of three factors.[80] One factor was that with the end of the cold war, "the actual foundation of the 'Cold War alliance' already had experienced changes."[81] The second reason was that European unification gave European nations control over their own destiny.[82] The third reason was that the United States' policies clashed with the historical trend toward multipolarization.[83]

In "Two Views on World Order Come into Conflict," Huang Yong wrote, "After the passing of more than ten years [since the elder Bush proclaimed a new world order], the US and European countries, especially Germany and France, these traditional allies, not only have not come together on the question of world order, but the gap in understanding between the two sides is even larger."[84] Consistent with other articles, Huang stated that the U.S. goal was to "preserve its position as the sole superpower."[85] Again, keeping to a widely held line of analysis in the Chinese press, Huang wrote, "European countries hold that multipolarization is a basic feature of the international politics of the future and is a world-wide trend that cannot be resisted."[86] As in so many other commentaries, Huang characterized U.S. policies as narrowly focused on its own self-interests, contrasting that with European countries that support international law and the role of multilateral organizations like the UN.[87]

With the start of the U.S. led war on Iraq, there were articles that discussed many of the factors that were now in play that could lead to a restructuring of the Middle East. One which appeared in the *New People's Evening News* on March 20, 2003, examined various scenarios, some favorable to U.S. goals; others, inimical to its interests.[88] Many of the commentaries and discussions provided a recapitulation of the general approach to the prewar coverage with additional elaboration. In one such article from the *People's Daily* on March 21, 2003, Gu Ping attacked the U.S. initiated war declaring, "This is a war that lacks legality," before summarizing the previous efforts made within the UN framework to resolve the Iraqi crisis.[89] Gu went on to write, "This is a war lacking in moral force" and then described the widespread opposition to the war within the "human community."[90] Further, Gu emphasized that the war would result in human suffering, instability, and disruptions that could extend beyond the region.[91] Gu concluded that China could best contribute to world peace through an internal unity that would enable it to "protect its own peaceful life."[92]

Conclusion

This study has found that the prewar coverage in the Chinese press as represented by five newspapers can be understood in terms of two narratives. One concerned the attempts of most of the international community to resolve the Iraq problem within the framework of international law and

234 / LOUIS MANGIONE

multilateral organizations like the UN. Though their efforts failed in the Iraqi crisis due to the intransigence of the United States and its allies, their commitment to such a framework was presented as the only approach compatible with the goals of worldwide peace, stability, and development. The other narrative was about the world's only superpower and its goal of imposing on the rest of the world an order that would primarily serve its own interests. In this narrative, the United States' use of force was seen as a component in a larger strategy. According to many commentaries and analyses found in the newspapers under study, this strategy was ultimately destined to fail because no nation was powerful enough to resist the historical trend toward a multipolar world.

Notes

1. I would like to thank Yao Guosong for his help in gathering material for this study and for his comments on an earlier draft. All errors and inadequacies in this study are my own.
2. All quotations, titles of articles, and newspaper names given in this study are translations from Chinese.
3. "Inspections, Once Again [They] Discover Four Empty Shells," *Jinhua Evening News*, January 30, 2003, 12.
4. Ibid.
5. Ibid.
6. Ibid.
7. Wang Bo and Liang Youchang, "Inspectors Are Not Satisfied with Iraqi Cooperation," *Zhejiang Daily*, January 21, 2003, 9.
8. Ibid.
9. Ibid.
10. Ibid.
11. Xu Yong, "There's No Proof of Violations; Cooperation Is Not Sincere," *New People's Evening News*, January 28, 2003, 16.
12. Ibid.
13. Ding Gang, "A Gray Report," *People's Daily*, January 29, 2003, 3.
14. Ibid.
15. Ibid.
16. Ibid.
17. "Security Council Will Receive Iraqi Weapons Inspector's Report," *Zhejiang Daily*, January 28, 2003, 9.
18. Ibid.
19. Ibid.
20. Ibid.
21. Guo Lijun and Duan Jiyong, "The Background to America's Playing of the 'Intelligence King,' " *Zhejiang Daily*, February 7, 2003, 4.
22. Ibid.
23. Ibid.
24. "Powell's Speech Is to Move Public Opinion towards War against Iraq," *Zhejiang Daily*, February 7, 2003, 4.

25. Ibid.
26. Ibid.
27. Ding Gang, "Security Council Once Again Hears a Report on Iraqi Weapons Inspections," *People's Daily*, February 15, 2003, 3.
28. Ibid.
29. Ibid.
30. Ibid.
31. "Inspections' Voice Overwhelms the US and Britain," *Jinhua Evening News*, February 16, 2003, 8.
32. Ibid.
33. Ibid.
34. Ibid.
35. Ibid.
36. Ding Gang, "The Security Council's Authority Should Not Be Damaged," *The People's Daily*, February 28, 2003, 3.
37. Ibid.
38. Ibid.
39. Ibid.
40. Ding Gang, "Iraq Agrees to Destroy Samoud-2 Guided Missiles," *People's Daily*, March 1, 2003, 7.
41. "Iraq: Within a Week Will Submit a New Report," *New People's Evening News*, March 4, 2003, 16.
42. "Monitoring and Inspections Commission Chairman Positively Assesses the Iraqi Side's Cooperation," *Jinhua Evening News*, March 8, 2003, 3.
43. Gu Ping, "Strengthen Inspections, Work Hard for Peace," *People's Daily*, March 5, 2003, 3.
44. Ibid.
45. Jiang Guoqing, "International Law and the Iraq Question," *People's Daily*, March 8, 2003, 3.
46. Yan Feng and Tan Weibing, "Bush Warns Iraq the Game Is Already Over," *People's Daily*, February 7, 2003, 8 and in *Zhejiang Daily*, February 8, 2003, 8.
47. Rong Changhai, "The International Community Must Make Preparations for War," *Zhejiang Daily*, February 9, 2003, 9.
48. "Iraq Has Already Lost Its Last Opportunity," *Jinhua Evening News*, February 25, 2003, 16.
49. Zhu Mengkui, "Moving Actions by 'Tomorrow's Peace," *People's Daily*. January 10, 2003, 3.
50. Ibid.
51. "Saddam Welcomes Antiwar Marches," *New People's Evening News*, January 19, 2003, 8.
52. Liu Aicheng, "Ordinary People under the Shadow of War," *People's Daily*, March 6, 2003, 9.
53. Ibid.
54. Ibid.
55. Ibid.
56. Ibid.
57. Ibid.
58. Ibid.
59. Ibid.

60. Liu Aicheng, "Ordinary People under the Shadow of War," *People's Daily*, March 6, 2003, 9.
61. Ibid.
62. Wu Wenbin, "The Changes in the Iraqi People's Lives," *People's Daily*, January 16, 2003, 13.
63. Ibid.
64. Ibid.
65. Ibid.
66. "Dreams of Babylon, Iraq's Thousand-Year Detoxification," *Zhejiang Daily*, February 8, 2003, 6.
67. Ibid.
68. Ibid.
69. Ibid.
70. Ibid.
71. Ibid.
72. Wen Xian, "The US and Iraq Used to Be 'Allies,' " *People's Daily*, January 8, 2003, 3.
73. Ibid.
74. Ibid.
75. Liu Liang, " 'The Economic Hegemony' behind 'the War to Overthrow Saddam,' " *New People's Evening News*, Around the World section, March 7, 2003, 5.
76. Ibid.
77. Ibid.
78. Ibid.
79. Ibid.
80. "Europe and America Fight a Big 'Spit War' " (January 25, 2003). *Jinhua Evening News*, January 25, 2003, 8.
81. Ibid.
82. Ibid.
83. Ibid.
84. Huang Yong, "Two Outlooks on world Order Bring Forth Conflict," *Zhejiang Daily*, February 28, 2003, 9.
85. Ibid.
86. Ibid.
87. Ibid.
88. Rong Song, "Shuffling the Deck for the Structure of the Middle East," *New People's Evening News*, Around the World, March 21, 2003, 4.
89. Gu Ping, "Oppose War, Defend Peace," *People's Daily*, March 21, 2003, p. 5.
90. Ibid.
91. Ibid.
92. Ibid.

ACROSS THE GLOBE

CHAPTER FOURTEEN

THE COVERAGE OF DEBATES ON THE IRAQ WAR: THE CASE OF ZIMBABWE

Stenford Matenda

The Iraq war is by far one of the most significant events in the world this millennium. The event, as had been anticipated through out the world, had political, economic, and legal implications that were and are still being debated worldwide. The war marked the beginning of the U.S. policy of preemptive attacks and also a U.S. presence in the Middle East, one of the most volatile regions in the world. This event also had serious implications on the war against terrorism, which the United States had embarked on after September 11 attacks in 2001. Naturally, the war attracted media attention in virtually every country.

This chapter describes how the Zimbabwean media covered this significant world event with particular focus on how debates on the war were handled by the media. The coverage of these debates, however, can only be understood in the context of Zimbabwe's history and the events that were unfolding in Zimbabwe at that time.

Around March 2003, Zimbabwe was going through a period of severe economic decline and international isolation. Inflation was over 200 percent and there was a political crisis as a result of the rejection of the 2002 presidential election by the main opposition political party, the Movement for Democratic Change. Civil society groups and opposition parties attributed the economic decline to poor economic governance and a futile land-reform exercise by President Mugabe's government. On the other had, government attributed this economic malaise to the "smart sanctions," which were imposed by both Britain and the United States as well as by other western countries soon after the 2000 parliamentary elections.

The Zimbabwean Government at the time was being ostracized for serious abuses of human rights and violation of international democratic tenets. The United Kingdom and the United States had, a year earlier criticized the highly contested presidential elections as both not free and fair.

This position of the United States and Britain in relation to Zimbabwe and also the economic conditions prevailing in Zimbabwe at that time had far reaching implications as to how the media in Zimbabwe covered the debates before and after the Iraq war. However, before analyzing how the Zimbabwean media covered the war, it is important to first look at the structure of the media in Zimbabwe.

The Media in Zimbabwe

Public Media

As in most other African countries, the media in Zimbabwe both electronic and print can broadly be categorized as either publicly owned or privately owned. The public media is either owned by public corporations established through an act of parliament or by a notarial deed of donation and trust. The Zimbabwe Broadcasting Holdings (ZBH) was established through an act of parliament and is governed mainly by the Broadcasting Services Act (2001) as well as the Zimbabwe Broadcasting Corporation commercialization Act. At present the holding company has diverse interests in the broadcasting sector, which include four radio stations, an equipment maintenance company, a transmission company, and two television channels.

Currently the ZBH subsidiaries are the only legal radio and television broadcasters—even though the Broadcasting Services Act enacted in 2001 allows for the establishment of private radio and television broadcasters.

Table 14.1   ZBH subsidiaries in Zimbabwe

Name	Description
Radio Zimbabwe	A vernacular radio station broadcasting mainly in two languages—Shona and Ndebele.
Power FM	A youth station based in Gweru.
ZTV	A television station and is responsible for all content on TV except news and current affairs.
Newsnet	This is the news and current affairs arm of ZBH. This company is responsible for all news and other current affairs for all subsidiaries in ZBH.
On Air Systems	This is the equipment maintenance and transmission arm of ZBH.
NTV (National Television)	Second national television channel to broadcast in Ndebele and Shona.
SFM	This has been transformed into a talk radio station in the group.
National FM	Radio station that broadcasts in other minority languages in the country.

Table 14.2 Newspaper publication frequency in Zimbabwe

Newspaper	Frequency
Herald	Daily
Chronicle	Daily
Sunday Mail	Weekly
Sunday News	Weekly
Kwayedza	Weekly
Umthunywa	Weekly
Trends	Monthly
The Traveller	Monthly
The New Farmer	Monthly

Without legal instruments to guarantee independence from government and other pressure groups, most ZBH subsidiaries remain under firm control of the Department of Information and Publicity in the office of the president. This therefore means that government has both direct and indirect influence on the editorial policies of all broadcast institutions in Zimbabwe.

The Zimbabwe Newspapers Group is the largest publishing group in the country. It runs two daily newspapers, five weeklies, and two monthly magazines over and above other printing interests.

The Zimbabwe Government has indirect control over this group, as the Zimbabwe Mass Media Trust, a Trust created in 1980 to invest in the Media Sector, owns 51 percent of the shares. Over the years, government has managed to control the group and it has the prerogative of appointing the Board and senior editorial staff at the company. As is the case with the ZBH, government also controls the editorial policy of the group's newspapers.

The other group, which is wholly controlled and indirectly owned by the Government, is New ZIANA (Pvt) Ltd. This company has a total of eight weekly provincial newspapers and also owns a news agency. There are plans to expand this group by establishing a broadcasting arm, which will run a satellite television and a radio station. The government also has the support of the Voice, which is a weekly newspaper owned by the ruling party.

As has been shown above, the Zimbabwe government has tremendous influence in the media industry and this has a negative influence on the diversity of views, which the people of Zimbabwe can get on most issues.

The Private Media

The private media in Zimbabwe is not as pervasive as is the "public" media due to the legal framework that exists in the country. In fact, Zimbabwe has

Table 14.3   Private newspaper ownership in Zimbabwe

Name	Ownership	Language
The Financial Gazette	Modus Publications	English
The Zimbabwe Independent	Trevor Ncube	English
The Daily Mirror	Southern Africa Printing and Publishing House	English
The Sunday Mirror	Southern Africa Printing and Publishing House	English
The Tribune	Africa Media Group	English

one of the most repressive media legislations in the world. This legislation affects both investment in the country and also existing media institutions. The private media have been the worst victims of the media laws that govern the media in Zimbabwe. Except internationally based radio broadcasting such as the VOA's Studio 7 and the SW Radio Africa, there exists no independent broadcasting in Zimbabwe.

At the time, when the debates about the Iraq war were raging, there existed a vibrant private press in Zimbabwe. The largest circulating newspaper at that time, the *Daily News*, was still operational and was only closed down by the government in September 2003 after the paper failed to register with the country's media and information commission.

The *Daily News*, before its closure, was the major source of alternative opinions to those supplied by government-controlled media in Zimbabwe. At the same time, some weekly private newspapers such as the *Financial Gazette*, the *Independent*, the *Standard*, and the *Daily Mirror* are still available in the country. Even though, the private media has a significant presence on the Zimbabwean media market, its influence and impact cannot be compared to the public media.

Media Coverage of Debates over the War: Public Media

The Zimbabwean media's coverage of various issues surrounding the war was to a certain extent openly influenced by the ownership patterns of the media institutions in the country. As in most other countries world wide, the major issues that were raised by the media in Zimbabwe were the reasons for the war, whether the United States could win the war, and also the relevance of this event to the Zimbabwean context. But clearly, the issue that was debated extensively was why the United States and its allies wanted to wage a war against Saddam Hussein.

The U.S. position and reason for going to war was clearly stated by U.S. President George Bush in a story carried by the *Chronicle*:

> The gravest danger in the war on terror, the gravest danger facing America and the World, is outlaw regimes that seek and possess nuclear, chemical and biological weapons.[1]

This was mainly the reason why it was necessary to disarm and eliminate "rogue" regimes such as the one in Iraq. However, the media in Zimbabwe, particularly the "public" media was quite critical of this position.

The "public" media, as they do on most issues, took a cue from the government position and rejected that the impending war on Iraq had something to do with the war on terror.[2] The "public" media maintained that the war was unjustifiable and infringement of the sovereign rights of the Iraqi people.

Zimbabwe was one of the first two countries in Africa, along with South Africa, to openly condemn the American intentions of waging a war against Iraq.[3] The public media proffered a variety of reasons against the impending war in Iraq. *Chronicle* carried a comment and aptly summarizes the public media's position and the reasons why Government did not support the war.

> They want a change of government in that country [Iraq] in the same way they are trying to topple president Mugabe because of the land reforms. We wish to remind them that the power to remove or retain a head of state in a country rests with the people of that country.[4]

One point, which should be noted, is that the Zimbabwean government did not arrive at this point of view without taking into account its experiences and the situation that existed in Zimbabwe. To the Zimbabwe government and hence the public press, the Iraq war provided the justification they needed to prove to the Zimbabwean electorate and the international community that the United States and Britain had no respect for the sovereignty of other nations. The ruling Zanu PF party had been criticizing British and U.S. comments on Zimbabwe's elections as interference with the internal affairs of Zimbabwe. President Robert Mugabe's statements at the Non-Aligned Movement (NAM) Summit, published by the public press and electronic media, alluded to this fact. Mugabe was quoted in both the *Herald* and the *Chronicle* saying:

> To support the US administration's zest for aggression on Iraq, is to support a proposed inhuman campaign, which is sure to see many lives lost. We, the

hunted game are for slaughter. The charter of the United Nations and its sacrosanct tenets of international peace, the sovereignty of nations and non-Interference in domestic affairs of states are being desecrated by the day.[5]

To the public media and also, to a larger extent, to the *Sunday Mirror* (a private newspaper), the reason for the war in Iraq was not that Iraq possessed weapons of mass destruction and not even Saddam's dictatorship as the United States alleged. The *Sunday Mirror* noted that

Sadam's brutal oppression is just window dressing. . . . Iraq has had more than a decade to pass its chemical and biological weapons to the Palestinian terror group to use against Israel—a country Iraq hates as much as the United States and has not done so.[6]

The public media also criticized the United States' stance and maintained that its decision to go to war was just as a ploy to get access to the vast oil resources in that country. Commentators on the Newsnet program— *The war on Iraq*, argued that Saddam Hussein had courted U.S. anger when he threatened not to sell Iraqi oil to Western countries including America.

The other reason cited by the public media as one of the reasons why the United States wanted to invade Iraq, was the need by the United States. to gain ideological and political threshold in the Middle East region. The political editor of the *Sunday Mail*, Munyaradzi Huni wrote in one of his stories that

America knows defeating Sadam Hussein is the first and biggest step in conquering the Moslems around the world. All the talk about weapons of mass destruction is just propaganda to justify the killing of innocent lives in Iraq. . . . Mr. Bush and Mr. Blair are using force to spread their wings of imperialism.[7]

The *Sunday Mirror* described the hegemonic interests of the United States in the Middle East as one of the major reasons why the U.S. was threatening to depose the Iraqi government. The paper noted the double standards by the Bush Administration as the major indication of the United States' intention to gain political and ideological control in that region.[8] For example, the United States chose to ignore the Palestinian cause. This raised serious questions on the United States of the double standards in that region. The Scrutator columnist in the *Sunday Mirror* observed:

Less obvious to many in the United States, is the contrast in their country's response between that, which confronts Iraq on the one hand, and on the other the virtual endorsement of Israel's war on terror against the Palestinians, not to mention the fact that the Jewish state itself possesses nuclear arms and weapons of mass destruction.[9]

American policy toward North Korea was also a proof of the double standards of the United States. North Korea, at that time, had indicated clearly that she had nuclear weapons of mass destruction and yet the U.S. policy toward this country was to solve that problem by diplomatic means.

The other topical issue on the war was the role of the United Nations in international affairs. The public media widely criticized the United States for its intentions to go to war without the consent of the United Nations Security Council. Another commentary in the *Chronicle* raised this issue of the authority of the United Nations:

> The UN Security Council should have the mandate to declare war . . . No country must be allowed to take law into its own hands. What they (the US and Britain) are doing is introducing chaos into international affairs. And we condemn that in the strongest sense.[10]

The United States was portrayed as having absolute disregard of the United Nations and no respect of international law.

As a result of this position, the public press and the *Mirror* tended to give more coverage to international groups that opposed the war. The papers gave a lot of coverage to what radical antiwar people in Iraq and other countries were saying about the war. Such groups, established particularly in the West, were receiving huge coverage. They included the Act Now to Stop War and End Racism (ANSWER), United for Peace and Justice, and other protest groups that were against the war.[11]

These newspapers also gave a lot of coverage to the Iraqi Government, and the Iraqi people, particularly, when they vowed to resist any invasion of their country.

The Private Media's Coverage of the War

The coverage of the war by the private media, particularly the *Daily News*, the *Independent* and the *Standard* was slightly different from the public media. While they covered most of the events occurring in the Middle East as they unfolded, these newspapers linked what was happening to the problems that were being faced in Zimbabwe.

To most of these newspapers, Saddam Hussein was a dictator who needed to be eliminated, as was President Mugabe's regime. Several writers actually applauded Blair for having a consistent policy against dictators like Saddam Hussein and President Mugabe.[12] Most opposition groups and the main opposition party, the Movement for Democratic Change, as well as some other civil society groups labeled Mugabe as a dictator who needed to be eliminated at all cost and, if necessary, through an international intervention such as the one taking place in Iraq.

Another letter to the editor, clearly illustrated the *Daily News*' position on the issue of dictators in general and Mugabe's government in particular:

> In modern times, the Middle East has produced some of the vilest leaders who use religion as a pretext for committing heinous crimes against mankind. A typical example is Saddam Hussein of Iraq, a repulsive, evil man of the worst kind. But in Africa, we have had brutal dictators such as Idi Amin, Kamuzu Banda, Mobutu Sese Seko, Jean Bedel Bokassa and our very own president Mugabe, right here in Zimbabwe.[13]

Most stories and letters published by local authors on the Iraq war tried to contextualize the war to the Zimbabwean situation. Some even went further to urge the United States and Britain to come to Zimbabwe as soon as they have restored democracy in Iraq.

Furthermore, the private media also provided a platform for criticizing government stance toward Iraq. Most stories noted that the government was worried about the deaths of Iraqis while it was responsible for the death of many Zimbabweans.

The *Daily News* carried one letter, which clearly illustrated this:

> It's a shame that the Minister of Propaganda is accusing the Americans of causing the deaths of innocent Iraqis. This concern is being shown at a time when the Zanu PF government is sending armed soldiers and Green Bombers to beat up, rape, and kill defenceless citizens of its own country. What strategy is that?[14]

Role of Global News Agencies in the Coverage of the Iraq War

Media organizations in Zimbabwe do not have the financial resources required to send reporters to international news sites such as Iraq. This is in line with global trends where international agencies are becoming more critical as some national papers cut down on foreign correspondents. The costs involved in sending foreign correspondents to foreign countries such as Iraq also forced media houses in the country to rely almost entirely on international news agencies for stories on the Iraq war. Hence almost 98 percent of the print media stories studied between January and March 20, 2003 were provided by either Reuters or Agence France Presse (AFP) with only very few provided by the Associated Press, which are among the four dominant global news Agencies in the world. The situation was, however different for television news. While reporters relied on established global sources such as CNN and BBC for footage, they managed to rewrite stories using their own interpretations and local views on the events to ensure they aligned with the editorial policy of the ZBH.

This dominance of global news agencies raises fundamental but old concerns about the domination of world news distribution by Western global news agencies. Conceptions and ideological interpretations of the current political developments therefore were being determined largely by those agencies. The major cultural and ideological ramifications of this situation led to the New World Information and Communication Order debates of the 1980s.[15]

In Zimbabwe the Public media relied mostly on AFP while the privately owned media used mostly Reuters. While analysis of the coverage of the war by these news agencies is not the subject of this paper, it can be said that Reuters gave clear preference to official voices while AFP went further and provided alternative voices that were mostly against the war and which the public media preferred.

Conclusion

From the foregoing remarks, it is clear that the media in Zimbabwe covered the debates over the war in Iraq by contextualizing the event. The public media, due to ownership and control dynamics, tended to criticize the war. Largely, the United States and British intentions were criticized as interference with the sovereignty of Iraq, violation of international law, undermining United Nations authority. The alleged need on the part of the Americans to gain control of the Iraqi oil resources was also emphasized. On the other hand, the private media to some extent justified the war maintaining that Saddam Hussein was a dictator who needed to be eliminated, as should be all other dictators anywhere in the world. This chapter also noted the continued dominance of the global news agencies, in the provision of news to countries such as Zimbabwe. This is a result of the under-capitalization of media institutions in developing countries in general and in Zimbabwe in particular, which has far reaching ideological and cultural implications.

Notes

1. Associated Press Iraqi Has weapons of Mass destruction: Bush, *Chronicle*, February 2, 2003, 6.
2. For analysis on the influence of media control in Zimbabwe see Thomas Bvuma, 1998: "Having it both ways: Dual Policy, An Analysis and Evaluation of Zimbabwe

Government Policy, 1980–1998," M.Phil. dissertation, Department of Media and Communication, Oslo, 8–15.

3. Itayi Musengeyi, "President Lambastes the United States over Iraqi," *Chronicle* and *Herald*, February 5, 2004, 1.
4. Comment, "Only the people of Zimbabwe have the power to effect regime Change", *Chronicle*, February 6, 2003, 4.
5. Comment, *Herald*, February 6, 2003, 7.
6. Comment, "Iraq debate: War mongers shamed again," *The Sunday Mirror*, February 2, 2004, 8.
7. Munyaradzi Huni, "Time to curb US bully tactics," *The Sunday Mail*, March 23, 2003, 9.
8. Comment, *Sunday Mirror*, February 2, 2004, 9.
9. The Scrutator, "Imminent war against Iraq: The ironies and contradictions," *The Sunday Mirror*, March 9, 2003, 9.
10. Comment, "Only the United Nations can declare war," *Chronicle*, March 15, 2003, 5.
11. Associated Press, Iraqis warn the United States, *Chronicle*, March 15, 2003 and *Herald* February 26, 2003.
12. Denford Magora, "Blair's policy against dictators consistent," Letter to the Editor, *The Daily News*, April 28, 2003, 9.
13. Dr Mudzingwa, "Mugabe among the worst dictators, letter to the Editor," *The Daily News*, April 30, 2003, 8.
14. D. Muposeki, "Mugabe killing own people," *Daily News*, April 30, 2003, 8.
15. For Detailed discussion on Nwico see Hamid Mowlana, *Global Communication in Transition: The End of Diversity?* (London: Sage, 1996), 63–66; Ali Muhammad, "Communication and the globalisation process in the Developing World," in *International Communication and Globalisation: A critical Introduction*, ed. Ali Mohammadi (London: Sage, 1997).

CHAPTER FIFTEEN

TURN ON, TUNE IN: LANGUAGE OF WAR IN IRAQ (CHILE, MEXICO, AND SPAIN)

Mariadelaluz Matus-Mendoza

This chapter does not aim to put on trial either the media or the countries that opposed or supported the war. It rather presents evidence of the images of war in Iraq that the editorials portrayed in March and April 2003, in Chile, Mexico, and Spain. This study explores quantitatively and qualitatively Spanish newspaper editorials and OpEd articles. "Op-ed articles are opinion pieces published on the page opposite to editorials."[1] A major newspaper was selected in each of these countries: *El Universal* in Mexico City, *La Segunda* in Santiago, Chile, and *El País* in Madrid, Spain. The selection was based on access to newspapers through Lexis-Nexis[2] and ABYZ News Link.

These three countries were chosen for two reasons. First, they were temporary members of the Security Council of the United Nations at the time when the United States made its case to begin a war against Iraq. Second, Spain supported the war against Iraq whereas Chile and Mexico did not. Spain supported the war in spite of the fact that its citizens rejected the idea. Even though Chile and Mexico did not have to vote to support the war, interesting messages were expressed in the editorials and OpEd articles in their newspapers. In an attempt to present the real national public opinion on the war in each country the editorials chosen for analysis here were written by journalists who did not work for the United Press. Because any type of media reflect the prevailing ideology,[3] this paper aims to draw away from "the interactive process between the [American] government and the media in which those in government frame and the media respond by addressing the issues in the ways they are framed by those in government."[4]

Spain, Chile, and Mexico are classified as neither the wealthiest nor the poorest countries in the world. Spain owns the best economies of these countries. Spain does not depend as much as Chile and Mexico on its imports and exports to the United States. In contrast, Chile and Mexico have as their primary business partner the United States. This partnership might be considered a blessing or a curse depending on the decisions that Chile and Mexico have to face.

Spain has a Parliamentary Monarchy. The United Nations ranks this country eleventh in social development. It is a member of the European Union and NATO. According to some, the Republic of Chile has a stable economic dynamism unparalleled in Latin America. "Chile is moving closer to Spain and Australia in terms of their standard of living."[5] Their primary export partners are to the European Union, United States, and Japan. Their import partners are from the United States, the European Union, and Argentina. Despite many efforts to improve the standard of living of Mexicans, more than 40 percent of the 100 million Mexicans live below the poverty level.[6] The United Mexican States has signed North American Free Trade Agreement Treaty (NAFTA) with Canada and the United States hoping to access a market of about 800 million consumers. However, decisions made by the Mexican government when signing NAFTA might have harmed more than benefited Mexican industries and farmers. Currently, Mexico's primary export partners are to the United States and Canada. Their import partners are from the United States, Germany, and Japan.

Even though language in the media has been studied from different perspectives, this study draws on pragmatics to analyze the editorials and OpEd articles. The following are some of the tendencies in analyzing language used in the media. Some authors have criticized the media accusing them of destroying the language.[7] Others explain the forces that interact in the production of radio and television programs.[8] Another group suggests how to approach that language to analyze it.[9] The influence that the language in the media exerts on the public's language usage has also been widely discussed.[10] Verschueren, Jucker, and Schmidt and Kess[11] have studied pragmatics and the mass media.

This paper combines pragmatics[12] and a variationist approach. Speech acts or locutionary acts are the central concern of pragmatics, that is, what a person does with words in a specific situation concentrating on the speaker's intentions and purposes. In making a meaningful utterance or speech act, one usually makes an illocutionary act. Here, the emphasis relies on one[13] of the characteristics of the illocutionary act[14]—that of being successful by getting one's illocutionary intentions recognized.[15] The variationist approach allows analyzing quantitatively the illocutionary acts of the selected here representatives, that is, these illocutionary acts present some state of affairs, in this case, stating, asserting, and explaining.[16]

Analysis

Editorials and OpEd articles were selected from three major newspapers in Chile, in Mexico, and in Spain from March 1 to April 30, 2003. In general, the newspapers in Chile did not devote too much space to discuss the war in Iraq; out of the three newspapers originally reviewed (*Estrategia*, *El Mercurio*, and *La Segunda*), one offered more editorials on the war in Iraq than the others. In search of consistency with the newspaper ideology, only one paper was selected, *La Segunda*. Newspapers have owners and owners have their own agendas[17] though "ideologies and opinions of newspapers are usually not personal, but social, institutional or political."[18] Forty-one editorials were from *La Segunda*, which is published in Santiago, Chile. Eighty-six were from *El Universal*, published in Mexico City. Seventy-one editorials were from *El País*, published in Madrid, Spain.

The editorials and OpEd articles were coded according to the prevailing illocutionary acts expressed. Six factor groups were created to compute the different illocutionary acts found in the editorials. A factor group is made out of as many factors as necessary to establish distinctions within that factor group. Factor one contained the dependent variable for or against the war in Iraq: this constitutes the base to run the binominal program, Goldvarb 2001.[19] Factor two indicated the country where the article was written: Chile, Mexico, or Spain. Factor three called "image of the war" divided the portrayal of the war as either a problem of law and order[20] or as an economic enterprise. This factor also divided American politicians into "hawks" or "doves,"[21] and divided the portrayal of war as a game[22] or an invasion rather than liberation. As the fourth factor, the reasons to oppose or support the war were broken into several groups, first, a utilitarian position was considered, where Chilean, Mexican, or Spanish governments wanted to get some benefits in order to support the war. Second, American imperialism imposed by militarist[23] means was also examined as another reason for war. Third for war was economic interests of different countries in Iraq. The fourth one was the fear that the United Nations would disappear. The fear that the United States would retaliate against the countries that opposed the war was consideration number five. And, the sixth one was the idea that the "universal principles of solidarity and respect for life" opposed the war.[24] Factor five was related to George Bush. His image was classified into a businessman in search of opportunities, "the epitome of Good and God,"[25] negligent, and the absence of any image at all. Factor six, the portrayal of the leaders of Spain, José María Aznar; of Chile, President Lagos; and of Mexico, President Fox, in the editorials were of a leader who: acted according to his people's decision; according to the Constitution; against his people's decision; according to Bush's wishes; as an indecisive leader; or the absence of any image at all.

Considering that only three newspapers were chosen for this analysis and no television or radio program were analyzed in this study, it would be fair to say that the observations made here are more suggestive than conclusive.

Results

Not surprisingly, the overall results of the first run of the program indicated that the majority of the editorials and OpEd articles rejected the war: 64 percent were against the war, and 35 percent supported the war. In general, the images of the war could be divided into two main groups: (1) as a problem of law and order with 75 percent occurrence and (2) the rest considering the war as business enterprise (10 percent), American politicians as predators (6 percent), war as a video game (5 percent), or an invasion rather than a war of liberations (2 percent). Although it is advised statistically to collapse, to combine, or to delete elements in the factor groups to avoid knockouts in the program Goldvarb 2001, the decision was taken to keep the very small number of factors to provide an accurate portrayal of the war.

Combining factor group three, image of the war, and factor two, country of origins of the editorial or OpEd articles, clearly delimited the countries where each illocutionary act was more frequent. Mexico led describing the war as a matter of breaking the international law and order as seen below:

> The war in Iraq will have very serious consequences for the judicial international order. The fact that the war takes place as a unilateral operation of the United States and its allies is very serious . . . From that disagreement the international order, born after the Second World War, will be deadly wounded.[26]

One might think that Mexican economic dependency would prevent the Mexican government from criticizing Washington. However, according to some authors,[27] Mexico has been more daring since the 1980s when more oil resources were discovered in the country. Sometimes, Mexico openly criticized Washington. Other times, as it is shown later on, Mexican government oscillated between a dangerous game to please Mexican businesspeople and Mexican lawmakers or to please Washington. Chile was the least confrontational of the three countries in expressing its disapproval to the war:

> Why do we deceive ourselves? Certain countries have always preferred to decide on their own in the international arena without constraining their decisions neither to bothersome vote nor to the second class countries' control. Nobody is defending Hussein. This is rather a defense of the international

law, the international order that will not be preserved with invasions that are a reminder of the Second World War.[28]

This quote illustrated the fact that the war was seen as an invasion. Another quote from *El País* might best summarize this opinion: "We shouldn't call an unjust invasion using the euphemism of preventive war that Bush attempts to drag us."[29] Considering the description of the war, mainly editorials from Mexico described the war as a show, as a video game or as a reality show:

> American military went to Iraq to make a war as if they were playing Nintendo. Real soldiers had to die for them to understand that the war was real and the lives do not recharge as it occurs in a videogame. At the end, there will not be a Game Over Liberator.[30]

Considering the reasons to reject or support the war in Iraq, the highest percentage of occurrences belongs to the American imperialism category with 50 percent, followed by the fear of disappearance of the UN group with 21 percent, the economic motivation reasons with 11 percent, the fear of the United States' retaliation category with 8 percent, the respect for life group with 7 percent, and the utilitarian position reasons with 2 percent.

Combining factor two, the country where the editorial was written, and factor four, the reasons to support or reject the war, it was interesting to observe that mainly Spain and Mexico offered American imperialism as the principal reason to oppose to the war. Even though Mexico has a less stable economy than Spain, they had a higher number of tokens (in this case, the illocutionary acts): 48 compared to 45. One might think that the economic dependence on the United States would have prevented this line of thought from prevailing in editorials. The Spanish and Mexican positions might be explained by two different circumstances. On one hand, Spain does not depend economically on the United States as much as Mexico does. On the other hand, Mexico has experienced American imperialism as history annals indicate. The United States invaded Mexico in 1846 arguing a border dispute. As a result, Mexico lost California, New Mexico, and parts of Arizona, Colorado, and Utah.[31] This historical event was brought up on several occasions in the editorials that explained the war in Iraq as the result of the American policy of extending its influence and power. The following quotation referred to James Polk who was the American President from 1845 to 1849 and who exerted his policy of extending the United States' empire to the south of their then existent borders:

> James Polk created a dispute among American and Mexican soldiers on the border with Mexico. Polk stated that, "I have done as much as my honor

allows me to avoid the war. However, all my efforts have been in vain. All our attempts to preserve peace have faced Mexico's insult and resistance."[32]

Aznar's assertion addressing the Spanish Parliament seemed to be a deja vu to justify his support of the United States, "we have done everything that is possible for the peace."[33] *El País* frequently stated that "Bush's hegemony vocation is clearly based upon the imperialist logic and the available military resources though it is not based on the supposed moral justification that he always claims."[34]

The fear of the disappearance of the UN from the international arena dominated in Chile's and Mexico's discourse. Editorials constantly affirm that "the unilateral action of Washington would practically finish with UN and would deadly wound the European Union."[35]

> It is truth that several spokesmen of the American Government have declared that the United Nations Security Council does not need to give permission or endorsement to the United States to disarm Iraq through a war. However, it is equally true that it is not an easy decision that might have bigger consequences. One of those, maybe the most important, is that it would put in danger the existence of the UN as an international institution that guarantees international peace and legality.[36]

However, few editorialists in Spain expressed this concern while most of the texts still criticized Aznar's alignment with the United States. They expressed their rejection of Aznar's decision to separate Spain from Europe and Latin America by favoring the United States in their war against Iraq.

In contrast with the Desert Storm, when the oil consumption or oil company interests were ranked as one of the main causes of the war[37]; this time, the economic motivation reason for the war was detected in a small number of articles (11 percent). Spain and Mexico explained the war based on the economic benefits that the United States would obtain not only from the control over the oil reserves, but also from the process of reconstruction of Iraq. Reference to the Vice President Dick Cheney and his involvement in several companies that would directly benefit from the war prevailed in the discourse. The companies were Lockheed Martin, Boeing, Raytheon Systems, Starmet, Loral Vought, Textron Defense Systems, Bechtel, and Halliburton. This list of companies sometimes seemed to be a broker's investment portfolio. These companies constitute a large spectrum of economic activities; they provide supplies to the U.S. army through "Carlyle and United Defense Industries or they would rebuild Iraq."[38]

> Nobody knows yet what is going to happen and American companies such as Kellos, Brown and Rooty [it is said it was chaired by Vice-President

Dick Cheney] have already won invitations to be in charge of the reconstruction of the country.[39]

Much of this argument was based on the fact that "The American oil reserves are being exhausted, and many other oil reserves in other countries that do not belong to OPEC are beginning to dry out."[40] In this light the war seemed to have created the land of opportunity to "give British and American oil companies a good opportunity to access directly the Iraq oil for the first time in 50 years, a gain that exceeds hundreds of thousands of dollars."[41] Considering the "rain of millions of dollars"[42] that the United States would make with the war in Iraq, any other reason weakened in the eyes of the reader.

The following two explanations to oppose the war were extremely close in percentage of occurrences: fear of retaliation (8 percent) and humanitarian reasons (7 percent). Both Chile and Mexico expressed this fear of retaliation through either conciliatory comments or blatant proposals "to sell" the possible vote for the war. Undoubtedly the NAFTA treaty between the United States and Mexico, and the signing of a trade agreement between the United States and Chile played a major role here. Chile and Mexico sought their seat in the Security Council in the United Nations. Both Chilean and Mexican editorialists lashed out at politicians who put their countries in danger seeking a seat in the Security Council, "The seat obtained in the Security Council would transform into a lethal electric chair."[43]

> The Chilean ambassador to the UN has avoided major announcements concerning the possible war in Iraq. She must safeguard the national dignity as much as possible and must avoid creating conflicts that damage the signing of the Free Trade Agreement with the United States.[44]

The conciliatory comments in Chile and in Mexico transformed into blaming the government officials for being part of the Security Council game in the United Nations as the date to cast a possible vote approached. "If there is going to be a war against Iraq, we should accelerate the process voting in favor so that we can take as much economic and political advantage as possible."[45]

The Chilean ex-ambassador to the United Nations, Hernán Felipe Errazúz, questioned the benefits of voting against the war in Iraq stating that a vote like that would only create uncertainty in Chile's future in terms of its relationship with the United States. He also assured:

> Chile should only be concerned with how Chile would vote if the United States and England propose another resolution. . . . [W]e assumed risks and we are about to make a greater mistake that goes against our principles

and interests. Chile shouldn't take a position in favor of Hussein . . . We cannot think that this decision of voting against the war will not bring consequences to the national interest and our bilateral relationship. Chile and the United States share principles of democracy and economic freedom. We are about to sign the Free Trade Agreement . . .[46]

The humanitarian concern for human life seems to be the least important reason to dissent with the war in Iraq, "We ask, following the logic of the 'Just Cause': Is it morally legal to kill hundreds of Iraqis with the only purpose to stop Saddam."[47] The discourse defending human life recognizes the death toll on either side of the armed conflict; it oscillates from presenting American soldiers as the perfect, athletic, and handsome Americans who go to war with their walkman while driving tanks, to the constant reference to the innocent civilians who would perish and perished during the war.[48] There also seemed to be a criticism of the American media that portrayed the war in Hackett's words as "patriotic cheerleaders."[49] However, American media did not mention the children's death rate, "Occidental deaths are only pondered while the bombarded civilians are ignored."[50]

Factor five deals with the image of George Bush portrayed in the editorials; the highest percentage of occurrences (54 percent) belonged to the Bush as an instrument of God and Good category. Bush seemed to believe that his moral legitimacy was provided by the values of Western democratic capitalism. He thought that, America was the one that would bring democracy to the world and light to the oppressed nations.[51] The next categories, in the order of percentages of occurrences, were the absence of image, Bush's portrayal as a business entrepreneur, and the negligent Bush category with 36, 8, and 1 percent respectively. When combining factor two, the country where the editorial was written, with factor five, Bush's image, Mexican editorialists led portraying Bush as having a special relationship with God.

> Bush has denounced the axis of evil. He has declared the XXI century the new American century and has assumed in the name of his country the responsibility not only to protect the sovereignty of his country but also to extend freedom to all the nations that is God's gift to humanity to guarantee the end of the terrible threats to the civilized world. He has also proclaimed himself the guarantor of human life and hope.[52]

Drawing on the Judaic/Christian/Islamic myths of a chosen people in exile, and of a new beginning in the Promised Land, Bush has appointed himself to direct humanity into better times. *El País* states, "one should recognize that Bush is more religious than Saddam; he is more primitive of the two presidents from the psychological point of view."[53] The editorial continued comparing Texas with Iraq in terms of the heat, oil wealth, and weekly executions.

Only editorials in Spain and in Mexico showed Bush as a business entrepreneur who sought economic benefits from the war in Iraq. "Earnings of Enron, Chrysler and Dupont that have flustered George Bush and his hawks to the White House do not allow them to see what happens in the world."[54]

An unusual image of an American president appeared in *El Universal*: a negligent politician unable to do politics. Even though statistically not significant[55] because it created empty cells in the data for Chile and Spain, the decision was taken to leave this aspect to illustrate maybe Mexico's fear to deal with Bush or "because words are only an escape to the frustration that everybody feels with this war."[56] Another editorial called Bush "the evil President" just to rhetorically retract this statement arguing that "evilness implies to be somewhat intelligent."[57] The most striking editorial was a long monologue supposedly uttered by Bush:

> I am not sure of my public speech abilities. To read is very difficult for me . . . Words are a pain in the neck. Sometimes I say things that I shouldn't. Literature is not for me. Books cause me an allergic reaction. What I care about is money . . . For me, history is a hit parade . . . And now everybody has to obey me, the English butler and the Spanish go-between, everybody.[58]

The last line in the previous quotation links perfectly with the last factor group that was explored in the editorials: the image that readers had of their political leaders (Aznar in Spain, President Lagos in Chile, and President Fox in Mexico). The descriptions were grouped in the following way: a leader who acted according to his people's decision; according to the Constitution; against his people's decision; according to Bush's wishes; an indecisive leader, and absence of image. The highest percentage of occurrences belonged to the absence of the leader's image category in the editorials with 75 percent. The next two categories—the leader acting according to Bush's wishes and the leader acting according to the Constitution—are very close in percentage: 8 and 7 percent respectively. Finally, the leader acting according to his people's decision, against his people's decision, and being indecisive categories offered just 3 percent each. Not surprisingly, editorials in Spain blamed Aznar as acting as Bush's puppet, "We know that the Spanish Government will do whatever President Bush decides."[59] Aznar was constantly accused of lying and of trying to manipulate the public opinion using euphemisms while referring to the war, for example, as not a war, but "an armed conflict" or "a democratic alternative" instead of "invasion."

Bush, Blair and Aznar juggle with their arguments to justify the decision they have already taken. They chose their arguments to support the war from a basket of tricks where words like disarmament, war against terrorism, change of regime and even humanitarian assistance pervade.[60]

Before considering the image of the leader acting according to the Constitution of his country category, it is important to indicate that only Mexican editorials dealt with this issue. The reason is that Mexican Constitution specifically prescribes the autonomy for each country to decide its own destiny: Mexico must not intervene in other countries' political decisions. Mexican editorials either praised or criticized President Fox because he took a stand against the war in Iraq. However, some editorials blamed him because he did not seem to have been absolutely clear in his position. At that time, he underwent a surgery and some editorialists suggested that Fox hid in the hospital to avoid meeting with George Bush senior. According to the press releases, Fox did have a surgery and couldn't meet with former President Bush. An editorial praising Fox assured that "Fox did not allow himself to be pressured by the sectors [of economy] that preferred doing business [with the U.S.] rather than to act according to what the Mexican Constitution prescribes in terms of the international law."[61] Fox's decision to declare his opposition to the war, in general, was seen as a matter of patriotism[62]; that is, if he had supported the war in Iraq he might have been considered a traitor. Understandably, these opinions were related to the issue of being able to act according to the Constitution "that prescribes without errors the exterior policy that our country should follow."[63]

Aznar was the only leader who acted against his people's will; both President Lagos and President Fox have acted according to their people's decisions, but they also were described as being a little bit indecisive. Editorialists called Aznar a manipulator, liar, and Bush's puppet among other epithets. "It would mean to insult President Aznar's intelligence to believe that he is convinced by the American argument of the Iraqi threat."[64] Before and during the war plenty of editorialists suggested that Aznar deceived his people.

Thank you, Aznar, because you have made us to be ashamed of being Spaniards . . . Mr. José María Aznar, I demand your resignation; it is illegal that you hold the Presidency of the Spanish Government, at least morally, because the majority of the Spaniards are against you; because you have covered us with shame, ignominy and indignity. And you have systematically deceived us.[65]

This quotation exemplifies the anger toward Spain's president of the government. The criticisms of President Lagos and of President Fox were, in general, less aggressive. For example, a member of the Chilean government denied that "Chile could have been 'ambiguous' at the UN."[66] Another editorial questioned whether the Chilean government took a stand against the war or simply never expressed its rejection of the war, "the government disagreed with Washington in reference to increase the time so that Baghdad would completely disarm . . . but never dismissed the war as a possibility."[67]

The very low percentages of occurrence suggested that the three categories discussed just above were not too important in the overall coverage of the pre-war debate. However, they showed some criticism directed against Chilean and Mexican presidents. The following quotation summarizes President Lagos' and President Fox's difficult position in relation to the war in Iraq.

> Mexico's and Chile's hesitation in front of this terrible farce can only be interpreted as obedience to the United States. This ambiguity is also reflected in Fox's conjectures that the war is a fact. This weakens his declared position of finding a peaceful solution . . . A responsible politician should refrain from saying that we can not do anything to avoid the war.[68]

One editorialist said earlier that nobody wanted to commit political hara-kiri in terms of our relations with our neighbors to the north.

Conclusion

As a word of caution, in spite of the limitations of this study, it was possible to see what Spanish-speaking countries were exposed to in the print media. This doesn't mean that this paper should be considered representative of the Spanish-speaking point of view; this is rather a glimpse of how people perceived the war and its protagonists in Chile, Mexico, and Spain. The illocutionary acts used throughout the editorials and OpEd articles portrayed the war in Iraq as a problem of law and order that could put in jeopardy the existence of the United Nations. The war was also depicted as an imperialist action commanded by George Bush who embodied in his opinion the rightfulness of Good and God. Not surprisingly, Spanish language editorials harshly criticized José María Aznar, the president of the Spanish government. Contrastingly, President Lagos of Chile and President Fox of Mexico sometimes were depicted as hesitant in taking a position in relation to the war. However, their attitude might be due to the economic dependency that these two countries have on the United States. It is important to highlight that these two economically small countries, in spite of being afraid of retaliation, as it was suggested in some editorials, dared oppose the war. They didn't boast their opposition, but they didn't sell their UN votes as it was suggested to them either. Thus, it seemed that even "the second class countries"[69] could take a stand and defend their right to disagree with their powerful business partner. In terms of the effects of the media on the public, it was interesting to observe that in Spanish-speaking countries journalists used their right dissent and tried to provide a perspective different from the one provided by the United States media.

The statistical program Goldvarb 2001 showed the distribution of the different illocutionary acts that articulated the support or opposition to the war in Iraq. Keeping all the images seen in the editorials and OpEd articles in the analysis allowed the reader to compare what the American media offered with what international media portrayed. After all, "the media perceptions and impressions directly affect the public opinion."[70] Or maybe, "the news media do not tell people what to think; they can tell the audience what topics to think about."[71] In any case, the reader has the possibility to compare and decide.

Notes

1. T. A. Van Dijk, "Opinions and Ideologies in the Press," in *Approaches to Media Discourse*, ed. Allan Bell and Peter (Garret Malden, Massachusetts: Blackwell Publishers, 1998), 21.
2. Even though Lexis-Nexis lists more newspapers, the files were not updated; many newspapers published in Spanish speaking countries were available up to 1999. Thus the access to the papers was somewhat limited.
3. Jef Verschueren, *International News Reporting: Metapragmatic Metaphors and the U-2* (Philadelphia: John Benjamins Publishing Company, 1985).
4. D. Porpora, *The Debate Over Central America. How Holocausts Happen: The United States in Central America* (Philadelphia: Temple University Press, 1990), 160.
5. P. Goodwin, Jr. *Latin America* (Connecticut: McGraw-Hill, 2003), 71.
6. P. Goodwin, Jr. *Latin America* (Connecticut: McGraw-Hill, 2003).
7. J. Jacoby, W. D. Hoyer, and D. A. Sheluga, *Miscomprehension of Televised Communications* (New York, NY: The Educational Foundation of the American Association of Advertising Agencies, 1980). See also J. M. Lope Blanch, *Los medios de información y la lengua española* (México: Universidad Nacional Autónoma de México, 1988). See also M. Parra, *Difusión internacional del español por radio, televisión y prensa* (Santafé de Bogotá: Publicaciones del Instituto caro y Cuervo, series Minor XL, 1999).
8. J. Corner and S. Harvey, eds., *Television Times, a Reader* (New York, NY: Arnold, 1996). See also E. Goffman, *Forms of Talk* (Philadelphia, PA: University of Pennsylvania, 1981). See also Karol J. Hardin, *Pragmatics of Persuasive Discourse in Spanish Television Advertising* (The United States: SIL International & University of Texas at Arlington, 2001).
9. Allan Bell, *The Language of the News Media* (Oxford, U.K. & Cambridge, MA: Blackwell, 1991). See also L. Elías-Olivares, R.Cisneros and J. Gutiérrez, eds., *Spanish Language Use in Public Life in the United States* (New York: Mounton

Publishers, 1985). See also C. Geraghty and D. Lusted, eds., *The Television Studies Book* (New York: Arnold, 1998). See also J. L. Martínez Albertos, *Lenguaje periodístico* (Madrid: Parafino, S.S., 1989). See also M. C. Mata and S. Scarafia, *Lo que dicen las radios, una propuesta para analizar el discurso radiofónico* (Quito, Ecuador: RN Industria Gráfica, 1993).

10. Lázaro Carreter, *El idioma del periodismo ¿lengua especial? El idioma español en las agencias de prensa* (Madrid: Fundación Germán Sánchez Rimpérez, 1981). See also M. Parra, *Difusión internacional del español por radio, televisión y prensa* (Santafé de Bogotá: Publicaciones del Instituto caro y Cuervo, series Minor XL, 1999). See also J. M. Lope Blanch, *Los medios de información y la lengua española* (México: Universidad Nacional Autónoma de México, 1988). See also Allan Bell, *The Language of the News Media* (Oxford, U.K. and Cambridge, MA: Blackwell, 1991).

11. Jef Verschueren, *International News Reporting: Metapragmatic Metaphors and the U-2* (Philadelphia: John Benjamins Publishing Company, 1985). See also A. H. Jucker, *News Interviews: A Pragmalinguisitc Analysis* (Philadelphia: John Benjamins Publishing Company, 1986). See also Rosemarie Schmidt and Joseph F. Kess, *Television advertising and televangelism discourse* (Philadelphia: John Benjamins Publishing Company, 1986).

12. In linguistics pragmatics is the study of the use of context to make inferences about meaning R., Fasold. *The Sociolinguistics of Language* (Cambridge, MA: Blackwell Publishers, 1994).

13. The other two characteristics of illocutionary acts are first; uttering the right explicit performative sentence (with the right intentions and beliefs and under the right circumstances) successfully performs an illocutionary act. Second, "illocutionary acts are central to linguistic communication. Our normal conversations are composed in large part of statements, suggestions, requests, proposals, greetings and the like" Adrian Akmajiam Richard A. Demers and Robert M. Harnish, "Pragmatics: The Study of Language Use and Linguistic Communication," in *Linguistics: An Introduction to Language and Communication* (Cambridge, MA: MIT Press, 1981), 269.

14. Linguists' interest in pragmatics has increased in the last couple of years. The theoretical background presented here might be considered the pick of the iceberg. For further reading on locutionary act and illocutionary acts see Karol J. Hardin, *Pragmatics of Persuasive Discourse in Spanish Television Advertising* (The United States: SIL International & University of Texas at Arlington, 2001). See also J. L. Mey, *Whose Language? A Study in Linguistic Pragmatics* (Philadelphia: John Benjamins Publishing Company, 1985). See also D. Jo. Napoli, "Semantics." In *Linguistics An Introduction* (New York: Oxford University Press, 1996).

15. Adrian Akmajiam, Richard A. Demers and Robert M. Harnish, *Linguistics: An Introduction to Language and Communication* (Cambridge, Massachusetts: MIT Press, 1981), 267–302.

16. J.Searle, *Speech* Acts (Cambridge, England: Cambridge University Press, 1975).

17. A. J. López Cáceres, in *Entre la Pluma y la pantalla: reflexiones sobre-literatura, cine y periodismo* (Calí, Colombia: Universidad del Valle, 2003), 41–61.

18. T. A. Van Dijk, "Opinions and Ideologies in the Press," in *Approaches to Media Discourse*, ed. Allan Bell and Peter (Garret Malden, Massachusetts: Blackwell Publishers, 1998), 22.

19. Goldvarb 2001 is an application for a multivariate analysis that runs in windows that was created for linguistic analysis.

20. R. A. Hackett, "The Press and foreign policy dissent: the case of the Gulf War," in *News Media and Foreign Relations: A Multifaceted Perspective*, ed. Abbas Malek (Norwood, NJ: Ablex, 1994), 197, 144.

21. Stephen Earl Bennett, "The Persian Gulf War's Impact on American's Political Information." *Political Behaviour* 16:2 (1994): 183.

22. A. Ball, "Political Language and the Search for an Honorable Peace: Presidents Kennedy and Johnson, Their Advisers, and Vietnam Decision Making," in *Beyond Public Speech and Symbols, Explorations in the Rhetoric of Politicians and the Media*, ed. Christ'l De Landtsheer and Ofer Feldman (Westport, Connecticut: Praeger, 2000), 41.

23. R. A. Hackett, "The Press and foreign policy dissent: the case of the Gulf War," in *News Media and Foreign Relations: a Multifaceted Perspective*, ed. Makek Abbas (Norwood, NJ: Ablex Publishing Corporation, 1997).

24. Ibid., 145.

25. Ibid., 153.

26. "Morirá la ONU en Bagadad," *El Universal*, Wednesday, March 19, 2003 <http://www.el-universal.com.mx/pls/impreso/editorial_histo_maquillado. despliega?var_id>

27. B. Kirkwood, *The History of Mexico* (Westport, Connecticut: Greenwood Press, 2000).

28. "Relaciones con E.U.," *La Segunda*, Wednesday March 19, 2003 <http:// web.ABYZNewsLinks.com.ezproxy.library.drexel.edu>

29. "Guerra preventiva o invasión," *El País*, March 14, 2003 <http://web.lexis-nexis.com/universe/document?_m=2ac020b940 cdeac0e7b76da373130725>

30. "Jugar al fútbol no a la guerra," *El País*, Wednesday, April 9, 2003 <http://web. lexis-nexis.com/universe/document?_m=2ac020b940 cdeac0e7b76da373130725>

31. B. Kirkwood, *The History of Mexico* (Westport, Connecticut: Greenwood Press, 2000).

32. "Semejanzas entre Kames Polk y George Bush," *El Universal*, Thursday, March 20, 2003 <http://www.eluniversal.com.mx/pls/impreso/editorial_histo_maquillado.despliega?var_id>

33. "Justificar lo injustificable," *El País*, Sunday, March 16, 2003 <http://web. lexis-nexis.com/universe/document?_m=2ac020b940 cdeac0e7b76da373130725>

34. "El honor de España," *El País*, Wednesday, March 12, 2003 <http://web.lexis-nexis.com/universe/document?_m=2ac020b940cdeac0e7b76da373130725>

35. Emmanuel Carballo, "Una guerra puramente estadounidense," *El Universal*, Tuesday, March 18, 2003 <http://web.ABYZNewsLinks.com.ezproxy.library. drexel.edu>

36. "Una nueva propuesta en pos del consenso en la ONU," *El Universal*, Friday, March 14, 2003 <http://www.el-universal.com.mx/pls/impreso/ editorial_histo_maquillado.despliega?var_id>

37. R. A. Hackett, "The Press and foreign policy dissent: the case of the Gulf War," in *News Media and Foreign Relations: a Multifaceted Perspective*, ed. Makek Abbas (Norwood, NJ: Ablex Publishing Corporation, 1997).

38. Rodolfo Echeverría Ruiz, "Guerra y terrorismo," *El Universal*, Friday, April 4, 2003 <http://www.el-universal.com.mx/pls/impreso/editorial_histo_maquillado. despliega?var_id>

39. Rodolfo Aziz Nasiff, "Ronda el fantasma de Vietnam," *El Universal*, Tuesday, April 1, 2003 <http://www.el-universal.com.mx/pls/impreso/editorial_histo_maquillado.despliega?var_id>

40. "La energía después de Sadam," *El País*, Sunday, March 2, 2003 <http://web.lexis-nexis.com/universe/document?_m=2ac020b940cdeac0e7b76da373130725>

41. "La energía después de Sadam," *El País*, Sunday, March 2, 2003, <http://web.lexis-nexis.com/universe/document?_m=2ac020b940cdeac0e7b76da373130725>

42. "Olor a dólares," *El País*, Saturday, March 22, 2003 <http://web.lexis-nexis.com/universe/document?_m=2ac020b940cdeac0e7b76da373130725>

43. "La burguesia se reparte el mundo," *El Universal*, Sunday, March 8, 2003 <http://www.el-universal.com.mx/pls/impreso/editorial_histo_maquillado.despliega?var_id>

44. "Espionaje norteamericano," *La Segunda*, Thursday, March 6, 2003 <http://web.ABYZNewsLinks.com.ezproxy.library.drexel.edu>

45. "Decir no con claridad y consecuencia," *El Universal*, Saturday, March 15, 2003 <http://www.el-universal.com.mx/pls/impreso/editorial_histo_maquillado.despliega?var_id>

46. "Chile anunció un costo innecesario," *La segunda*, Friday, March 14, 2003 <http://web.ABYZNewsLinks.com.ezproxy.library.drexel.edu>

47. "¿Causa justa?," *La Segunda*, Wednesday, March 19, 2003, <http://web.ABYZNewsLinks.com.ezproxy.library.drexel.edu>

48. Sara Sefchovich, "Las necesidades primordiales del ejército yanquí," *El Universal*, Thursday, April 3, 2003 <http://www.el-universal.com.mx/pls/impreso/editorial_histo_maquillado.despliega?var_id>

49. R. A. Hackett, "The Press and foreign policy dissent: the case of the Gulf War," in *News Media and Foreign Relations: a Multifaceted Perspective*, ed. Makek Abbas (Norwood, NJ: Ablex Publishing Corporation, 1997), 142.

50. "Alto al exterminio," *El Universal*, Tuesday, April 8, 2003 <http://www.el-universal.com.mx/pls/impreso/editorial_histo_maquillado.despliega?var_id>

51. R. A. Hackett, "The Press and foreign policy dissent: the case of the Gulf War," in *News Media and Foreign Relations: a Multifaceted Perspective*, ed. Makek Abbas (Norwood, NJ: Ablex Publishing Corporation, 1997).

52. "El énfasis declarativo," *El Universal*, Sunday, March 16, 2003 <http://www.el-universal.com.mx/pls/impreso/editorial_histo_maquillado. despliega?var_id>

53. "En el Palacio final," *El País*, Tuesday, March 11, 2003 <http://web.lexis-nexis.com/universe/document?_m=2ac020b940cdeac0e7b76da373130725>

54. Gerardo Urizueta, "Nos imponen Guerra sin fin y sin límites," *El Universal*, Saturday, March 22, 2003 <http://www.el-universal.com.mx/pls/impreso/editorial_histo_maquillado.despliega?var_id>

55. It is advisable to delete or to collapse elements in each factor or even factor groups to avoid the creation of empty cells. This could result when there are elements that are either uninteresting or misleading, or they are in very small numbers in each cell.

56. Juan María Alponte, "El destino manifiesto y la dramatica muerte de las Naciones Unidas," *El Universal*, Monday, March 24, 2003 <http://www.el-universal.com.mx/pls/impreso/editorial_histo_maquillado.despliega?var_id>

57. Víctor Flores Olea, "Las derrotas de Geroge W. Bush," *El Universal*, Sunday, March 30, 2003 <http://www.el-universal.com.mx/pls/impreso/editorial_histo_maquillado.despliega?var_id>

58. "Monologo recitado un lunes de marzo en la Casa Blanca," *El Universal*, Thursday, March 20, 2003 <http://www.el-universal.com.mx/pls/impreso/editorial_histo_maquillado.despliega?var_id>

59. "¿Quién está al mando?," *El País*, Friday, March 14, 2003 <http://web.lexis-nexis.com/universe/document?_m=2ac020b940cdeac0e7b76da373130725>

60. *"Bandos y bandazos,"* *El País*, Tuesday, March 11, 2003 <http://web.lexis-nexis.com/universe/document?_m=2ac020b940cdeac0e7b76da373130725>

61. "Palabras valientes," *El universal*, Thursday, March 20, 2003 <http://www.el-universal.com.mx/pls/impreso/editorial_histo_maquillado.despliega?var_id>

62. "Campaña a favor de la paz," *El Universal*, Friday, March 7, 2003 <http://www.el-universal.com.mx/pls/impreso/editorial_histo_maquillado.despliega?var_id>

63. "El presidente cumplió con su deber legal y con sus gobernados," *Universal*, Monday, April 10, 2003 <http://www.el-universal.com.mx/pls/impreso/editorial_histo_maquillado.despliega?var_id>

64. "¿Quién está al mando?," *El País*, Friday, March 14, 2003 <http://web.lexis-nexis.com/universe/document?_m=2ac020b940cdeac0e7b76da373130725>

65. "Vergüenza," *El País*, Sunday, March 23, 2003 <http://web.lexis-nexis.com/universe/document?_m=2ac020b940cdeac0e7b76da373130725>

66. "Canciller Alvear destaca actitud responsible de Chile," *La Segunda*, Friday, March 14, 2003 <http://web.ABYZNewsLinks.com.ezproxy.library.drexel.edu>

67. "El PS y el incidente de Ginebra," *La Segunda*, Monday, March 31, 2003 <http://web.ABYZNewsLinks.com.ezproxy.library.drexel.edu>

68. "De cara a la historia," *El Universal*, Tuesday, March 11, 2003 <http://www.el-universal.com.mx/pls/impreso/editorial_histo_ maquillado.despliega?var_id>

69. "Relaciones con E.U.," *La Segunda*, Wednesday, March 19, 2003 <http://web.ABYZNewsLinks.com.ezproxy.library.drexel.edu>

70. D. Bonafede, "The President, Congress, and the Media in Global Affairs," in *News Media and Foreign Relations: a Multifaceted Perspective*, ed. A. Malek (Norwood, NJ: Ablex Publishing Corporation, 1997), 95.

71. K. H. Jamieson, *Everything You Think Your Know About Politics . . . And Why You're Wrong* (United States: Basic Books, 2000), 12.

Notes on Contributors

Alexander G. Nikolaev is an assistant professor of communication in the Department of Culture and Communication at Drexel University (Philadelphia, PA, U.S.A.). He earned his doctorate from the Florida State University where he also taught for four years. His areas of research interest and expertise include such fields as public relations, political communication, organizational communication, international communication, international negotiations, international news coverage, and discourse analysis. He authored several articles in these areas in trade and scholarly journals as well as some book chapters in the United States and overseas. He also has years of practical work experience in the fields of journalism and public relations in the United States and Eastern Europe. His current research focuses on international political rhetoric, international news coverage, international negotiations, and transformation and applications of the two-level-game theory.

Ernest A. Hakanen, Ph.D. is an associate professor of communication and head of graduate program in the Department of Culture and Communication at Drexel University (Philadelphia, PA). He earned his doctorate from Temple University. He has published scholarly articles in a variety of fields such as journalism, psychology, information science, sociology, and communication. He edited *Mass media and society* with A. Wells and is on the editorial board of *Popular Communication*. His ongoing research is in public affairs reporting and telecommunications history.

Ronald Bishop is an associate professor in the communication program at Drexel University. He teaches courses in media law, sports journalism, global journalism, and the cultural history of fame. His research interests include news media portrayals of activism, journalism history, America's fascination with collecting, and textual and narrative analysis. His work has appeared in the *Journal of Communication, Journalism and Communication Monographs, the Journal of Communication Inquiry, and the Journal of Popular Culture*. He holds a Ph.D. in communication from Temple University.

Judith Brown first qualified as a nurse and nurse teacher, and worked as an aid worker in Eastern Europe, Africa, and the Middle East, where she managed health programs. During this time she became aware of the different perspectives from which people from other cultures viewed the world, which led her to undertake a Ph.D. at the Institute of Arab and Islamic Studies at Exeter University resulting in *The Image of Arabs in the British Media*. She is also a Director of Arab Media Watch, a media-monitoring organization in Britain that aims for fair and accurate coverage of Arab issues.

Daniela V. Dimitrova received her Ph.D. in Mass Communication from the University of Florida. She is an Assistant Professor at Iowa State University where she teaches Multimedia Production and Communication Technology courses. Her research interests focus on new media adoption and political communication. Dr. Dimitrova's research has been published internationally.

William A. Dorman is Professor Emeritus of Government and Journalism at California State University, Sacramento, where he has taught such courses as American Foreign Policy and War and Peace and the Mass Media. Professor Dorman has written extensively on foreign affairs and on press performance and he is coauthor with Mansour Farhang of *U.S. Press and Iran: Foreign Policy and the Journalism of Deference* (U.C. Press, 1987). He was a member of the scholarly team that produced a highly regarded study of the 1991 war with Iraq, *Taken by Storm: The Media, Public Opinion, and U.S. Foreign Policy in the Gulf War* (Chicago, 1994).

Brian J. Foley is an Assistant Professor of Law at Florida Coastal School of Law. He has published scholarly work on international law and the use of force. He received his J.D. from Boalt Hall School of Law, University of California, Berkeley, and his A.B. from Dartmouth College.

Philip Hammond is Senior Lecturer in Media at London South Bank University. He is coeditor, with Edward S. Herman, of *Degraded Capability: The Media and the Kosovo Crisis* (Pluto Press, 2000), and is currently writing a book on Media, War, and Postmodernity to be published by Routledge.

Steven Livingston is the director of the School of Media and Public Affairs at George Washington University and an associate professor of media and international affairs. He is also the chair of the Public Diplomacy Institute at George Washington University.

Lea Mandelzis is the head of Marketing Communications Studies at the School of Communications, Sapir Academic College in Israel and supervisor for seminar projects in the Department of Communications Studies at the Open University. Her fields of interest include discourse analysis in conflicts, security peace and political discourses in the news, media representations and images, sociopolitical communications and international communications. Dr. Mandelzis has presented and published a number of articles on news discourses and is a council member of the International Peace Research Association (IPRA).

Louis Mangione is an associate professor in the Center for Critical Languages at Temple University where he has held a faculty position since 1985. His training is in linguistics and his academic interests include semantics, language teaching, and various aspects of Asian Studies. Recently, he has become interested in software packages designed to promote the learning of Chinese and their application in language courses. He has made a number of trips to China, where he has taught short term at Zhejiang Normal University, pursued various academic projects, and traveled. He is currently working on a study of traditional ballads from the Wenzhou and Jinhua districts of Zhejiang Province.

Stenford Matenda is a lecturer and acting chairman of the Department of Journalism and Media studies at the National University of Science and Technology

(NUST) in Zimbabwe. Before joining the academia, he worked at the Zimbabwe Broadcasting Holdings, first as a producer and later as a senior Radio News Writer. He holds a Bachelor's degree in Psychology, a postgraduate Diploma in Media and Communication, and a Masters degree in Media and Communication all from the University of Zimbabwe. His research interests are in the media in Africa and Health Communication in the African context.

Mariadelaluz Matus-Mendoza is a language Educator and Sociolinguist. At present, she is the Assistant Professor of Spanish in the Department of Culture and Communication at Drexel University. Her research interests lie generally in relating linguistic variation and movement as seen in migration and social movement. Dr. Matus-Mendoza is also interested in language in the media, Second Language acquisition, and bilingualism. She is the author of *Linguistic Variation in Mexican Spanish as Spoken in Two Communities—Moroleón, Mexico and Kennett Square, Pennsylvania* (Mellen Press, 2002).

Chanan Naveh is Senior Lecturer and the academic counselor at the School of Communication Sapir Academic College, and is the head of Radio Professional studies at the College. He also teaches at the International Relations Department, Hebrew University, Jerusalem. Until recently Dr. Naveh worked as a Senior Managing Editor—News Department, Israeli Radio, and The Voice of Israel. Dr. Naveh's fields of interest include Media and foreign policy, international communication, the Internet as an international media environment, and International regimes and media. He published papers in these fields and presented papers in international and Israeli academic conferences on these topics.

Anne-Marie Obajtek-Kirkwood is assistant professor of French at Drexel University, Philadelphia. Her centers of interest and research are French and Francophone twentieth century and current novels, literary and filmic representations of the Occupation and other events or features of French civilization and culture, autobiography, minorities in France, feminist issues, and film. She has published on Simone de Beauvoir, Patrick Modiano, Jean-Noël Pancrazi, Mélina Gazsi, Geneviève Brisac, Viviane Forrester, Yvonne Baby. Her latest article, "Quand La Banlieue se fait chambre d'écho d'une actualité hors frontières . . ." appeared in the Spring issue of Contemporary French and Francophone Studies. She is currently preparing an anthology on multiple forms of exile and exclusion.

M.G. Piety is an Assistant Professor of Philosophy at Drexel University. She received her Ph.D. from McGill University. She has published numerous scholarly articles in professional journals as well as in the *Times Literary Supplement* and the *Times Higher Education Supplement*. She is a regular columnist for *ASK*, the new journal of the College of Arts and Sciences of Drexel University.

Lucas Robinson is a researcher and lecturer at Agder University College, in Kristiansand, Norway. He holds a master's degree in media and public affairs from George Washington University, and a BA in peace and conflict studies from the University of Toronto.

Iman Roushdy-Hammady was born in Cairo, Egypt. She studied German literature and linguistics, completed a B.A. in economics (1987), and an M.A. in anthropology/sociology (1990) at the American University in Cairo, and a Ph.D. in medical anthropology and middle-eastern studies at Harvard University (2001). Her research on endemic cancer in Turkey and Europe appeared in The Lancet (2001), three publications in print in Culture, Medicine, and Psychiatry, and an article in print in the Encyclopedia of Women and Islamic Cultures. Roushdy Hammady was assistant member in the Division of Population Science at Fox Chase Cancer Center, Philadelphia, PA (2002–04). She taught courses on Arabic and German languages and cultures at Drexel University, Philadelphia, PA (2004), combining language, anthropology, literature, music, and film. She teaches Arabic diction since 1997 as faculty in the Arab American Arts Institute, NY. She knows different Altaic, Endo-European, Romance, and Semitic languages. She recently took a research position in the Department of Psychiatry and Behavioral Sciences at Duke University Medical Center, Durham, NC.

Simone Schlichting-Artur is a German native and has spent half her life in Germany and the other half in the United States. She studied Art History, Philosophy and Languages in Marburg, Germany and holds a B.A. in International Area Studies and an M.A. in Science, Technology and Society from Drexel University in Philadelphia. For many years she worked as a German language instructor at Drexel University, Temple University, and University of Pennsylvania in Philadelphia. Since 2001, she has been the Director of Modern Languages and the Senior Lecturer of German at Drexel University. She is also pursuing her Ed.D. in the Educational Leadership Program at the University of Pennsylvania. Her research focus is on language hegemony and power relations established through foreign language acquisition.

BIBLIOGRAPHY

Akmajiam, A., R. A. Demers, and R. M. Hernish. *Linguistics: An Introduction to Language and Communication*, 267–302. Cambridge, MA: MIT Press, 1981.

Al-Saqr (The Eagle). Film. Arabic. Directed by Salah Abu-Sayf. Egypt, 1950.

Al-Watan al-Akbar (The Greater Homeland). Arabic. Composed by Mohammed Abd-al-Wahháb, 1964.

American Dynasty: Aristocracy, Fortune and the Politics of Deceit in the House of Bush. New York: Viking, 2004.

Amír al-Intiqám (The Prince of Revenge). Film. Arabic. Shády Abd-al-Salám. Egypt. ART Arab Radio Television. 1950.

Anderson, P. *The Origins of Postmodernity.* London: Verso, 1998.

Appleton, J. "Back to Baudrillard." *spiked,* http://www.spiked-online.com/Articles/00000006DD41.htm (accessed April 10, 2003).

Arian, A. "Israeli Public opinion on National Security." *Memorandum No. 61, July 2002.* Tel Aviv: The Jaffe Center for Strategic Studies, Tel Aviv University, 2002. available: http://www.tau.ac.il/jcss/memoranda/memo61.pdf

Augé, Marc. *An Anthropology for Contemporaneous Worlds.* Stanford, CA: Stanford University Press, 1999.

Augé, Marc. *Journal de guerre.* Paris: Editions Galilée, 2002.

Augé, Marc. *Non-lieux. Introduction à une anthropologie de la surmodernité.* Paris: Seuil, 1992.

Auletta, K. "Fortress Bush," *The New Yorker,* January 19, 2004.

Awdat al-Ibn al-Dál [Return of the stray son]. Arabic, with French subtitles. Directed by Youssef Chahine, 1970.

Bailyn, B. *The Ideological Origins of the American Revolution.* Cambridge, MA: Belknap Press, 1992.

Ball, M. A. "Political Language and the Search for an Honorable Peace: Presidents Kennedy and Johnson, Their Advisers, and Vietnam Decision Making." In *Beyond Public Speech and Symbols, Explorations in the Rhetoric of Politicians and the Media,* ed. Christ'l De Landtsheer and Ofer Feldman, 31–53. Westport, CT: Praeger, 2000.

Baudrillard, J. *The Gulf War Did Not Take Place.* Bloomington: Indiana University Press, 1995.

BBC News. "Australia's Iraq War Case Damned." 2004, http://news.bbc.co.uk/2/hi/asia-pacific/3915759.stm (accessed July 29, 2004).

Bell, Allan. *The Language of the News Media.* Oxford, UK and Cambridge, MA: Blackwell, 1991.

Bennett, Stephen Earl. "The Persian Gulf War's Impact on American's Political Information." *Political Behaviour* 16, no. 2 (1994): 179–201.

Bennett, W. L. Toward a Theory of Press–State Relations. *Journal of Communication* 40, no. 2 (1989): 103–125.

Bennett, W. L. "The News About Foreign Policy." In *Taken by Storm: The Media, Public Opinion, and U.S. Foreign Policy in the Gulf War*, ed. W. L. Bennett and D. L. Paletz, 12–40. Chicago and London: University of Chicago Press, 1994.

Bennett, W. L. and David L. Paletz, eds. *Taken By Storm: The Media, Public Opinion, and U.S. Foreign Policy in the Gulf War*. Chicago: University of Chicago Press, 1994.

Ben-Zvi, A. "The Foreign and Security Policy of the Bush Administration in Historical Perspective." In *In the Wake of the War in Iraq*, ed. S. Feldman and M. Grundman, 23–34. Tel Aviv: The Ministry of Defense Publishing House, 2004 (Hebrew).

Best, S. and D. Kellner. *The Postmodern Adventure*. London: Routledge, 2001.

Betts, R. K. "Suicide From Fear of Death?" *Foreign Affairs*, January/February 2003.

Blix, H. *Disarming Iraq*. New York: Pantheon, 2004.

Bonafede, D. "The President, Congress, and the Media in Global Affairs." In *News Media and Foreign Relations: A Multifaceted Perspective*, ed. A. Malek, 95–120. Norwood, NJ: Ablex Publishing Corporation, 1997.

Bovard, J. *Terrorism and Tyranny: Trampling Freedom, Justice and Peace to Rid the World of Evil*. New York: Palgrave/Macmillan, 2003.

Branigin, W. and D. Priest, "Senate Report Blasts Intelligence Agencies' Flaws," *The Washington Post*, July 9, 2004, http://www.washingtonpost.com/ac2/wp-dyn/A38459-2004Jul9 (accessed September 13, 2004).

Brock, D. *The Republican Noise Machine: Right-Wing Media and How It Corrupts Democracy*. New York: Crown Publishers, 2004.

Brown, S. "From the 'Death of the Real' to the Reality of Death: How Did the Gulf War Take Place?" *Journal for Crime, Conflict and the Media*, 1, no. 1 (2003), http://www.jc2m.co.uk/Issue1/Brown.pdf (accessed December 19, 2003).

Bush, G. W. The President's State of the Union Address. Washington, DC, 2002, http://www.whitehouse.gov/news/releases/2002/01/20020129–11.html (accessed February 9, 2005).

Bush, George W. "Remarks by the President at 2002 Graduation Exercise of the United States Military Academy, West Point, New York," http://www.whitehouse.gov/news/releases/2002/06/20020601–3.html

Bvuma, Thomas. *Having it Both Ways: Dual Policy, An Analysis and Evaluation of Zimbabwean Government Policy, 1980–1998*, MPhil Thesis, University of Oslo, Norway, 1998.

Campbell, D. *Writing Security*. Minneapolis: University of Minnesota Press, 1992.

Campbell, Richard. *60 Minutes and the News: A Mythology for Middle America*. Urbana, IL: University of Illinois Press, 1991.

Carey, James. "Introduction." In *Media, Myths, and Narratives: Television and the Press*, ed. James Carey, 1–13. Newbury Park, CA: Sage, 1988.

Carey, James. "The Chicago School and the History of Mass Communication Research." In *James Carey: A Critical Reader*, ed. Eve Munson and Catherine Warren, 14–33. Minneapolis, MN: University of Minnesota Press, 1997.

Carey, James. "The Press, Public Opinion, and Public Discourse: On the Edge of the Postmodern." In *James Carey: A Critical Reader*, ed. Eve Munson and Catherine Warren, 228–260. Minneapolis, MN: University of Minnesota Press, 1997.

Carreter, Lázaro. *El idioma del periodismo ¿lengua especial? El idioma español en las agencias de prensa.* Madrid: Fundación Germán Sánchez Rimpérez, 1981.

Carter, D. T. *Politics of Rage: George Wallace, the Origins of the New Conservativism, and the Transformation of American Politics.* Baton Rouge, LA: Louisiana State University Press, 2000.

Chari, Tendai. *Media and Communication in Zimbabwe and Africa.* Harare: Zimbabwe Open University, 2003.

Chari, Tendai and Wallace Chuma. *Introduction to Global Media Structures.* Harare: Zimbabwe Open University, 2002.

Chermak, S., F. Bailey, and M. Brown. *Journalism After September 11.* Westport, CT: Praeger, 2003.

Chesterman, S. "Ordering the New World: Violence and its Re/Presentation in the Gulf War and Beyond." *Postmodern Culture* 8, no. 3 (May 1998), http:// www.iath.virginia.edu/pmc/text-only/issue.598/8.3chesterman.txt (accessed May 10, 2004).

Chipman, J. "Remarks." In *Strategic Survey 2003/4,* International Institute for Strategic Studies, May 25, 2004, http://www.iiss.org/showdocument.php? docID=364 (accessed July 16, 2004).

Clarke, R. A. *Against All Enemies: Inside America's War on Terror.* New York: Free Press, 2004.

Clausen, Lisbeth. "Global news communication strategies—9.11.2002 around the world." *Nordicom Review* no. 3. Göteborg: Nordicom, 2003, http://www.nordicom. gu.se/reviewcontents/ncomreview/ncomreview203/105-116.pdf (accessed August 1, 2004).

Cohen, B. *The Press and Foreign Policy.* Princeton, NJ: Princeton University Press, 1963.

Control Room. Film. English and Arabic with English subtitles. Middle East and U.S. production; Directed by Jehane Noujaim, 2004.

Corner, J. and S. Harvey, eds. *Television Times, a Reader.* New York: Arnold, 1996.

Coulter, A. *Treason: Liberal Treachery from the Cold War to the War on Terror.* New York: Crown Forum, 2003.

Cranberg, G. "Colin Powell and Me: Tracking the Secretary's Crucial UN Speech." *Columbia Journalism Review* 1 (January/February 2004): 60–61.

D'Angelo, Paul. "News Framing as a Multiparadigmatic Research: A Response to Entman." *Journal of Communication* 52 (2002): 870–888.

Dadge, D. *Casualty of War: The Bush Administration's Assault on a Free Press.* New York: Prometheus Books, 2004.

Dananír Film. Arabic. Directed by Ahmad Badrakhán. 1940. Egypt. ESC Egyptian Satellite Channel, News.

de Beer, Arnold S., and John C. Merrill. *Global Journalism: Topical Issues and Media Systems,* 4th ed. Needham Heights, MA: Allyn & Bacon, 2004.

de Smaele, H. "The Applicability of Western Media Models on the Russian Media System." *European Journal of Communication* 14, no. 2 (1999): 173–189.

Der Derian, J. *Virtuous War: Mapping the Military–Industrial–Media–Entertainment Network.* Boulder, CO: Westview Press, 2001.

Dickey, C. and J. Barry. "Has the War Made Us Safer?" *Newsweek,* 2004, http://www.msnbc.msn.com/id/46661300/site/newsweek/ (accessed September 13, 2004).

Dor, D. *Newspapers Under the Influence*. Tel Aviv: Babel, 2001 (Hebrew).

Dorman, W. A. and S. Livingston. "The Establishing Phase of the Persian Gulf Policy Debate." In *Taken by Storm: The Media, Public Opinion, and U.S. Foreign Policy in the Gulf War*, ed. W. L. Bennett and D. L. Paletz, 63–81. Chicago and London: University of Chicago Press, 1994.

Dreyfus, R. "The Pentagon Muzzles the CIA." *American Prospect* 13, no. 22 December 16, 2002.

Elías-Olivares, L., R. Cisneros, and J. Gutiérrez, eds. *Spanish Language Use in Public Life in the United States*. New York: Mounton Publishers, 1985.

Entman, R. *Projections of Power: Framing News, Public Opinion, and U.S. Foreign Policy*. Chicago: University of Chicago Press, 2004.

Entman, Robert M. "Framing U.S. Coverage of International News: Contrasts in the Narratives of the KAL and the Iran Air Incidents." *Journal of Communication* 41 (1991): 6–27.

Entman, Robert M. "Framing: Towards Clarification of a Fractured Paradigm." *Journal of Communication* 43, no. 4 (1993): 51–58.

Eriposte. "Gallup International Poll," January 2003, http://www.eriposte.com/war_peace/iraq/world_support/gallup_intl_2003_by_country.gif (accessed July 29, 2004).

Evron, Y. "Strategic Theories and its Implementation: The War on Iraq as a Case Study." In *In the Wake of the War in Iraq*, ed. S. Feldman and M. Grundman, 35–46. Tel Aviv: The Ministry of Defense Publishing House, 2004 (Hebrew).

Fairclough, N. *Language and Power*. London: Longman, 1989.

Fasold, R. *The Sociolinguistics of Language*. Cambridge, MA: Blackwell Publishers, 1994.

Fidá'i Song. Arabic. Performed by Abd-al-Halim. Egypt. 1968.

Fishman, M. *Manufacturing the News*. Austin: University of Texas Press, 1980.

Foucault, M. *The Archaeology of Knowledge*, trans. A. M. Sheridan Smith. London: Tavistock Publications, 1972.

Foucault, M. "Disciplinary Power and Subjection." In *Power*, ed. S. Lukes, 229–242. New York: Pantheon Books, 1986. First published in Michel Foucault, *Power/Knowledge: Selected Interviews and Other Writings 1972–1977*, ed. and trans. Colin Gordon. New York: Pantheon Books, 1980.

Foucault, M. *The Will to Knowledge. The History of Sexuality: 1*, trans. Robert Hurley. England: Penguin, 1998.

Foucault, M. "Truth and Power." In *Orientalism, a Reader*, ed. A. L. Macfie, 41–43, Edinburgh: Edinburgh University Press, 2000. From a conversation with Michel Foucault. First published in Michel Foucault, *Power/Knowledge: Selected Interviews and Other Writings 1972–1977*, ed. and trans. Colin Gordon. New York: Pantheon Books, 1980.

Frank, T. *What's the Matter With Kansas: How Conservatives Won the Heart of America*. New York: Metropolitan Books, 2004.

Friedland, L. A. and M. Zhong. "International Television Coverage of Beijing Spring 1989: A Comparative Approach." *Journalism and Mass Communication Monographs* 156 (April 1996): 1–60.

Friedrich, R. Der Brand: *Deutschland im Bombenkrieg 1940–1945*. Berlin: Prpyläen Verlag, 2003.

Gamson, W. A. "The Social Psychology of Collective Action." In *Frontiers in Social Movement Theory*, ed. A. D. Morris and C. McClurg Mueller, 53–76. New Haven: Yale University Press, 1992.

Gamson, William and Anthony Modigliani. "The Changing Culture of Affirmative Action." In *Research in Political Sociology*, ed. R. G. Braungart and M. M. Braungart, vol. 3, 137–177. Greenwich, CT: JAL, 1987.

Gandy, Oscar. "Epilogue." In *Framing Public Life*: Perspectives on Media and Understanding of the Social World, ed. Stephen Reese, Oscar Gandy, Jr., and August Grant, 355–378. Mahwah, NJ: Lawrence Erlbaum, 2001.

Gans, H. *Deciding What's News*. New York: Pantheon, 1979.

GeographyIQ. "Australia—Foreign Relations," 2003, http://www.geographyiq. com/countries/as/Australia_relations_summary.htm (accessed July 29, 2004).

Geraghty, C. and D. Lusted, eds. *The Television Studies Book*. New York: Arnold, 1998.

Gershkoff, A. and S. Kushner. "The 9/11-Iraq Connection: How the Bush Administration's Rhetoric in the Iraq conflict Shifted Public Opinion." Paper presented at the Annual Meeting of the Midwest Political Science Association, Chicago, April 2004, http://www.princeton.edu/~agershko/GershkoffKushner IraqPaperJuly142004.pdf (accessed July 21, 2004).

Gilbert, A., R. Walensky, M. Murphy, P. Hirschkorn, and M. Stephens. *Covering Catastrophe: Broadcast Journalists Report September 11*. New York: Bonus Books, 2002.

Gitlin, T. *The Whole World Is Watching: Mass Media in the Making and Unmaking of the New Left*. Berkeley: University of California Press, 1980.

Gitlin, T. "From Put-Down to Catch-Up; the News and the Anti-War Movement." *The New American Prospect* 14, March 1, 2003, http://www.prospect.org/print/ V14/3/gitlin-t.html (accessed May 8, 2004).

Glenn, Ian. *Media Coverage of Iraq War in South Africa*, Unpublished paper, University of Cape Town, 1991.

Goffman, E. *Forms of Talk*. Philadelphia, PA: University of Pennsylvania, 1981.

Goffman, Erving. *Frame Analysis: An Essay on the Organization of Experience*. New York: Harper Colophon, 1974.

Good, Byron. "The Heart of What's the Matter: The Semantics of Illness in Iran." *Culture, Illness, and Psychiatry* 1 (1977): 25–58.

Goodwin, P. Jr. *Latin America* Connecticut: McGraw-Hill, 2003.

Graber, D. *Processing Politics: Learning from Television in the Internet Age*. Chicago: University of Chicago Press, 2001.

Gramsci, A. *Selection from Prison Notebooks*, trans. Quinton Hoare and Geoffrey Nowell-Smith. London: Lawrence and Wishart, 1971.

Gramsci, A. *A Gramsci Reader; Selected Writings 1916–1935*, ed. D. Forgacs, trans. Quinton Hoare and Geoffrey-Nowell-Smith. London: Lawrence and Wishart, 1988.

Gray, C. H. *Postmodern War: The New Politics of Conflict*. London: Routledge, 1997.

Greenberg, B. S. *Communication and Terrorism: Public and Media Responses to 9/11*. Norwood, NJ: Hampton Press, 2002.

Hachten, W. A. and J. Scotton, *The World News Prism: Global Media in an Era of Terrorism*. Ames, IA: Iowa State Press, 2002.

Hackett, R. A. "The Press and Foreign Policy Dissent: The Case of the Gulf War." In *News Media and Foreign Relations: A Multifaceted Perspective*, ed. Makek Abbas, 141–160. Norwood, NJ: Ablex Publishing Corporation, 1997.

Hall, S. "The Question of Cultural Identity." In *Modernity and Its Futures*, ed. Hall S. D. Held, and T. McGrew. Cambridge, UK: Polity Press in association with the Open University, 1996.

Hammond, P. "Postmodernity goes to War." *spiked*, June 1, 2004, http://www.spiked-online.com/Articles/0000000CA554.htm (accessed June 1, 2004).

Hardin, Karol J. *Pragmatics of Persuasive Discourse in Spanish Television Advertising.* The United States: SIL International and University of Texas at Arlington, 2001.

Harel, A. and A. Isacharoff, *The Seventh War.* Tel Aviv: Miskal/Yedioth Ahronoth Books and Hemed Books, Israel, 2004 (Hebrew).

Hartley, J. "Invisible Fictions: Television, Audiences, Paedocracy, Pleasure." In *Television Studies: Textual Análisis*, ed. G. Burns and R. J. Thompson, 223–243. New York: Praeger, 1989.

"Has Iraq War Made U.S. Safer? That's Questionable," *USA Today*, 2004, http://www.usatoday.com/news/opinion/editorials/2004–07–15-our-view_x.htm

Hastie, R. and B. Park. "The Relationship Between Memory and Judgment Depends on Whether the Task Is Memory-Based Or On-Line." *Psychological Review* 93 (1986): 258–268.

Heartfield, J. *The "Death of the Subject" Explained.* Sheffield, UK: Sheffield Hallam University Press, 2002.

Hedges, C. *War is a Force That Gives Us Meaning.* New York: Public Affairs, 2002.

Hendrix, B. "Not a Safer World," *Radio Netherlands Wereldomroep*, September 10, 2004, http://www.rnw.nl/hotspots/html/us040910.html (accessed September 13, 2004).

Hentoff, N. *The War on the Bill of Rights and the Gathering Resistance.* New York: Seven Stories Press, 2003.

Hiro, H. *Secrets and Lies: Operation "Iraqi Freedom" and After.* New York: Nation Books, 2004.

Hodges, S. D. and T. D. Wilson. "Effects of Analyzing Reasons on Attitude Change: The Moderating Role of Attitude Accessibility." *Social Cognition* 11 (1993): 353–366.

Houston, D. A. and R. H. Fazio. "Biased Processing As a Function of Attitude Accessibility: Making Objective Judgments Subjectively." *Social Cognition* 7 (1989): 51–66.

Huang, K. S. "A Comparison between Media Frames and Audience Frames: The Case of the Hill-Thomas Controversy." Paper presented at the Annual Conference of the International Communication Association, Chicago, May 1996.

Iraq War Timeline. *Fact Index Website.* Available: http://www.fact-index.com/ir/iraq_disarnament_2001_2003.html

Iraq War Timeline. *Infoplease Website.* Available: http://www.infoplease.com/ipa/A0909792.html

Iyengar, S. "The Accessibility Bias in Politics: Television News and Public Opinion." *International Journal of Public Opinion Research* 2 (1990): 1–15.

Iyengar, Shanto. *Is Anyone Responsible?* Chicago: University of Chicago Press, 1991.

Jacoby, J., W. D. Hoyer, and D. A. Sheluga. *Miscomprehension of Televised Communications.* New York: The Educational Foundation of the American Association of Advertising Agencies, 1980.

Jamieson, K. H. *Everything You Think You Know About Politics . . . And Why You're Wrong.* United States: Basic Books, 2000.

Jamieson, Kathleen Hall and Paul Waldman. *The Press Effect: Politicians Journalists, and the Stories That Shape the Political World.* New York: Oxford University Press, 2002.

Jehl, D. "Iraq Study Finds Desire for Arms, but not Capacity." *The New York Times*, September 17, 2004.

Jensen, R. "Highjacking Catastrophe: A Review." *Counterpunch* September 13, 2004 http://counterpunch.org/jensen09132004.html (accessed September 13, 2004).

Johnson D. "Senior Official Tells Lawmakers of Iraq and Al-Qaeda Ties." *New York Times On the Web*, February 11, 2003, http://www.nytimes.com

Jonsson, C. "International Negotiations and Cognitive Theory: A Research Project." In *Process of International Negotiations*, ed. F. Mautner-Markhof, 257–276. Boulder: Westview Press, 1989.

Jucker, A. H. *News Interviews: A Pragmalinguisitc Analysis*. Philadelphia: John Benjamins Publishing Company, 1986.

Kagan, Robert. *Of Paradise and Power. America and Europe in the New World Order*. New York: Alfred A. Knopf, 2003.

Kahn, Jean-François. "La guerre en Irak: un an après." Librairie Gaïa, http://www.librairie-gaia.com/CML/KahnJF/Kahn.htm#Conférence (accessed July 28, 2004).

Kamhawi, Rasha. "Television News and the Palestinian Israeli Conflict: An Analysis of Visual and Verbal Framing." Paper presented at the Visual Communication division at the Association for Education in Journalism and Mass Communication (AEJMC), Miami Beach, Florida, 2002.

Kampmark, B. "Wars that Never Take Place: Non-Events, 9/11 and Wars on Terrorism." *Australian Humanities Review*, Issue 29 (May–June 2003), http://www.lib.latrobe.edu.au/AHR/archive/Issue-May-2003/kampmark.html (accessed January 10, 2005).

Kierkegaard, S. *Works of Love*, trans. Howard V. Hong and Edna H. Hong. Princeton, NJ: Princeton University Press, 1995.

Kinder, D. R. and L. M. Sanders. "Mimicking Political Debate with Survey Questions: The Case of White Opinion on Affirmative Action for Blacks." *Social Cognition* 8 (1990): 73–103.

Kirkwood, B. *The History of Mexico*. Westport, CT: Greenwood Press, 2000.

Kirmayer, Laurence J. Landscapes of Memory: Trauma, Narrative, 1996 Dissociation. *Tense Past: Cultural Essays in Trauma and Memory*, 173–197. New York: Routledge.

Kleinman, Arthur. "Pain and Resistance: The Delegitimation and Relegitimation of Local worlds." In *Pain as a Human Experience: An Anthropological Perspective*, ed. M.-J. DelVecchio Good et al., 169–197. Berkley, LA and Oxford: University of California Press, 1994.

Koch, A. *Power, Morals and the Founding Fathers: Essays in the Interpretation of the American Enlightenment*. Ithaca, NY: Cornell University Press, 1961.

Krugman, P. *The Great Unraveling: Losing Our Way in the New Century*. New York: W.W. Norton & Company, 2003.

Kull, S. "Misperceptions, the Media, and the Iraq War." Report of the Program on International Policy Attitudes, http://www.pipa.org/OnlineReports/Iraq/Media_10_02_03_Report.pdf (accessed October 28, 2003).

Kull, S. "Misperceptions, the Media and the Iraq War." Maryland, Program on International Policy Attitudes (PIPA), 2003, http://www.pipa.org/OnlineReports/Iraq/Media_10_02_03_Report.pdf (accessed February 9, 2005).

Kull, S., C. Ramsay, and E. Lewis. "Misperceptions, the Media, and the Iraq War." *Political Science Quarterly* 118, no. 4 (December 1, 2003): 569–598.

Kull, S. "U.S. Public Beliefs on Iraq and the Presidential Election." Report of the Program on International Policy Attitudes, http://www.pipa.org/ OnlineReports/Iraq/IraqReport4_22_04.pdf (accessed May 3, 2004).

Kurz, A. and T. Maltz "Stressed Routine—The Israeli Public at the Eve of War." In *In the Wake of the War in Iraq*, ed. S. Feldman, and M. Grundman, 161–168. Tel Aviv: The Ministry of Defense Publishing House, 2004 (Hebrew).

Lá ará, lá asma', lá atakallam (I don't see, don't hear, don't talk). Arabic. Program on ART. Presented by Mona Zaki. 2003.

Laïdi, Z. *A World Without Meaning: The Crisis of Meaning in International Politics*. London: Routledge, 1998.

Landay, J. M. "The *Apparat*: George W. Bush's backdoor political machine," http://www.mediatransparency.org/stories/apparat.html (accessed September 13, 2004).

Langer, G. "Was It Worth It? Poll: More Americans Think Iraq War Raises Risk of Anti-U.S. Terror." *ABC News*, September 8, 2004, http://abcnews.go.com/ sections/wnt/World/poll030908_iraq.html (accessed September 13, 2004).

Lapham, L. "Tentacles of Rage: The Republican Propaganda Mill, a Brief History." *Harpers*, September 2004.

Lasorsa, D. L. "Review of *Measuring Bias on Television*, by Barrie Gunter." *Journal of Communication* 48, no. 3 (1998): 161–163.

Layton, C. "Miller Brouhaha." *AJR* 6, August/September 2003, http://www.ajr.org/ article.asp?id=3057 (accessed July 15, 2004).

Lehman-Wilzig, S. and A. Schejter. "Israel." In *Mass Media in the Middle East: A Comprehensive Handbook*, ed. Y. R. Kamalipour and H. Mowlana. Westport, CT: Greenwood Press, 1994, 109–125.

Livingston, S. *The Terrorism Spectacle*. Boulder, CO: Westview Press, 1994.

Livingston, S. *Clarifying the CNN Effect*. Joan Shorenstein Center on the Press, Politics and Public Policy, Harvard University, 1997, http://sparky. harvard.edu/ presspol/publications/pdfs/70916_R-18.pdf (accessed June 10, 1999).

Livingston, S. and W. L. Bennett, "Gatekeeping, Indexing and Live-Event News: Is Technology Altering the Construction of News?" *Political Communication* 20, no. 4 (2003): 363–380.

Lope Blanch, J. M. *Los medios de información y la lengua española*. México: Universidad Nacional Autónoma de México, 1988.

López Cáceres, A. J. *Entre la Pluma y la pantalla: reflexiones sobre literatura, cine y periodismo*, 41–51. Calí, Colombia: Universidad del Valle, 2003.

Lule, Jack. *Daily News, Eternal Stories*. New York: Guilford, 2001.

Lyotard, J.-F. *The Postmodern Condition: A Report on Knowledge*. Manchester, UK: Manchester University Press, 1984.

Maertens, T. "Asserting This War Has Made Us Safer Won't Make It So," *Minneapolis Star Tribune*, July 27, 2004.

Malanczuk, P. *Akehurst's Modern Introduction to International Law*, 7th edn. London and New York: Routledge, 1997.

Manaev, O. "The Disagreeing Audience: Change in Criteria for Evaluating Mass Media Effectiveness with the Democratization of Soviet Society." *Communication Research* 18, no. 1 (1991): 25–52.

Martínez Albertos, J. L. *Lenguaje periodístico*. Madrid: Parafino, S.S., 1989.

Massing, M. "Now They Tell Us." *New York Review of Books* 51, no. 3, February 26, 2004.

Mata, M. C. and S. Scarafia, *Lo que dicen las radios, una propuesta para analizar el para analizar el discurso radiofónico*. Quito, Ecuador: RN Industria Gráfica, 1993.

McCombs, M. and D. Shaw. "The Agenda Setting Function of the Media". *Public Opinion Quarterly* 36 (1972): 176–187.

McQuail, D. *Mass Communication Theory: An Introduction*, 3rd edn. Thousand Oaks: Sage, 1994.

McQuail, Denis. *Communication Theory: An Introduction*, 3rd edn. London: Sage, 1994.

Mearsheimer, J. J. and S. M. Walt, "Can Saddam Be Contained? History Says Yes." Paper. Cambridge, MA: Belfer Center for Science and International Affairs, November 2002, http://bcsia.ksg.harvard.edu/publication.cfm?program= CORE&ctype=paper&item_id=361.

Mey, J. L. *Whose Language? A Study in Linguistic Pragmatics*. Philadelphia: John Benjamins Publishing Company, 1985.

Miller, M. C. *The Bush Dyslexicon*. London: Bantam Books, 2001.

Moeller, S. *Media Coverage of Weapons of Mass Destruction*. Maryland: Centre for International and Security Studies, University of Maryland, March 9, 2004, http://www.cissm.umd.edu/documents/WMDstudy_full.pdf (accessed July 7, 2004 and February 9, 2005).

Mooney, C. "Did Our Leading Newspapers Set Too Low a Bar for a Preemptive Attack"? *Columbia Journalism Review* 2, March/April 2004, http://cjr.org/issues/ 2004/2/mooney-war.asp (accessed July 15, 2004).

Mooney, C. "The Editorial Pages and the Case for War." *Columbia Journalism Review*, 29 (March/April 2004).

Mowlana, Hammid. *Global Information and World Communications*. London: Sage Publications, 1996.

Muwātin wa-mukhbir wa-harāmī (A citizen, a detective, and a thief). Film. Arabic. Directed by Dawud Abd-al-Sayyid. Egypt, 2001.

Napoli, D. Jo. "Semantics." In *Linguistics an Introduction*, 449–553. New York: Oxford University Press, 1996.

Nelson, T. E., R. A. Clawson, and Z. M. Oxley. "Media Framing of a Civil Liberties Conflict and its Effect on Tolerance." *American Political Science Review* 91 (1997): 567–583.

Neuman, R. W., M. R. Just, and A. N. Crigler, *Common Knowledge: News and the Construction of the Political Meaning*. Chicago: The University of Chicago Press, 1992.

Norris, C. *Uncritical Theory: Postmodernism, Intellectuals and the Gulf War*. London: Lawrence and Wishart, 1992.

Norris, Pippa. "The Restless Search: Network News Framing of the Post-Cold War World." *Political Communication* 12 (1995): 357–370.

Not Necessarily the News, *Harpers,* September 2004.

O'Neill, B. "Rewriting Basra." *spiked*, April 9, 2003, http://www.spiked-online. com/Articles/00000006DD3A.htm (accessed April 9, 2003).

O'Sullivan, T., J. Hartley, D. Saunders, M. Montgomery, and J. T. Fiske. *Key Concepts in Communication and Cultural Studies*. London: Routledge, 1994.

Overholser, G. "If Only They Knew Cowed Media Can't Keep Americans Informed." *Columbia Journalism Review* 6, November/December 2002, http://www.cjr.org/issues/2002/6/voice-over.asp (accessed July 15, 2004).

Palmer, N. *Terrorism, War and the Press.* Cambridge, MA: Joan Schornstein Center, 2003.

Pan, Z. and G. M. Kosicki. "Framing Analysis: An Approach to News Discourse." *Political Communication* 10 (1993): 55–75.

Parra, M. *Difusión internacional del español por radio, televisión y prensa.* Santafé deBogotá: Publicaciones del Instituto caro y Cuervo, series Minor XL, 1999.

Pew Research Center For The People & The Press. Unusually High Interest in Bush's State of the Union: Public Priorities Shifted by Recession and War. January 17, 2002. http://www.pewtrusts.com/ideas/ideas_item.cfm?content_item_id=886&content_type_id=18&issue_name=Public%20Opinion%20and%20Polls&issue=11&page=18&name=Public%20Opinion%20Polls%20and%20Survey%20Results (accessed February 9, 2005).

Phillips, K. *Wealth and Democracy: A Political History of the American Rich.* New York: Broadway Books, 2003.

Polling Report.com. Iraq, page 7. http://www.pollingreport.com/iraq7.htm (accessed February 9, 2005).

Porpora, D. "The Debate over Central America." In *How Holocausts Happen: The United States in Central America*, 153–170. Philadelphia: Temple University Press, 1990.

Preparations? *Ynet website*, November 5, 2002. http://www.ynet.co.il.

Price, V., D. Tewksbury, and E. Powers. "Switching Trains of Thought: The Impact of News Frames on Readers Cognitive Responses." Paper presented at the Annual Conference of the Midwest Association for Public Opinion Research, Chicago, November 1995.

Price, V., D. Tewksbury, and E. Powers. "Switching Trains of Thought: The Impact of News Frames on Readers Cognitive Responses." *Communication Research* 24 (1997): 481–506.

Program on International Policy Atitudes (PIPA). *Conflict With Iraq.* Washington, DC. http://www.americans-world.org/digest/regional_issues/Conflict_Iraq/linkstoTerr.cfm (accessed February 9, 2005).

Rampton, S. and J. Stauber. *Weapons of Mass Deception: The Uses of Propaganda in Bush's War on Iraq.* New York: Tarcher/Penguin, 2003.

Rep. King Calls France "Second-Rate," Suggests Separate Alliance. February 11, 2003. Associated Press. Fox News.com—Politics—Rep. King Calls France "Second-Rate," Suggests Separate Alliance. http://www.foxnews.com/story/0,2933,78289,00.html (accessed July 14, 2004).

Rhodebeck, L. A. "Framing Policy Debates on Old Age." Paper presented at the Annual Conference of the Midwest Political Science Association, Chicago, April 1998.

Ricks, T. E. and V. Loeb. "Bush Developing Military Policy of Striking First: New Doctrine Addresses Terrorism," *Washington Post*, June 10, 2002.

Rosen, Jay. *What are Journalists For?* New Haven, CT: Yale University Press, 1999.

Roushdy-Hammady, Iman "Recombination and Forensics: Cancer Risk among 2001 Two Cappadocian Communities in Turkey, Sweden and Germany." Committee on Middle Eastern Studies, PhD Thesis, Department of Anthropology, Harvard University, Cambridge, MA September, 2001.

Roushdy-Hammady, Iman "Introduction. Contested Etiology and Fragile Castles: An Ethnography of Cancer Risk and Cancer Research in Two Parts." *Culture, Medicine, and Psychiatry*. In press (a).

Roushdy-Hammady, Iman "Contested Etiology: Cancer Risk among Two Anatolian Populations in Turkey and Europe." *Culture, Medicine, and Psychiatry*.

Said, E. *Orientalism*. London: Penguin, 1995. In press (b).

Scheper-Hughes, Nancy. *Death without Weeping: The Violence of Everyday Life in Brazil*. Berkeley and Los Angeles, California, University of California Press, 1992.

Scheufele, D. A. "Framing As a Theory of Media Effects." *Journal of Communication* 49, no. 1 (1999): 102–122.

Schlesinger Jr., A. "The Making of a Mess." *The New York Review of Books* 51, no. 14 (September 23, 2004).

Schmidt, Rosemarie and Joseph F. Kess. *Television Advertising ant Televangelism Discourse Analysis of Persuasive Language*. Philadelphia: John Benjamins Publishing Company, 1986.

Searle, J. *Speech Acts*. Cambridge, England: Cambridge University Press, 1969.

Sennet, R. *The Corrosion of Character: The Personal Consequences of Work in the New Capitalism*. New York: W.W. Norton & Company, 1998.

Shapiro, Samantha M. "The War Inside the Arab Newsroom." *The New York Times*, January 2, 2005, http://www.nytimes.com/2005/01/02/magazine/02ARAB. html?ex=1106570919&ei=1&en=746d59b9793559b4 (accessed January 17, 2005).

Shoemaker, P. J., and S. D. Reese. *Mediating the Message: Theories of Influence on Mass Media Content*, 2nd edn. White Plains, NJ: Longman, 1996.

Sigal, L. *Reporters and Officials*. Lexington, MA: D.C. Heath, 1973.

Speech on Iraq. CBS NEWS, March 17, 2003, http://www.cbsnews.com/ stories/2003/03/17/iraq/main544377.shtml

Spurlin, P. M. *The French Enlightenment in America: Essays on the Times of the Founding Fathers*. Athens, GA: University of Georgia Press, 1984.

Suskind, P. *The Price of Loyalty: George W. Bush, the White House, and the Education of Paul O'Neill*. New York: Simon and Shuster, 2004.

Suter, Keith. "Australia's Involvement in the Iraq War." *Contemporary Review*, November 2003, http://www.findarticles.com/p/articles/mi_m2242/ is_1654_283/ai_111858199 (accessed July 29, 2004).

Tankard, J. W. "The Empirical Approach to the Study of Media Framing." In *Framing Public Life: Perspectives on Media and Understanding of the Social World*, ed. S. Reese, O. Gandy, and A. Grant, 95–106. Mahwah, NJ: Lawrence Erlbaum, 2001.

Taylor, Phillip. *War and the Media: Propaganda and Persuasion in the Gulf War*, Manchester, UK: Manchester University Press, 1992.

The 9/11 Commission, *The 9/11 Commission Report*, Washington, DC, 2004, http://www.9-11commission.gov (accessed February 9, 2005).

The Australian. "Demographics," 2004, http://newsmedianet.com.au/home/titles/ title/Demographics.jsp?titleid=5 (accessed July 22, 2004).

The National Security Strategy of the United States of America, September 17, 2002, http://www.whitehouse.gov/nsc/nss.html

The Sydney Morning Herald. "Polls Apart on Whether This Is A Conflict Worth Waging," April 1, 2003, http://www.smh.com.au/articles/2003/03/31/ 1048962700473.html (accessed July 29, 2004).

The World Messenger "British, Scottish, Irish, Welsh Casualties In Iraq," 2003, http://www.worldmessenger.20m.com/brits.html (accessed July 29, 2004).

Thussu, Daya Kishan. "Managing the Media in an Era of Round-the-Clock News: Notes from India's First Tele-War." *Journalism Studies* 3, no. 2 (2002): 203–212.

Tomlison, John. *Cultural Imperialism*. London: Pinter Publications, 1991.

Topoushian, Mayda. "Interpreting the Constructed Realities of the 1991 Gulf War: A Comparative Textual Analysis of Two Arab and Two North American Newspapers." PhD diss., Concordia University, Canada, 2002.

Trotsky, L., J. Dewey, and G. Novak. *Their Morals and Ours: Marxist Versus Liberal Views on Morality*. New York: Pathfinder Press, Inc., 1973.

Tuchman, G. *Making News: A Study in the Construction of Reality*. New York: Free Press, 1978.

Tversky, A. and D. Kahneman. "Availability: A Heuristic for Judging Frequency and Probability." *Cognitive Psychology* 5 (1973): 207–222.

Uhler, W. C. "Preempting the Truth." *Bulletin of the Atomic Scientists*, September/ October 2004.

Unfit to Print *New York Review of Books* 51, no. 11, June 24, 2004.

United Nations, *Historical Review of Developments relating to Aggression*. United Nations Publication, 2003.

United Nations Charter, http://www.un.org/aboutun/charter/index.html

Van Dijk, T. A. *News as Discourse*. London: Lawrence Erlbaum, 1988.

Van Dijk, T. A. "Opinions and Ideologies in the Press." In *Approaches to Media Discourse*, ed. Allan Bell and Peter Garret, 21–43. Malden, MA: Blackwell Publishers, 1998.

Verschueren, Jef. *International News Reporting: Metapragmatic Metaphors and the U-2*. Philadelphia: John Benjamins Publishing Company, 1985.

Viguerie, R. A., D. Franke, and T. LaHaye. *America's Right Turn: How Conservatives Used New and Alternative Media to take Power*. Chicago: Bonus Books, 2004.

Walzer, M. *Arguing About War*. New Haven, CT: Yale University Press, 2004.

Wa-nalqá al-ahibbah (Knowing the Beloveds). Arabic. Program on ART. Presented by 'Amr Khálid. 2003.

Wilson, J. *The Politics of Truth: Inside the Lies that Led to War and Betrayed My Wife's CIA Identity*. New York: Carroll & Graf, 2004.

Wood, G. *The Creation of the American Repubic 1776–1787*. Chapel Hill, NC: University of North Carolina Press, 1998.

Yaar, E. and T. Hermann. *The Peace Index: February 2003*. Tel Aviv: The Tammy Steinmatz Center for Peace Research, Tel Aviv University. 2003. Available: http://spirit.tau.ac.il/socant/peace/peaceindex/2003/files/feb2003e.doc

Zelizer, B. and S. Allan. *Journalism after September 11*. New York: Routledge, 2002.

INDEX

DATE DUE